Praise for
One Gospel, Many Cultures: Doing Theology in Context

"This new collection derived primarily from evangelical scholars working in the South Asian context provides new impetus to reconsider Christian faith in relationship to the plurality of religious and faith traditions, especially in India but also beyond. The authors make their case especially through in-depth dialogue with the scriptural traditions that the gospel resounds through *many* cultural frames, not just one, and therefore invite ever more dialogical postures and practices for Christian witness amid the many religio-cultural realities of the human condition."

—Amos Yong, professor of theology and mission,
Fuller Seminary

"Taking the discussion on the relationship between the gospel and culture to another level, this book is definitely an essential read for theologians, missiologists, and ministry practitioners. Not only do the essays offer a clear methodology for decontextualizing gospel truths and reclothing them in new cultural contexts, but they also incisively demonstrate this practical outworking in biblical texts and in engaging current theological and missiological issues. The arguments are cogent and well balanced, the complexities sensitively nuanced and boldly addressed. This truly is an indispensable resource."

—Sooi Ling Tan, dean,
Asia Graduate School of Theology Alliance

"For centuries the church of the Global South has struggled to make practical sense of the relationship of the gospel and culture. We have either vilified our cultures as fundamentally antithetical to the values of the gospel or we have sanctified their every manifestation as consonant with the message of Christ. To borrow Ken Gnanakan's words, 'The truth must be discovered somewhere in between.' *One Gospel,*

Many Cultures turns to a global team of eminent scholars to mount a renewed argument: only a culturally coherent gospel can be transformatively embraced and lead to lifestyles shaped by the culture of the kingdom of Christ."

—Ivor Poobalan, principal, Colombo Theological Seminary, Sri Lanka, and co-chair, Theology Working Group, Lausanne Movement

"This book is a beautiful tapestry of the gospel message in the multicultural context of India. The authors posit the power of culture as a primary vehicle for communicating the gospel. Cultural expressions of the gospel do not diminish its transforming power. Instead, the expression articulates the intellectual and affective dimensions that reveal the loving presence of the risen Savior among every people-group. The writers show how people see, hear, and experience God in their context when the gospel of Jesus Christ wears the cultural garment. These scholarly reflections embolden Indian believers to be unapologetically Christian in their diverse cultures. I recommend this compendium to anyone seeking to effectively communicate the gospel in the church."

—Emmanuel Bellon, vice president, Executive Network, ScholarLeaders International

"Culture shapes people's perception and expression of the gospel; thus, communication and application of the gospel must take into consideration local cultural contexts to be meaningful and relevant. *One Gospel, Many Cultures* addresses this need, providing principles and examples of the crucial task of contextualizing the gospel in diverse cultures. A highly recommended reading for all serious students of theology in India and even all across Asia!"

—Dr. Theresa Roco Lua, general secretary, Asia Theological Association, and director of Global Theology, World Evangelical Alliance

One Gospel, Many Cultures

Doing Theology in Context

Edited by
ARREN BENNET LAWRENCE

Fortress Press
Minneapolis

ONE GOSPEL, MANY CULTURES
Doing Theology in Context

Cover image: Brown wooden door, copyright Rahul Pande (@rahulxpande) | Unsplash
Cover design: Savanah N. Landerholm

Print ISBN: 978-1-5064-8539-3
eBook ISBN: 978-1-5064-8540-9

Dedicated to
the late Dr. Ken Gnanakan,
former general secretary of the Asia Theological Association.
A theologian, educationist, environmentalist, and musician.

Contents

Foreword

ROGER E. HEDLUND

To the organizers and contributors to this writing project, I express my appreciation for the honor of being asked to write a foreword to this significant volume. Books are many on the subject of gospel and culture. The subject is vast with widely differing opinions. The authors and compilers of this compendium are to be appreciated for their sensitivity to a largely Indian context and audience. As the well-known Asian scholar Wesley Ariarajah reminds us, "The relationship between gospel and culture has been an issue of contention from the very beginnings of the church."[1] In South Asia, the Saint Thomas Christians, the Nestorians, and other early arrivals apparently made "many accommodations to the local cultures." This, however, changed radically during the missionary era of the seventeenth to nineteenth century, "when Christianity was accompanied by colonialism and the assumed superiority of Western culture." In the postcolonial era, many in South Asia felt the need to reaffirm their local cultures, leading to a third phase of "indigenization and inculturation" involving the adaptation of local cultural symbols, art forms, and concepts to "incarnate" the gospel in every culture.[2]

Gospel and mission are indivisible, yet appropriate methodologies are indispensable. Keith Ferdinando says, "For this reason storying is increasingly adopted as a particularly effective approach to gospel communication, since it sets the central events of Jesus' life, death and resurrection in the context of the biblical storyline as a

---

1. Wesley Ariarajah, "Gospel and Culture," in the *Oxford Encyclopaedia of South Asian Christianity*, ed. Roger E. Hedlund et al. (New Delhi: Oxford University Press, 2012), 282.
2. Ariarajah, 283.

whole, so that their meaning can be properly grasped."[3] The Christian understanding of salvation "is distinctive in that it comes from God by his grace as a gift which cannot be earned."[4] Salvation is "the central theme of biblical revelation, and Christian missionary witness is guided by the salvific vision of Christ."[5]

Several chapters in this volume relate especially to the task of incarnating the gospel in our many contemporary human cultures. In chapter 1 in this volume, "One Gospel in Many Cultures," late professor Ken Gnanakan states, "There is no cultureless gospel, or cultureless Christianity, or even cultureless scriptures." He quotes Paul G. Hiebert's reminder, "While affirming that Scripture is divine revelation, it is important to keep in mind that the Scriptures themselves were given to humans in particular historical and socio-cultural contexts."[6] Later in his chapter, Gnanakan refers to the late African theologian Kwame Bediako's critique of the impact of the West, and specifically of Western mission, on African culture and identity as something that "should be read."[7] Many from the West exhibited a sense of cultural superiority and brought a Western cultural package along with the gospel. Gnanakan confesses that Evangelicals "have had a love-hate relationship with culture." Fortunately, there has been considerable progress in our understanding of culture as Gnanakan documents, citing the *Willowbank Report* and the work of the Lausanne Committee for World Evangelization (LCWE). Gnanakan also devotes attention to the difference between Hinduism and Hindutva and the need to redefine the Indian Christian culture in light of the current conflicts threatening the democratic principles of India's constitution and secular fabric.

Fuller Seminary professor Wilbert R. Shenk clearly states that "the gospel is the dynamic center of the biblical narrative, the heart

3. Keith Ferdinando, "Gospel," in *Dictionary of Mission Theology*, ed. John Corrie (Nottingham, UK: InterVarsity, 2007), 141.

4. Parush R. Parushev, "Salvation," in Corrie, *Dictionary of Mission Theology*, 353.

5. Parushev, 352.

6. Paul G. Hiebert, *The Gospel in Human Contexts: Anthropological Explorations for Contemporary Mission* (Grand Rapids, MI: Baker Academic, 2009), 29.

7. Kwame Bediako, *Theology and Identity* (Oxford: Regnum Studies in Mission, 1969), 227–66.

of the Christian faith. The term means to announce good news as well as the content of the good news, that is, God's redemptive action in Jesus Christ for the salvation of humankind."[8] God does for us what we cannot do for ourselves, providing the means for our redemption. It is our responsibility to respond to God's gracious invitation. Moreover, everyone receives the gospel message through a particular culture, with its language and customs that filter the information received. Shenk adds that in the seventeenth century, the Pietist movement brought spiritual awakening to a largely nominal European church by preaching individual conversion and personal salvation.[9]

In chapter 7 in this volume, "The Gospel and Truth Predicates in a Hindu Context," Professor Aruthuckal Varughese John, having cited Semitic claims for the exclusive conception of truth in Christianity, finds similar truth claims in some Hindu traditions. He says, "After all, the doctrinal claims of the Hindu scriptures are intended to be taken as true. To suggest otherwise would be discourteous." He then continues, "Indic religionists, similar to their Semitic counterparts, have articulated responses such as certitude, doubt, trust, fallibility, and the like with respect to their religious beliefs. Rational and logico-semantic articulations are eminently manifest within the robust Hindu philosophical schools. We may thus surmise that a belief, religious or otherwise, articulated in a language possesses truth predicates."

Therefore, it follows that disagreements about truth claims are possible, provided both parties recognize the category in question. Varughese John states, "This means not that the Indic religionists do not desire truth predicates in religious beliefs but rather that the multiple parallel traditions with alternate doctrines make it impossible to create a single creed." Some overlap is inevitable. Eclecticism is part of the Hindu culture. According to Varughese John, the Brahmo Samaj is a case in point: "Influenced by Christian missionaries,

---

8. Wilbert R. Shenk, "Gospel," in the *Global Dictionary of Theology: A Resource for the Worldwide Church*, ed. William A. Dyrness and Veli-Matti Kärkkäinen (Downers Grove, IL: InterVarsity, 2008), 356–58.

9. Shenk, 357.

Hindu reformers like Raja Ram Mohan Roy appropriated the critique of idol worship, sati, and child marriage and incorporated these changes within his neo-Hindu reformed movement of Brahmo Samaj." For Varughese John, the historicity of the four Gospels is essential to the proclamation of the message, in contrast to the mythical nature of Hindu beliefs. Persuasion rather than coercion is characteristic of Christianity. The Christian understanding of truth "cannot be severed from historical events surrounding Jesus." Moreover, "the veracity of religious beliefs will elude a probing believer, as they cannot be validated."

Varughese John suggests the possibility of bridges to Christ from specific Hindu traditions. The growing Hindu Krista Bhakta movement "initiates a way for the gospel to refine the culture." According to Varughese John, "The cultural continuity with the Hindu traditions that the *Krista Bhakta* movement endorses does not view Hinduism as a rival. Rather, it envisages a continuity by recognizing the fulfillment of certain Hindu aspirations in the person of Jesus Christ. Further, if there are no specific creedal beliefs that essentially make one a Hindu, then one's devotion to Christ should not exclude a Christ devotee for that reason from being *Hindu Krista Bhakta*. This message is pivotal in the context of alienating rhetoric within the society that seeks to vilify religious conversions as a form of betrayal."

Noted historian and theologian Jaroslav Pelikan, at the beginning of his brilliant exposition of *Jesus through the Centuries: His Place in the History of Culture*, declares Jesus of Nazareth the dominant figure in the history of Western culture for some twenty centuries.[10] Each epoch has tried to come to terms with his significance. As Pelikan says, "It was as a rabbi that Jesus was known and addressed by his immediate followers and by others."[11] His preaching ministry was launched as a rabbi in the Nazareth synagogue when he stood up and read these words from the sixty-fourth chapter of the scroll of Isaiah:

10. Jaroslav Pelikan, *Jesus through the Centuries: His Place in the History of Culture* (New Haven, CT: Yale University Press, 1985).
11. Pelikan, 11.

The Spirit of the Lord is upon me,
because he has anointed me to preach good news to the poor.
He has sent me to proclaim release to the captives
and recovering of sight to the blind,
to set at liberty those who are oppressed,
to proclaim the acceptable year of the Lord. (Luke 4:18–19 RSV)

Then in place of the customary sermon, Jesus closed the book, handed it back to the attendant, and sat down. "Today," said Jesus, "this scripture has been fulfilled in your hearing" (Luke 4:21 RSV). Jesus was no ordinary rabbi. He was, however, a teller of parables, as is clear from the four New Testament Gospel accounts. On the occasion of his so-called triumphal entry into Jerusalem (prior to Palm Sunday), Rabbi Jesus is introduced as "the *prophet* Jesus from Nazareth of Galilee" (Matt 21:11 RSV; emphasis added). Rather than merely one who predicts the future, the prophet Jesus is one who is "authorized to speak on behalf of Another"—a special status confirmed in the conclusion of the Sermon on the Mount: "And when Jesus finished these sayings, the crowds were astonished at his teaching, for he taught them as one who had authority, and not as their scribes. When he came down from the mountain, great crowds followed him" (Matt 7:28–8:1 RSV).

The New Testament writings also cite Jesus's miracles as "substantiation of his standing as rabbi-prophet." Furthermore, Jesus is portrayed as "the one prophet in whom the teaching of Moses was simultaneously fulfilled and superseded, as the one rabbi who both satisfied the law of Moses and transcended it."[12] According to the Fourth Gospel, "The law was given through Moses; *grace and truth came through Jesus Christ*" (John 1:17 RSV; emphasis added). Pelikan says, "The future belonged to the titles 'Christ' and 'Lord' as names for Jesus, and to the identification of him as the Son of God and the second person of the Trinity."[13]

---

12. Pelikan, 16.

13. Pelikan, 17. In addition to *Jesus through the Centuries*, the late Jaroslav Pelikan is the author of the five-volume series *The Christian Tradition: A History of the Development of Doctrine* (Chicago: University of Chicago Press), vol. 1, *The*

In chapter 6 in this volume, entitled "Culture Dynamics in the Johannine Community Context," Professor Johnson Thomaskutty scrutinizes two contrasting worldviews, that of Jesus rooted in God versus that of the Jews in relation to Abram and Moses. Utilizing the interdisciplinary deliberations of H. Richard Niebuhr's fivefold classification of the relationship between Christ and culture yields insights into the dynamics at work in the contemporary Indian context.[14] Thomaskutty states that the Fourth Gospel "portrays Jesus as the incarnated Word, the agent of God, the savior of the world, and the glorious child of God. This portrait of Jesus introduces a conflicting situation between the traditional Judaism and the newly emerged Christian community." This created a situation in which the Johannine community confronted opposition and "existed as a resistance movement" within the synagogue.

In his analysis, Thomaskutty stresses the transformative power of the gospel. Through Jesus's initiative, many people were brought to new levels of life: "The Johannine community was composed of a transformed group of people with a new culture, morality, and principles. The newness motif of the Gospel demonstrates the transformative lifestyle that Jesus emphasized over against the existent social and cultural norms. . . . Over against a culture that was hate oriented and exclusive, Jesus's transformative model introduces a love-centered and inclusive pattern that accommodates people irrespective of their race, caste, color, gender, and national identity." As Thomaskutty points out, initially there is an "element of clash between Christ and culture," but this is followed by various stages of adjustment in which "that which is corrupted by human sinfulness and selfishness can be transformed by the initiative of Christ and the gospel." Finally, given the present level of uncertainty in India today, Thomaskutty believes that

---

Emergence of the Catholic Tradition (100–600), 1975; vol. 2, *The Spirit of Eastern Christendom (600–1700)*, 1977; vol. 3, *The Growth of Medieval Theology (600–1300)*, 1980; vol. 4, *Reformation of Church and Dogma (1300–1700)*, 1985; vol. 5, *Christian Doctrine and Modern Culture (since 1700)*, 1991; and other titles.

14. See H. Richard Niebuhr, *Christ and Culture* (San Francisco: Harper & Row, 1951).

the Christian identity in India should be demonstrated in dialogical and intertextual relationships with the surrounding socioreligious and politico-cultural realities so that the Christians can stand *against* the odds and the injustices of the cultural phenomena, accommodate the cultural values and be part *of* the prevailing realities of our neighbors. . . . An "insider" and "outsider" dynamism can be identified through the means of the aforementioned ways and means. By enabling a boundary mark between the "insider" and the "outsider," Christian communities can transform the culture by extending invitations to outsiders so that they may embrace the paradigmatic inside group. As the Covid-19 pandemic grips the people across the globe, the church as a community of the reformed . . . should foster the virtue of solidarity in the midst of turbulent situations.

In chapter 3 in this volume, "'The God of the Nations' (Rom 3:29): A Pharisee's Confession?," Professor Andrew B. Spurgeon argues that the apostle Paul, prior to conversion, was committed to the exclusivity of Judaism. However, Paul's encounter with the Jewish Messiah changed Paul's theology. Paul wrote, "God shows no partiality. All who have sinned without the law will also perish without the law, and all who sinned under the law will be judged by the law" (Rom 2:11–12 RSV). Spurgeon notes, "Since God judged Jews who possessed the law by the law and nations apart from the law (since they did not have the law), he was a fair and universal judge, the God of all nations."

Later, as recorded in the Acts of the Apostles, upon the occasion of the conversion of the devout gentile centurion Cornelius, the apostle Peter also came to a similar conclusion: "God shows no partiality, but in every nation any one who fears him and does what is right is acceptable to him" (Acts 10:34–35 RSV). Upon witnessing the outpouring of the Holy Spirit upon these gentiles, Peter "commanded them to be baptized in the name of Jesus Christ" (Acts 10:48 RSV). This leads Spurgeon to declare, "The same is true now: God isn't exclusively the God of the Christians. He is still the God of the nations." Spurgeon cites the example of E. Stanley Jones, the

Methodist missionary to India, who said it beautifully: "If we present Christianity as a rival to other religions, it will fail. . . . There are many religions. There is but one gospel. We are not setting a religion over against other religions, but a gospel over against human need, which is the same everywhere. The greatest service we can give to anyone in East or West is to introduce him to the moral and spiritual power found in Christ. India needs everything. We humbly offer the best we have. The best we have is Christ."[15] And as Spurgeon concludes, "Any gospel we proclaim that omits Jesus Christ, his rule as the Lord and king, his resurrection, or trusting/believing in him is not a gospel at all." Moreover, "one gospel, many cultures" simply means we "retain the *purity* of the gospel in the *plurality* of cultures"—that is, one God for all nations.

Scholars Richard Fox Young and Jonathan A. Seitz speak of Asia's pluriform Christianity—that is, a multiplicity of Christianities.[16] In another recent publication, Havilah Dharamraj argues that the evangelist John presents Jesus as the new Torah, "one in whom is invested all of its authority. Thus, we could say in contrast to the sacred texts of other religions, the primary agent of divine revelation in the Christian faith is not the Bible per se, but rather Jesus Christ."[17] The Bible operates as an instrument of transformation by pointing to Jesus as "the only means by which fellowship with God becomes available to anyone, and beyond that, by calling into being that fellowship." Furthermore, Dharamraj calls attention to "a triune God seeking to reconcile to himself all the peoples of the earth."[18]

Asian theologian Simon Chan makes note of the "great importance placed on the family in Asia," for which "the Trinity as the divine family takes on a special significance. The ideal Asian family

15. E. Stanley Jones, "Report on the New India," *Christian Century* 64 (1947): 556.
16. Richard Fox Young and Jonathan A. Seitz, *Asia in the Making of Christianity: Conversion, Agency, and Indigeneity, 1600s to the Present*, Social Sciences in Asia 35 (Leiden: Brill, 2013), 26.
17. Havilah Dharamraj, "On the Doctrine of Scripture: An Asian Conversation," in *Asian Christian Theology: Evangelical Perspectives*, ed. Timoteo D. Gener and Stephen T. Pardue (Carlisle, UK: Langham, 2019), 47.
18. Dharamraj, 57.

is an ordered relationship with differentiated roles and recipro-
cal responsibilities that reflect the order of the Trinity."[19] An Asian
Christian theology "may be phrased in different ways, but it runs
through diverse Christian traditions, including Catholicism, Orthodoxy, evangelicalism and Pentecostalism," and always with a "common spiritual heritage in terms of the givenness of the gospel, which
cannot be compromised."[20] Chan further observes that "contextual
theologies emerge as the church lives out its given script in new situations. In other words, theology is first a lived experience of the
church before it is a set of ideas formulated by church theologians."[21]
It also is to be noted that "local cultures do shape the way the faith is
received and expressed, but for a local theology to be authentically
Christian, it must have substantial continuity with the larger Christian tradition."[22]

To conclude this foreword to gospel and culture, I refer to some
thoughts from Vinoth Ramachandra, secretary for dialogue and
social engagement for the International Fellowship of Evangelical
Students (IFES), based in Singapore, regarding following Jesus as
Lord in the changing landscape of today's Asia. Vinoth calls us to
engage in "integral mission," in which we bring together our theology and our practice: being and doing, spiritual and physical,
individual and social, prayer and politics, justice and mercy. For
Ramachandra, "integral mission springs out of an integral gospel.
The good news of the in-breaking reign of God in Jesus to heal,
renew and recreate his broken world is far, far bigger than a message
of individual salvation."[23] Our mission today is to express "what the
Lordship of Jesus Christ means in our rapidly changing economic,
cultural and political contexts."[24] How so? Ramachandra suggests,
"The primary way the church witnesses in the world is by simply

19. Simon Chan, *Grassroots Asian Theology: Thinking the Faith from the Ground Up* (Downers Grove, IL: InterVarsity, 2014), 66.
20. Chan, 10, 11.
21. Chan, 15.
22. Chan, 11.
23. Vinoth Ramachandra, *Church and Mission in the New Asia: New Gods, New Iden- tities* (Singapore: Trinity Theological College, 2009), 16.
24. Ramachandra, 25.

being the church: a radically new community in which social, cultural and economic barriers between peoples are broken down and men and women learn to love their traditional and personal enemies."[25] So be it. "Your kingdom come . . . on earth as it is in heaven" (Matt 6:10 NIV). Amen.

---

25. Ramachandra, 24.

Introducing One Gospel, Many Cultures

PAUL PREMSEKARAN CORNELIUS

"The church is the village, and the village is the church" is a popular phrase in the Northeast Indian state of Nagaland. This is generally accompanied by another phrase that describes Christian faith and practice as "cultural Christianity." Both of these speak to the question of the relationship between the gospel and culture(s). The Nagaland context, of course, is one of a kind, where the line between Christian belief and cultural practice is blurred to the extent that one is not distinguishable from the other. This is typically one end of the spectrum, which is seen in several parts of the world, especially in the so-called Christian countries or leftover empires of erstwhile Christendom. On the other end of the spectrum is the belief that no interaction between the gospel and human culture is possible. Such a view, in most instances, is expressed by some denominations that maintain that no possible relationship between the two can exist.

Both positions emanate from an impoverished view and understanding of Scripture and, also, the God of all creation and cultures. On the one hand is the heady conflation of the Christian faith with one's culture; on the other is the wholesale rejection of culture. The first runs the danger of leading to a compromised gospel, while the second logically results in the isolation and irrelevance of the gospel in our contexts. A more appropriate reading of Scripture, however, suggests that neither of these positions is tenable and that there is a third approach that provides a balanced interaction between the two.

I. What Is the Issue?

Nowhere is the question of the relationship between the gospel and culture more relevant than in the majority world. Followers of Christ are faced with this enigmatic challenge every day and in all walks of life. An encounter, some years ago, with an auto rickshaw driver in the city of Chennai brings this into sharp relief. As I got into his vehicle, I noticed a picture of Jesus with a bleeding heart on his windscreen. I, naturally, asked him if he was a Roman Catholic, but his response stopped me dead in my tracks. He said, "Sir, I am *Hindu*, but I follow *Christ!*" The story of how his wife and mother-in-law were freed from demonic possession when a pastor prayed for them and how they put faith in Christ is not unique and is one among the hundreds of stories we hear in India. What was new—and refreshing, I may add—was how he identified himself both as a follower of Christ and as a Hindu. As I probed deeper, I realized he viewed himself as a Hindu from a cultural perspective and as a follower of Christ from a faith perspective. Questions began to flood my mind. Are these two positions mutually exclusive? What does it mean to be a Hindu culturally and yet come under the lordship of Christ? How would the church consider him? How would the church disciple such a person without causing him to lose both his cultural identity and his faith identity?

Generally speaking, our understanding of the gospel (i.e., Jesus Christ) is one colored by a "Christianized" version. By *Christianized*, I refer to theological perspectives that are heavily influenced by the Christendom construct and its adherents. This Christianized portrayal of the gospel—where to be "Christian" is to be accepting of a Western culture and lifestyle—has, over the years, been the dominant force in evangelism and cultural engagement. The underlying assumption is that to be Christian is to appropriate a narrative from the West, which in itself is contextual to a particular worldview. Historically, the "Latinization" of the gospel was prevalent in the early missionary endeavors to Asia, beginning from the sixteenth century. Examples of the wholesale rejection of anything local and the imposition of all things foreign abound.[1] Such a position represents a monocultural understanding and presentation of the gospel. Herein lies the problem, for this view does not take into account the "translatability" of the gospel.[2] It is imperative that we understand that the idea of translation is embedded in the biblical view of "incarnation." Perhaps this is where we must begin.

2. Where Do We Start?

I often begin my class on gospel and culture with this simple question: "Was Jesus a Christian or a Jew?" Students, more often than not, do a double take, unsure of how to respond. Slowly, however, as the realization of what I am emphasizing sinks in, sheepish grins emerge on their faces. This is a powerful reminder that it is good for us to step back every once in a while, pause, and reorient ourselves with the right frame of reference. This frame of reference cannot be anything other than a proper understanding of the gospel presented in and through the person and work of Jesus Christ. In fact, Richard Niebuhr approaches the issue of the nature of the gospel by asking the question, "Who is Jesus?" This, surely, is the crux of the issue. As much as a faith perspective provides a theological response, the historical reality of a man who lived in Palestine as Jesus clarifies the human aspects of culture and context.

Our view of incarnation, therefore, is central to making sense of the interface between the gospel and the plurality of cultures it encounters. John's statement in his prologue, "The Word became flesh and dwelt [pitched his tent among humankind] among us" (John 1:14 RSV), sets the tone for any discussion on the gospel and culture. This assertion goes hand in hand with Philippians 2:7–8 RSV,

---

1. Paul Cornelius, "Christianity in Asia: Movement and Maturity in Mission" (paper presented at the ATA Triennial General Assembly, Chongshin University, South Korea, July 25–29, 2016).
2. See Lamin Sanneh, *Translating the Message: The Missionary Impact on Culture* (Maryknoll, NY: Orbis, 1989).

where Paul clearly states that Christ was born in the "likeness of men" and was "found in human form." Most students of the Bible would emphasize Christ becoming like and identifying with humanity in its broadest application. While this is not a wrong interpretation, it unfortunately ignores the more nuanced reading that must include the particularities of the cultural context in which the gospel took human form. That the gospel (i.e., Jesus) took root in the Jewish culture and worked itself out in the lives of people who came in touch with it is critical for us to appreciate.

The more rooted the gospel is in a culture, the more influence it has in the transformation of deeply embedded worldviews and lifestyles. Alan Hirsch describes this as a downward rooting and outward influencing process.[3] Conceivably, this is partly what "[the emptying of] himself," in respect of Jesus, involved (Phil 2:7). A phrase in the movie *Avatar* throws light on this notion of emptying: "You cannot fill a vessel that is already full!" In effect (for those who have seen the movie and know the context), to be rooted in a culture is to strip one's self of the cultural trappings and thought patterns that are familiar and put on the unfamiliar in order to make sense of and become relevant to the host culture. In essence, this is what the incarnation is. Admittedly, this understanding has limitations, given the finiteness of human understanding, but perhaps it offers us a way forward. The incarnation exemplifies for us how the pure essence of the gospel in the person of Jesus Christ took deep root in the midst of a people and culture. The gospel then became an influence from the inside out, shaping, changing, and transforming worldviews and behavior. Here is where the relevance and effectiveness of the gospel are evident.

3. What Does This Volume Say?

For the serious theologian and pastor, first, the task is to deconstruct the version of the gospel that came in the garb of another culture to the biblical essential. It calls for a stripping away of the contextual

---

3. Alan Hirsch, *The Forgotten Ways: Reactivating the Missional Church* (Grand Rapids, MI: Brazos Press, 2006), 127–48.

and cultural trappings to which the gospel is bound. It is, in effect, a decontextualizing of a gospel that was already contextualized to a particular audience. Second, it calls for a reclothing of that essential truth in ways that becomes relevant, understandable, and meaningful to the new cultural context in which it is birthed. This is no easy task, given the already prejudiced notions of the gospel in many of our contexts. This particular volume does not shy away from this undertaking. The contributions of several fine theologians, biblical scholars, and practitioners are part of an already vibrant conversation. The reader of this volume will soon realize that all the writers hold Scripture in high regard and in no way compromise this bedrock of the Christian faith. The contributions that make up this book address the issue from biblical, theological, and missiological perspectives. Matters of contextualization are interwoven into the fabric of the content.

In this volume, Ken Gnanakan launches the conversation with a comprehensive overview of the core issues surrounding the notions of culture and the gospel. He provides broad brushstrokes on the dynamic between the two and clearly provides the conceptual and historical backdrop to the rest of the contributions. It is important to note his assertion that "there is no such thing as one Christian culture." While Gnanakan takes a positive view of culture, he also provides a solid affirmation of the gospel. He argues for a nuanced approach to the gospel and its engagement with culture(s). As "evangelicals," Gnanakan reminds us that we have generally been suspicious of and cautious in our approach to culture. This approach to culture(s), he reminds us, was evident in the writings of secular authors. But there has been a shift in the last six decades or so, beginning with the Lausanne gathering in 1974. He concludes by stating, "The gospel is only comprehensible within cultures, as diverse or as fallen as they are."

The next five contributions offer the reader with a strong biblical framework, providing several specific examples of how the biblical writers engaged with their culture(s). Manoja Kumar Korada, Andrew B. Spurgeon, Eric R. Montgomery, Arren Bennet Lawrence, and Johnson Thomaskutty demonstrate serious engagement with the text, arguing for a strong biblical imperative toward the plurality of cultures as a biblical given, thereby prompting a closer look at how the gospel must respond to this lived reality.

Manoja Kumar Korada addresses the issue of plurality from the Old Testament and asks, "Why does the narrator of Genesis reject a global monoculture but retain the 'many'?" Andrew B. Spurgeon's chapter, "'The God of the Nations' (Rom 3:29): A Pharisee's Confession?," forcefully argues for a deep and meaningful engagement with Indian culture, all from Paul's experience and witness to Yahweh in the plurality of his own context. Spurgeon builds his case from the New Testament, emphasizing that God was not only the God of the Jews but "the God of the nations." He founds his thinking on several premises, beginning with God as the creator of all and moving to his salvific work on the cross, which is available to all. Similarly, Eric R. Montgomery uses Galatians and how Paul addresses the triple cultural identity that his readers faced. Parallels are drawn to the present readers' situation and context, especially in relation to the religious and cultural practice of applying the bindi in India. Arren Bennet Lawrence does a careful study of Paul's use of the Torah to guide Paul's response to cultural practices in Corinth. He emphasizes both how Paul affirmed certain practices and how he stood firm against other practices that were opposed to his strong belief in the Torah. Johnson Thomaskutty adeptly uses Richard Niebuhr's *Christ and Culture* categories as a framework to describe Jesus's interactions and engagement in John's Gospel. Jesus, as the one "from above," demonstrates an active engagement with the ones "from below" not only in demonstrating a clash of cultures but also in appropriating and becoming part of "humanness," thereby bringing transformation in all aspects of human culture and lived experience.

The chapters by Aruthuckal Varughese John and Prabhu Singh Vedhamanickam bring significant theological and missiological insights from the Indian context. Varughese John dives deep into a discussion of truth predicates in a Hindu context and the gospel's response in the context of discussions surrounding identity and conversion. Vedhamanickam offers broad brushstrokes from an anthropological and missiological perspective, a nuanced understanding of culture and the misconceptions that attend it, and approaches that the church can use in its engagement in the Indian context.

In the final piece, Darrell Bock presents the reader with a solid biblical exposition of the type of engagement that a Christ follower must embrace. Clear biblical standards on tone, attitude, and approach provide Christ followers a meaningful way to engage with the culture and context they find themselves in.

These excellent contributions present ways of taking this important conversation further. While almost all the authors are rooted primarily in the Indian context, their reflections and theologizing speak to the diversity of contexts across the globe. Uniquely, too, as much as Richard Niebuhr's categories provide a basic framework for understanding the interface between the gospel and culture, the authors take it further by either providing a solid application of these categories or, as is the case with Vedhamanickam, suggesting categories that are born out of the Indian experience. Either way, this volume is relevant both for the Indian and also the global church.

There is no doubt in my mind that this conversation will always be ongoing and one that future generations of Christ followers will engage with in the realities of their contexts. I am reminded of an interaction on Facebook that illustrates this well. A few years ago, a friend had posted a picture of silhouetted hands raised in worship with the following comment: "Finally, this generation has discovered what true worship is!" As I reflected on his comment, I realized how flawed his thinking was. I responded by posting the following assertion: "Every generation must discover for itself what authentic worship is!" This volume does not presume to provide the answers to the critical and nuanced issues of how the gospel relates to culture(s) for all time. But what it does, from this generational point of view, is demonstrate and suggest ways for meaningful and fruitful engagement with our lived realities.

Till God's reign is established on all the earth!

Bibliography

Cornelius, Paul. "Christianity in Asia: Movement and Maturity in Mission." Paper presented at the ATA Triennial General Assembly, Chongshin University, South Korea, July 25–29, 2016.

Sanneh, Lamin. *Translating the Message: The Missionary Impact on Culture.* Maryknoll, NY: Orbis, 1989.

I

One Gospel in Many Cultures

KEN GNANAKAN

1. The Gospel and Culture

The gospel, the Bible asserts, came into a real world, within real history. Therefore, one of the first consequences must be that there is no such thing as one Christian culture or a pure gospel culture separated from alien cultures that we are located within. We are all part of our cultures, and in a real sense, the gospel is not actualized until it has become part of each of these varied cultures. In other words, the gospel touches human beings in their own cultures, as it touched the disciples in their culture when Jesus walked this earth. It is the one true gospel, becoming flesh in varied cultures.

Culture has undoubtedly been a bit of a controversial word with various attitudes, particularly when it comes to its identification with our faith. "We must not mix Christianity with culture," some naively maintain, while others are totally enslaved to their cultures. The truth, as always, must be discovered somewhere in between, as culture is an important aspect of human beings, and yet not all aspects of culture are to be condoned. The gospel comes to us in our cultures, whether they are good or bad.

There is an important corollary: there is no cultureless gospel, or cultureless Christianity, or even cultureless scripture. Our scripture is given within particular contexts, and we need to understand these contexts in order to truly interpret scripture. Scripture reveals God, and even God's "revelation is given within the particularities of history and locality."[1] Paul G. Hiebert says, "While affirming that Scripture is divine revelation, it is important to keep in mind that the Scriptures themselves were given to humans in particular historical and socio-cultural contexts. This is obvious to Old and New Testament scholars but is often overlooked by ordinary Christians. Differentiating between eternal truth and the particular contexts in the Bible is not an easy task, but is essential if we are to understand the heart of the Gospel, which is for everyone."[2]

2. What Is Culture?

But what is culture? Although culture has gone through an evolution in its understanding, in its basic form, it consists of the values, beliefs, behaviors, and other peculiarities common to the members of a particular group. People and groups define themselves, share their commonalities—language, food, habits, or customs—and declare their identities through whatever is characteristic of their "culture" and therefore their society. Sometimes culture and society are spoken about synonymously, as culture belongs to society and any society is empty without its culture. No wonder, Albert Camus said, "without culture, and the relative freedom it implies, society, even when perfect, is but a jungle."[3] The word *culture* also finds itself used in the sense of being "civilized" or of a higher order than the average. We sometimes speak of a highly "cultured gentleman." It is in this sense that Jawaharlal Nehru said, "Culture is the widening of the mind and of the spirit."[4]

The *Dictionary of Modern Sociology* defines culture as "the total, generally organised way of life, including values, norms, institutions, and artifacts, that is passed on from generation to generation

---

1. Paul G. Hiebert, *The Gospel in Human Contexts: Anthropological Explorations for Contemporary Mission* (Grand Rapids, MI: Baker Academic, 2009), 29.
2. Hiebert, 29.
3. Albert Camus, *The Myth of Sisyphus and Other Essays* (New York: Vintage, 1991), 212.
4. Quoted in A. R. Rather, *Theory and Principles of Education* (New Delhi: Discovery, 2004), 212.

by learning alone."[5] One of the oldest definitions of culture quoted in many works on the subject is by the British anthropologist Sir Edward Burnett Tylor (1832–1917) in the book *Primitive Culture*: "Culture is that complex whole which includes knowledge, belief, art, morals, law, customs and other capabilities and habits acquired by man as a member of society."[6]

Asians, Africans, and Latin Americans have been devastated by faulty notions of culture that have been handed down as part of the gospel. Charles H. Kraft writes, "One of the tragedies of American (including missionary) attempts to help other peoples is that we have so often shown little respect for their traditional customs."[7]

Culture in the popular sense refers to a whole way of life and is characteristic of every society. We begin to see the gospel really taking roots in all of society and culture, not distanced from these realities. And the gospel grows in our cultures because God sent his Son into this world—"the word became flesh," and he dwelt with us in our real history, with real people, in a real culture. This is the same gospel that moved from its Jewish roots into gentile cultures and then spread to all the world. This gospel encountered cultures, transforming them and societies that existed within them, not just converting individuals.

3. The Missionary Movement

Before we proceed further, it is helpful for us to identify a problem. The Western missionary enterprise was not an isolated happening. It was part of a whole movement of imperialistic culture that evolved over those centuries. For instance, I grew up watching the *Tarzan the Ape Man* movies and reading the comic books. Although first

---

5. T. F. Hoult, *Dictionary of Modern Sociology* (New York: Littlefield, Adams, 2006), 38.

6. Edward Burnett Tylor, *Primitive Culture: Researches into the Development of Mythology, Philosophy, Religion, Art, and Custom*, vol. 1 (Cambridge: Cambridge University Press, 1871), 1.

7. Charles H. Kraft, "Culture Worldview and Contextualization," in *Perspectives on the World Christian Movement: A Reader*, ed. Ralph D. Winter and Steven C. Hawthorne (Pasadena, CA: William Carey Library, 1999), 386.

published in 1912, the popularity of the character endured for several decades. Literary critics tell us that in reality, these representations were cleverly portraying Western caricatures of Africa. Tarzan—the perfectly built, strong, white man—had an ape as his companion, which was obviously superior to the native Africans, who were portrayed as the typical savages. Even the "Me Tarzan, me white man, me king of the jungle" slogan was an attitude of cultural superiority that excluded all those whose skin color or class status was Black.

And a popular novel by Joseph Conrad painted Congo as an essentially corrupting place inhabited by ruthless cannibals. His novel *Heart of Darkness*, inspired by his visit to the region in 1890, portrays Africa as "the other world," the antithesis of Europe and therefore of civilization, a place where Western civilization finds its stark—perhaps more rightly, "dark"—contrast.[8] Not just the people; even the River Congo was the very antithesis of the Thames. The novel explored the savage-versus-civilized relationship and the colonialism and racism that made imperialism possible.

Edward Said, the Palestinian American academic, political activist, and literary critic, thoroughly analyzes such cultural representations in colonial literature and uses the term *Orientalism* to consider how the West perceives of and represents the East. For Said, Orientalist scholarship is inextricably tied to the imperialist societies that produce it and contain an inherently political and imperialistic agenda. His book *Orientalism* (1977) has been influential not only in literary studies (English, comparative literature) but also in history, anthropology, sociology, Middle East studies, and comparative religion. One major premise in *Orientalism* is that culture, in many ways, prepares, precedes, imposes, and finally proceeds to imperial domination. Said argues that much of Western culture has been historically engaged in the Western project of empire building. Culture is the instrument of imperialism. Said emphasizes, "We cannot understand the power of imperialism until we understand the importance of culture."[9] One would agree that the degradation of the many Afri-

---

8. Joseph Conrad, *Heart of Darkness*, Dover thrift ed. (New York: Dover, 1990).
9. Edward Said, *Orientalism* (London: Penguin, 1977), 15.

can countries on the basis of culture is an embarrassing aberration in the Western missionary enterprise.

It is from this perspective that Kwame Bediako, the late Ghanaian theologian, and his critique of the impact of the West, specifically Western mission, on African culture and identity should be read.[10] He argues that the gospel was taken to Africa by many from the West who exhibited their cultural superiority. Bediako describes how the missionaries thought their enterprise was part of a benevolent Western movement that strived to elevate the condition of African peoples, and this meant that Africans must be given not only Christianity but also a total Western cultural package.[11]

A popular statement of the imperialistic mindset is summed up in Rudyard Kipling's well-known quote, "East is east and west is west and never the twain shall meet."[12] One should either impose the West on the East or allow the East to be separate from the West seems to be what is implied. However, with our global scene today, this view no longer holds any water. Each culture is unique. In fact, South Indian culture is one of the oldest and most influential. Globalization is making its influence, but the intricacies still remain. We need to see how the gospel binds our diverse cultures as one within God's ultimate kingdom culture rather than one superior culture imposing itself on others.

4. Culture and the Gospel

Charles H. Kraft, an influential missionary teacher on the subject, is one who has dared to enter into the whole culture debate. He has written extensively on the Bible and culture, communicating biblical Christianity in cultures, anthropology, cross-cultural Christian

---

10. Kwame Bediako, *Theology and Identity* (Oxford: Regnum Studies in Mission, 1969).
11. Bediako, 227–28.
12. Rudyard Kipling, Eileen Gillooly, and Jim Sharpe, "The Ballad of East and West," in *Poetry for Young People,* ed. Eileen Gillooly (New York: Sterling, 2000), 26.

theology, worldviews, and other related topics.[13] He writes, "Human beings are thoroughly immersed in culture. Each human individual is born into a particular society and immediately begins a lifelong training process (technically known as enculturation) by means of which he or she is thoroughly indoctrinated into that society's culture. . . . Values, attitudes, worldview and the majority of basic patterns of the society's cultures are made their own even before children become old. What then seems natural and normal to the rest of society seems natural and normal to them. What seems unnatural to the rest of society seems unnatural to them."[14]

The importance of culture is clearly spelled out, particularly the inseparability of human beings from their culture. Even the phrase "thoroughly immersed" seems inadequate, as it gives the impression that humans are on the outside and take a plunge into culture. We belong to our culture, and as Kraft himself describes, it is so much an integral part of our existence that "human beings, like fish, can live inside a culture but not outside of one."[15] Here are a few excerpts:

We cannot live without culture. It is that matrix within which we "live and move and exist" (Acts 17.28), the non-biological, non-environmental part of our lives that we learn from our elders, that we share with our community, and in which we are totally submerged from one end of life to the other.[16]

The way of Jesus is . . . to honor a people's culture, not to wrest them from it. Just as he entered the cultural life of first century Palestine

---

13. Charles H. Kraft and Marguerite G. Kraft, *Christianity in Culture: A Study in Dynamic Biblical Theologizing in Cross-Cultural Perspective* (Maryknoll, NY: Orbis, 1978); Charles H. Kraft, *Issues in Contextualization* (Pasadena, CA: William Carey Library, 2016); Charles H. Kraft, *Communicating Jesus' Way*, rev. ed. (Pasadena, CA: William Carey Library, 2013); Charles H. Kraft, *Worldview for Christian Witness* (Pasadena, CA: William Carey Library, 1997); Charles H. Kraft, *Anthropology for Christian Witness* (Maryknoll, NY: Orbis, 1996).

14. Charles H. Kraft, *Culture, Communication and Christianity: A Selection of Writings* (Pasadena, CA: William Carey Library, 2001), 21.

15. Kraft, 46.

16. Kraft, 45.

in order to communicate with them, so we are to enter the cultural matrix of people we seek to win.[17]

We are concerned about spelling out the whole gospel within the real world, and to help us place culture in this direction, Kraft elucidates some valuable characteristics.[18] These characteristics enable us to see the complexity, integration, continuity, and dynamic nature of culture that makes the gospel truly fleshed out, as it adapts itself within various cultures as naturally as possible. However, in contrast, we have entertained certain fixed aspects forced down into cultures, claiming that there is a universality to Christianity that is supracultural.

Importantly, there is a continuity to culture that connects us to the past as society evolves: "Culture is a legacy from the past. The customs we practice were developed by past generations . . . this fact provides cultural continuity from generation to generation. It also provides the present generation with wisdom from the past."[19] This continuity is important, reminding us that we do not break from our cultures but build on them, transforming them as the gospel enters in.

5. Christ and Culture

No discussion on culture in Christian circles is complete without some reference to Richard Niebuhr's celebrated book *Christ and Culture*. Niebuhr provides five views on culture: Christ against culture, Christ of culture, Christ above culture, Christ and culture in paradox, and Christ the transformer of culture. These categories show how Christians have attempted to deal with this "enduring problem," which is, to Niebuhr, the relationship between "Christianity and civilization."[20]

---

17. Kraft, 46.
18. Kraft, 53–59.
19. Kraft, 56.
20. Richard Niebuhr, *Christ and Culture*, reprint ed. (New York: Harper & Row, 2001), 1.

What Niebuhr refers to as the "enduring problem" is critical to his categorization. He asks, Because we know Christ is perfect/sinless, and if culture is created by humans, and since humans are imperfect/ sinful, how can Christ mingle with imperfection? Our response is also confused by passages in the Bible that suggest we should be away from the world and other verses that suggest we should be in the world. The value of Niebuhr's contribution is his description of Christian responses to culture in the five approaches.

The first position is "Christ against culture." Niebuhr sees this as a radical reaction in which all loyalty is given to Christ and all claims to loyalty by culture are rejected. This appears to be the position of the early Christians as well as those involved in monasticism. They separated themselves from the culture of the world. For Niebuhr, this view does not adequately recognize Jesus's and the Spirit's roles in creation. He says, "Their rejection of culture is easily combined with a suspicion of nature and nature's God . . . ultimately they are tempted to divide the world in the material realm governed by a principle opposed to Christ and a spiritual realm governed by the spiritual God."[21]

The second position is the "Christ of culture," where theological foundations for identifying Christ with the cultural achievements of Christians are identified. Here we see an engagement in social good as the best way to be an example of Christ. Those who hold this position "feel no great tension between church and world, the social laws and the Gospel."[22] However, there is an interesting tension: "On the one hand they interpret culture through Christ, where those aspects that are most like Jesus are given most honor. On the other hand, they interpret Christ through culture, selecting from his teaching that which best harmonizes with the best in civilization."[23]

The third position is that of "Christ above culture." Jesus Christ in this position is part of the culture but located above it as both an example and source. This position portrays Christ as the fulfillment

---

21. Niebuhr, 81.
22. Niebuhr, 83.
23. Niebuhr, 83.

of cultural aspiration and the restorer of the institutions of true society. This view does not consider Christ and culture in conflict; the conflict is between a holy God and a sinful man. Thomas Aquinas followed this approach.

The fourth approach, "Christ and culture in paradox," occurs when both Christ and culture are understood as good even though they remain irreconcilable. This strategy promises most fully to preserve the tension between the two sources of norms, as it works to generate an honest portrayal of our condition as Christians with dissonant values. This view will hold together "loyalty to Christ and responsibility for culture"[24] even though followers believe that this cooperation is not a happy balance. The conflict between Christ and culture enables us to see both sin and grace.

The fifth approach is "Christ the transformer of culture," and this was best represented by Augustine in *The City of God*.[25] Human nature is corrupt, but culture can, and must, be transformed. There is hope of transformation through Christ. The theological conviction comes from belief in God as creator, anticipating that there will be God's dramatic interaction with humankind in historical human events.[26] There is hope in transformation through the grace of God.

Niebuhr himself was aware that there was no final formulation— no single viewpoint, no final solution, no one formulation that might capture the right and proper relationship between human culture and Christ. The tension will continue. And all he does is show us all these approaches, providing us with the positive and the negative sides of both. The Evangelical church has matured, in a way, and is able to look objectively at the context today and apply biblical insights. There are signs of hope as many groups engage in culture and various cultural activities in a positive way. As we consider Niebuhr's discussion, we must accept that there is truth in each one of these.

---

24. Niebuhr, 149.
25. *De Civitate Dei*, translated in English as *The City of God*, is a book of Christian philosophy written in Latin by Augustine of Hippo in the early fifth century AD and one of his major works.
26. Augustine of Hippo, *The City of God* (New Delhi: Penguin, 2003), 194.

6. The *Willowbank Report*

Evangelicals, we must admit, have had a love-hate relationship with culture. And if Niebuhr's categorizations are to be the yardstick, our stance would range from "Christ against culture" to "Christ above culture." Some would individualize Christianity to an inner experience to such an extent that there is no interaction with culture, while others would argue for a pure Christian culture with claims that this is what can be found in the Bible. This attitude came through strongly, as we have seen, in the nineteenth century, when Christian culture was seen as being synonymous with Western culture.

This ongoing struggle is addressed in a document popularly referred to as the *Willowbank Report*. The statement came out of a consultation that followed the Lausanne Congress on World Evangelization 1974, when thirty-three theologians, anthropologists, linguists, missionaries, and pastors together from all six continents met in 1978 to study gospel and culture. One of the sentences in the preamble affirms the role of culture in the gospel, reading, "The process of communicating the gospel cannot be isolated from the human culture from which it comes, or from that in which it is to be proclaimed."[27]

Reading the document will reveal the major shift made by Evangelicals in their relation to society and culture. The Lausanne gathering in 1974 was a watershed event with its enduring Lausanne Covenant. And the *Willowbank Report* took the 1974 Lausanne findings even further. In the section entitled "The Biblical Basis of Culture," there is a reference to the earlier document: "Because man is God's creature, some of his culture is rich in beauty and goodness. Because he is fallen, all of it is tainted with sin and some of it is demonic." Importantly, there is the biblical justification for culture:

---

27. Lausanne Committee for World Evangelization, *The Willowbank Report: Consultation on Gospel and Culture*, Lausanne Occasional Paper 2, accessed March 2, 2020, https://www.lausanne.org/content/lop/lop-2. All subsequent quotations in this section of the chapter are from this source.

God created mankind male and female in his own likeness by endowing them with distinctive human faculties—rational, moral, social, creative and spiritual. He also told them to have children, to fill the earth and to subdue it (Gen. 1:26–28). These divine commands are the origin of human culture. For basic to culture are our control of nature (that is, our environment) and our development of forms of social organisation. Insofar as we use our creative powers to obey God's commands, we glorify God, serve others and fulfil an important part of our destiny on earth.

Now however, we are fallen. All our work is accompanied by sweat and struggle (Gen. 3:17–19), and is disfigured by selfishness. So none of our cultures is perfect in truth, beauty or goodness. At the heart of every culture—whether we identify this heart as religion or world-view—is an element of self-centredness, of man's worship of himself. Therefore a culture cannot be brought under the Lordship of Christ without a radical change of allegiance.

For all that, the affirmation that we are made in God's image still stands (Gen. 9:6; James 3:9), though the divine likeness has been distorted by sin. And still God expects us to exercise stewardship of the earth and of its creatures (Gen. 9:1–3, 7), and in his common grace makes all persons inventive, resourceful and fruitful in their endeavors. Thus, although Genesis 3 records the fall of humanity, and Genesis 4 Cain's murder of Abel, it is Cain's descendants who are described as the cultural innovators, building cities, breeding livestock, and making musical instruments and metal tools (Gen. 4:17–22).

There is an acceptance of the negative stance that once prevailed: "Many of us evangelical Christians have in the past been too negative towards culture. We do not forget the human fallenness and lostness which call for salvation in Christ." Despite this, there is "a positive affirmation of human dignity and human cultural achievement," acknowledging that "wherever human beings develop their social organisation, art and science, agriculture and technology, their creativity reflects that of their Creator."

In the section entitled "A Definition of Culture," there seemed to be a broad agreement with what most will affirm: "In the broadest sense, it means simply the patterned way in which people do things together. If there is to be any common life and corporate action, there must be agreement, spoken or unspoken, about a great many things." Referring to the broad spectrum the term covered, the statement also concurs, "This means that an accepted culture covers everything in human life." Importantly, it underlines the "world-view" that conditions our culture:

> At its centre is a world-view, that is, a general understanding of the nature of the universe and of one's place in it. This may be "religious" (concerning God, or gods and spirits, and of our relation to them), or it may express a "secular" concept of reality, as in a Marxist society.
>
> From this basic world-view flow both standards of judgement or values (of what is good in the sense of desirable, of what is acceptable as in accordance with the general will of the community, and of the contraries) and standards of conduct (concerning relations between individuals, between the sexes and the generations, with the community and with those outside the community).

We all belong to particular cultures. "The worst penalty that can be inflicted on the rebel is exclusion from the culturally defined social community," the group agrees. Hence, "participation in a culture is one of the factors which provide them with a sense of belonging. It gives a sense of security, of identity, of dignity, of being part of a larger whole, and of sharing both in the life of past generations and in the expectancy of society for its own future." The authors continue,

> Biblical clues to the understanding of the human culture are found in the threefold dimension of people, land, and history, on which the Old Testament focuses attention. The ethnic, the territorial, and the historical (who, where and whence we are) appear there as the triple source of economic, ecological, social and artistic forms of human life in Israel, of the forms of labour and production, and so of wealth and well-being. This model provides a perspective for interpreting all cultures.

Perhaps we may try to condense these various meanings as follows: Culture is an integrated system of beliefs (about God or reality or ultimate meaning), of values (about what is true, good, beautiful and normative), of customs (how to behave, relate to others, talk, pray, dress, work, play, trade, farm, eat, etc.), and of institutions which express these beliefs, values and customs (government, law courts, temples or churches, family, schools, hospitals, factories, shops, unions, clubs, etc.), which binds a society together and gives it a sense of identity, dignity, security, and continuity.

The *Willowbank Report* has a section that relates directly to our discussion of the gospel in culture. As it is clearly stated in the section entitled "The Bible and the Gospel," "The gospel is like a multifaceted diamond, with different aspects that appeal to different people in different cultures. The Bible proclaims the gospel story in many forms. It has depths we have not fathomed. It defies every attempt to reduce it to a neat formulation." Most importantly, "it is necessary to add that no theological statement is culture-free." The authors write,

In our desire to communicate the gospel effectively, we are often made aware of those elements in it which people dislike. For example, the cross has always been both an offense to the proud and folly to the wise. But Paul did not on that account eliminate it from his message. On the contrary, he continued to proclaim it, with faithfulness and at the risk of persecution, confident that Christ crucified is the wisdom and the power of God. We too, although concerned to contextualize our message and remove from it all unnecessary offense, must resist the temptation to accommodate it to human pride or prejudice. It has been given to us. Our responsibility is not to edit it but to proclaim it.

There are some clear reminders that no Christian witness can hope to communicate the gospel if he or she ignores the cultural factor. Sometimes people resist the gospel not because they think of it as false but because they perceive it as a threat to their culture, especially the fabric of their society and their national or tribal solidarity.

Despite this, "Jesus challenges many of the cherished beliefs and customs of every culture and society." But the problem of presenting a Western religion surfaces:

> The other problem is that the gospel is often presented to people in alien cultural forms. Then the missionaries are resented and their message rejected because their work is seen not as an attempt to evangelize but as an attempt to impose their own customs and way of life. Where missionaries bring with them foreign ways of thinking and behaving, or attitudes of racial superiority, paternalism, or preoccupation with material things, effective communication will be precluded.
>
> Sometimes these two cultural blunders are committed together, and messengers of the gospel are guilty of a cultural imperialism which both undermines the local culture unnecessarily and seeks to impose an alien culture instead.

There is a call for sensitive cross-cultural witnesses, which, it is felt, "will not arrive at their sphere of service with a pre-packaged gospel." There need to be attempts to recognize these elements and present the gospel in clarity: "We are not claiming that it will be easy, although some Global South cultures have a natural affinity to biblical culture. But we believe that fresh creative understandings do emerge when the Spirit-led believing community is listening and reacting sensitively to both the truth of Scripture and the needs of the world."

7. One Gospel and Many Cultures

The point we need to affirm is becoming clear: the gospel is only comprehensible within cultures, as diverse or as fallen as they are. It is one gospel, true and God-sent. But it is realized in different cultures. Arguments for one true, pure culture—implying, perhaps, a uniform gospel—are far from the reality. There is no culture-less gospel. There are cultural influences right within the church of the New Testament itself. Andrew F. Walls has been a proponent for advocating the legitimacy of Christianity in different cultures without placing one over the other. Culture is an inevitable factor when we speak of Christianity in its missionary context. In other words, we will have to look at the gospel within real cultures, within various cultures of our world, whether they are American, European, African, or Asian.

In an essay entitled "The Gospel as Prisoner and Liberator of Culture," Walls writes,

> Church history has always been a battleground for two opposing tendencies; and the reason is that each of the tendencies has its origin in the Gospel itself. On the one hand it is of the essence of the gospel that God accepts us as we are, on the ground of Christ's work alone, not on the ground of what we have become or are trying to become. But, if He accepts us "as we are" that implies He does not take us as isolated, self-governing units, because we are not. We are conditioned by a particular time and place, by our family and group and society, by "culture" in fact. In Christ God accepts us together with our group relations; with that cultural conditioning that makes us feel at home in one part of human society and less at home in another.[28]

Walls argues for this "indigenizing principle," which associates Christians with the particulars of their culture and group. But alongside this, there is "the pilgrim principle," which is in tension with the indigenizing principle. The adoption into Israel becomes a "universalizing" factor, bringing Christians of all cultures and ages together through a common inheritance, lest any of us make the Christian faith such a place to feel at home that no one else can live there, and bringing into everyone's society some sort of outside reference.[29]

---

28. Andrew F. Walls, "The Gospel as Prisoner and Liberator of Culture," in *The Missionary Movement in Christian History: Studies in the Transmission of Faith*, ed. Andrew F. Walls (New York: Orbis, 1996), 7.

29. Walter A. Elwell, *Evangelical Dictionary of Theology* (Grand Rapids, MI: Baker Academic, 1984), 294.

Walls touches upon a very important aspect. While we are all local through the indigenizing principle at work, we are also interacting with other cultures through the pilgrim principle. And eventually, the universalizing principle brings us all into a common culture within the kingdom of God. The gospel binds the church worldwide together through this universalizing principle, into a wholeness that is characteristic of this gospel.[30]

8. Culture and Contextualization

Walls refers to the indigenizing principle, and that leads us to a brief reference to the whole movement of indigenization. Indigenization was a missionary tool or strategy for the effective communication of the gospel in a form that would be acceptable to its hearers. This made the message as external as the missionaries themselves, and the concept, therefore, had its limitations. Contextualization takes us further. It came into use in 1972, when Shoki Coe and Aharon Sapsezian, directors of the Theological Education Fund (TEF), proposed the term to imply everything of indigenization but also to include all the struggles and injustices that were faced in the Global South as well as the process of secularity and its associated factors.[31]

Veteran missionary Bruce J. Nicholls suggests that missionaries from the Global South must understand four cultures: "the Bible's, the Western missionaries' who first brought the gospel, their own, and the people's to whom they take the gospel."[32] Recognizing this, Nicholls proposes that the gospel be contextualized—that is, presented in forms that are characteristic of the culture to which the gospel is taken. The problem is to find the right cultural forms and thus keep the gospel message both clear and biblical.

The gospel came into culture and, as we have seen, adapts to various cultures as God fleshes out the gospel to all people all over the world. In his classic work *The Gospel in a Pluralist Society*, the

---

30. Bruce J. Nicholls, *Contextualization: A Theology of Gospel and Culture* (Vancouver: Regent College, 1979), 32.
31. Nicholls, 21.
32. Nicholls, 7.

renowned missionary statesman Lesslie Newbigin, in a chapter entitled "Contextualization: True and False," makes very perceptive observations that will help us bring the gospel to focus within cultures. He says, "The gospel is addressed to human beings, to their minds and hearts and consciences, and calls for their response. Human beings only exist as members of communities which share a common language, customs, ways of ordering economic and social life, ways of understanding and coping with their world."[33] He adds,

> If the gospel is to be understood, if it is to be received as something which communicates truth about the real human situation, if it is, as we say, to "make sense" it has to be communicated in the language of those to whom it is addressed and has to be clothed in symbols which are meaningful to them. And since the gospel does not come as a disembodied message, but as the message of a community which claims to live by it and which invites others to adhere to it the community's life must be so ordered that it "make sense" to those who are invited. It must as we say, "come alive."[34]

The inevitable fact of cultural influences on the gospel message needs to be emphasized: "There is no such thing as a pure gospel if by that is meant something which is not embodied in a culture."[35] Newbigin comments,

> Every interpretation of the gospel is embodied in some cultural form. The missionary does not come with the pure gospel and then adapt it to the culture where she serves; she comes with a gospel which is already embodied in the culture by which the missionary was formed. And this is so from the very beginning. The Bible is a book which is very obviously in a specific cultural setting. Its language is Hebrew and Greek, not Chinese or Sanskrit. All the events it records, all the teachings it embodies are shaped by specific human

---

33. Lesslie Newbigin, *The Gospel in a Pluralist Society* (London: SPCK, 1989), 141.
34. Newbigin, 141.
35. Newbigin, 148.

cultures. And of course, it could not possibly be otherwise. Something which is not expressible in any human language, which is not embodied in any human way of living, which is not located in any specific time, or place, can have no impact on human affairs.[36]

9. Cross-Cultural or Intracultural Mission

Mission, at least by the Evangelicals, has widely been considered "cross-cultural," meaning that the message was taken from one culture to the other—and was, in earlier times, invariably from the West to the rest. In *Kingdom Concerns*, written in 1989, I discussed an aspect that could be crucial to a more holistic interpretation of the gospel within our cultures today.[37] This was the concept of intracultural mission.

Mission in the eighteenth and nineteenth centuries, in the heyday of Western missions, operated with an optimistic view of Western culture. It was the time of colonization and the accompanying attitude of cultural imperialism that prevailed. It cannot be denied that there were many positive results, and with men and women going to the "ends of the earth," many cultures were transformed. But Christianity was still perceived by many as a Western or even a "white" religion. Those like Mahatma Gandhi and Rabindranath Tagore spoke out in India, reminding Western missionaries as well as Indian Christians of the dangers of disparaging Indian culture.

The concept of cross-cultural mission needs to be reconsidered in order to bring wholeness to the mission movement today. This will also serve well to avoid the danger of an unintended cultural invasion. The concept is clear: the "missionary," it was thought, needed to get out of his or her culture in order to be true to this kind of mission. There is still a continuing conception with views that "Evangelism refers to same-culture witness . . . in contrast missions refers to cross-cultural witness and is the only way to reach people who have

---

36. Newbigin, 144.
37. Ken Gnanakan, *Kingdom Concerns: A Biblical Exploration towards a Theology of Mission* (Bangalore: Theological Book Trust, 1989).

no near-neighbour Christians who can evangelise them."[38] I have no problem with this, as long as we accept that the task of mission is for everybody.

Cross-cultural mission has biblical support. Jesus himself commanded his disciples to "go into all the world" (Mark 16:15). The apostle Paul declared to the church in Rome that he was "obligated both to Greeks and non-Greeks" (Rom 1:14 NIV). Why was he obligated? Paul's driving desire to take the gospel where God had called him is compelling. William Carey, C. T. Studd, David Livingstone, and many others went in response to such a compelling call. The concept of cross-cultural mission may be controversial in our contemporary context, but there is no denying the fact that the influence of the gospel has been taken far and wide because of this persuasive phase in the history of missions.

However, there is an equally strong motivation for mission to be considered within local cultural contexts. The Thessalonian Christians had become models to their own people, and the message had spread. Christian mission is no longer a matter of missionaries from the West going to the rest of the world. Rather, as we study the growth of Christianity in Latin America, Africa, and parts of Asia today, it is eclipsing that of the Western church through movements from within these countries. Christian mission today is truly global, with missionaries from all places going to all peoples. Veteran missiologist Samuel Escobar explores these new realities of our globalized world and sets forth a thoroughly biblical theology of missions, considering how God the Father, Son, and Holy Spirit are at work around the world.[39]

Similarly, Michael Nazir-Ali's book *From Everywhere to Everywhere* captures the essence of this new move in mission. It is no longer from the West to the East, and as he states, "There is no single

---

38. Timothy C. Tennent, *Invitation to World Missions: A Trinitarian Missiology for the Twenty-First Century*, Invitation to Theological Study Series (Grand Rapids, MI: Kregel, 2010), 371–72.

39. Samuel Escobar, *The New Global Mission: The Gospel from Everywhere to Everyone, Christian Doctrine in Global Perspective* (Downers Grove, IL: IVP Academic, 2003), 119–20.

missionary history of the church. Different families of churches, different geographical areas and particular clusters of churches may each have had their own missionary history."[40]

There is no doubt that the gospel crosses cultures, and in fact, it is a transworld phenomenon. But even more, the gospel penetrates local cultures. And this calls for the locals to be engaged in missions within their own cultures. This is what I refer to as "intracultural mission," which should be as much a motivation for missions as cross-cultural missions.

Within the climate of criticisms still being faced alongside increasing nationalistic temperaments, there is need for a truly biblical approach that will make Christianity accepted as a local religion, recognizable within local cultures. Apart from any cultural imperialistic attitude that needs to be obliterated, there is also the need for us to understand that there is no such thing as a universal Christian culture or even gospel that is contained in fixed forms. The gospel is a seed that needs to be planted in various cultural soils and allowed to grow naturally and produce fruit within varied conditions.

10. Indianization, Hinduization, and Hindutva

Christians are facing a threat from various conflicting forces in our country today. Right-wing influences are misinterpreting everything we claim and state. We've had the recent incident when the archbishop of Delhi called for a yearlong prayer campaign to save India from the "turbulent political atmosphere" that has threatened the democratic principles of its constitution and secular fabric.[41]

Wanting to impose a Hindu culture, groups like Bajrang Dal, Vishwa Hindu Parishad, Dharma Raksha Sena, and such others allegedly patronized by the Rashtriya Swayamsevak Sangh

---

40. Michael Nazir-Ali, *From Everywhere to Everywhere: A World View of Christian Mission* (London: HarperCollins, 1990), 30.

41. "Delhi Archbishop's Letter: Turbulent Political Atmosphere, Let's Pray for New Govt in 2019," *India Today*, May 22, 2018, https://www.indiatoday.in/india/story/delhi-archbishop-s-letter-turbulent-political-atmosphere-let-s-pray-for-new-govt-in-2019-1238564-2018-05-22.

(RSS)—and implicitly, the Bharatiya Janata Party (BJP)—seem to be telling us what we should be to be truly Indian. Whether it is cow slaughter or conversions, there is a deeper cultural threat lurking behind. It is the imposition of a Hindutva culture, not a Hindu culture. Is there a difference?

Member of Parliament Shashi Tharoor's recent book *Why I Am a Hindu* exposes this critical issue of our time—the difference between Hinduism and Hindutva.[42] While Hinduism has a distinct cultural ethos, a pluralistic base assimilating various trends, beliefs, even "gods" within a common civilization, Hindutva asserts that Indian nationalism is the same as Hindu nationalism and that non-Hindus must acknowledge their Hindu parentage or convert to Hinduism to return to their true cultural roots.

This tension needs to be carefully resolved. On the one hand, we need to redefine our Indian Christian culture, which is the crux of our problem, but on the other hand, we must guard against forces that are forcing us into cultural identities that are not the real secular, even the pluralistic Hindu, culture that our country is reputed to have.

II. One Gospel, Many Cultures

In conclusion, our task is clear, although complex. We have been blessed with the powerful gospel of our Lord Jesus, touched and transformed by it. But we live in India with varied cultures. Our first challenge is to grasp the meaning of this gospel within the Indian cultures as against a European or an American culture. For this we need to get to the Bible itself. We must sincerely ask, How is this one true gospel actualized in a Punjabi, a Naga, or a Kerala culture?

But amid all these challenges, how blessed we are to be bearers of this glorious gospel for the whole world longing to be one with God. And we are all longing for that day when we will be part of that "great multitude that no one could count, from every nation, tribe, people and language, standing before the throne and before

---

42. Shashi Tharoor, *Why I Am a Hindu* (New Delhi: Aleph, 2018).

the Lamb. They were wearing white robes and were holding palm branches in their hands. And they cried out in a loud voice: 'Salvation belongs to our God, who sits on the throne, and to the Lamb'" (Rev 7:9–10 NIV).

Bibliography

Augustine of Hippo. *The City of God*. New Delhi: Penguin, 2003.

Bediako, Kwame. *Theology and Identity*. Oxford: Regnum Studies in Mission, 1969.

Camus, Albert. *The Myth of Sisyphus and Other Essays*. New York: Vintage, 1991.

Conrad, Joseph. *Heart of Darkness*. Dover thrift ed. New York: Dover, 1990.

Elwell, Walter A. *Evangelical Dictionary of Theology*. Grand Rapids, MI: Baker Academic, 1984.

Escobar, Samuel. *The New Global Mission: The Gospel from Everywhere to Everyone, Christian Doctrine in Global Perspective*. Downers Grove, IL: IVP Academic, 2003.

Gnanakan, Ken. *Kingdom Concerns: A Biblical Exploration towards a Theology of Mission*. Bangalore: Theological Book Trust, 1989.

Hiebert, Paul G. *The Gospel in Human Contexts: Anthropological Explorations for Contemporary Mission*. Grand Rapids, MI: Baker Academic, 2009.

Hoult, T. F. *Dictionary of Modern Sociology*. New York: Littlefield, Adams, 2006.

Kipling, Rudyard, Eileen Gillooly, and Jim Sharpe. "The Ballad of East and West." In *Poetry for Young People*, edited by Eileen Gillooly, 26–27. New York: Sterling, 2000.

Kraft, Charles H. *Anthropology for Christian Witness*. Maryknoll, NY: Orbis, 1996.

———. *Communicating Jesus' Way*. Rev. ed. Pasadena, CA: William Carey Library, 2013.

———. *Culture, Communication and Christianity: A Selection of Writings*. Pasadena, CA: William Carey Library, 2001.

———. "Culture Worldview and Contextualization." In *Perspectives on the World Christian Movement: A Reader*, edited by Ralph D. Winter and Steven C. Hawthorne, 384–391. Pasadena, CA: William Carey Library, 1999.

———. *Issues in Contextualization*. Pasadena, CA: William Carey Library, 2016.

———. *Worldview for Christian Witness*. Pasadena, CA: William Carey Library, 1997.

Kraft, Charles H., and Marguerite G. Kraft. *Christianity in Culture: A Study in Dynamic Biblical Theologizing in Cross-Cultural Perspective*. Maryknoll, NY: Orbis, 1978.

Lausanne Committee for World Evangelization. *The Willowbank Report: Consultation on Gospel and Culture*. Lausanne Occasional Paper 2. Accessed March 2, 2020. https://www.lausanne.org/content/lop/lop-2.

Nazir-Ali, Michael. *From Everywhere to Everywhere: A World View of Christian Mission*. London: HarperCollins, 1990.

Newbigin, Lesslie. *Gospel in a Pluralist Society*. London: SPCK, 1989.

Nicholls, Bruce J. *Contextualization: A Theology of Gospel and Culture*. Vancouver: Regent College, 1979.

Niebuhr, H. Richard. *Christ and Culture*. Reprint ed. New York: Harper & Row, 2001.

Rather, A. R. *Theory and Principles of Education*. New Delhi: Discovery, 2004.

Said, Edward. *Orientalism*. London: Penguin, 1977.

Tennent, Timothy C. *Invitation to World Missions: A Trinitarian Missiology for the Twenty-First Century*. Invitation to Theological Study Series. Grand Rapids, MI: Kregel, 2010.

Tharoor, Shashi. *Why I Am a Hindu*. New Delhi: Aleph, 2018.

Tylor, Edward Burnett. *Primitive Culture: Researches into the Development of Mythology, Philosophy, Religion, Art, and Custom*. Vol. 1. Cambridge: Cambridge University Press, 1871.

Walls, Andrew F. "The Gospel as Prisoner and Liberator of Culture." In *The Missionary Movement in Christian History: Studies in the Transmission of Faith*, edited by Andrew F. Walls, 3–15. New York: Orbis, 1996.

2

Why Not Mono, but Many Cultures?

Rereading the Stories of Babel and Hagar in Genesis

MANOJA KUMAR KORADA

This chapter seeks to explain the reason why the narrator of Genesis rejects a global monoculture but promotes the "many." We begin with this statement of the problem because the plurality of culture, generally, has spelled troubles for the world regardless of its accrued benefits. Wars, genocides, and cultural hegemony are some of the ugly manifestations of cultural plurality. For instance, humanity in the past centuries has suffered two devastating world wars, a Jewish Holocaust, and numerous ethnic cleansings, and currently, we are witnessing projects of cultural homogenization in pockets of the globe. This, in some ways, justifies Samuel P. Huntington's thesis, "the clash of civilizations."[1] The stories of ancient cultures seem to corroborate the view that Huntington propounds, as the modern and postmodern racial-cultural conflicts also validate. The Old Testament provides multiple narratives of ethnic-cultural-national conflicts and bloodshed. Empires such as ancient Assyria and Babylon have attempted to enculturate their subjects through language, literature, religious philosophies, and dietary regimen (Dan 1:4–5).[2] In

---

1. Samuel P. Huntington, *The Clash of Civilizations* (New York: Touchstone, 1997).
2. There are competing scholarly views that argue for and against Assyrian cultural imperialism. For the two opposing views, see Simo Parpola, "National and Ethnic Identity in the Neo-Assyrian Empire and Assyrian Empire

fact, reading the first deplorable act of humanity in the postdiluvian world, one understands that Ham's sin of viewing Noah's nakedness is transposed to the nations (Gen 10) because Noah curses the nation of Canaan (Gen 9:25). In hindsight, therefore, one may ask, Should not have Yahweh allowed Babel's survival? Or, should not have Yahweh retained a monoculture (one people/ethnicity and language, etc.) even when he dispersed humanity all over the world, since this would have minimized human woes arising out of a multicultural setting? To flip the question, why does the narrator of Genesis reject a global monoculture but retain the "many"? This chapter answers it and argues that the narrator does so because the global monoculture subverts the divine speech/word of the creational paradigm and further prevents Yahweh's speech/word-centric engagement with humanity, whereas the "many" provides a space for it. We shall substantiate this proposal by examining Babel (an example of the global monoculture; Gen 11:1–9) and the story of Hagar (an example of the "many"; Gen 16). We have selected the story of Hagar because the blessing to nations through Abraham begins with Abraham's family itself, which is a microcosm of multiethnicity.

I. The Monoculture and an Absence of Divine Word to Babel (Gen 11)

Here the issue is speech *versus* speech. It is the language or speech-centric culture that subverts and prevents Yahweh's word or his speech-centric engagement. Otherwise, Babel could have taken a different turn.

I.I. The Language or Speech-centric Monoculture of Babel
The common language and speech in the Babel narrative form the basis of a monoculture (וַיְהִי כָל־הָאָרֶץ שָׂפָה אֶחָת וּדְבָרִים אֲחָדִים; Gen 11:1).[3]

Identity in Post Empire," *JAAS* 18, no. 2 (2004): 5–22; and Ariel M. Bagg, "Palestine under Assyrian Rule: A New Look at the Assyrian Imperial Policy in the West," *JAOS* 133, no. 1 (2013): 119–44.

3. Generally, scholarly observations do not go beyond the remark of "one language." See Gordon J. Wenham, *Genesis 1–15*, WBC 1 (Waco, TX: Word Books,

Victor P. Hamilton's explanation of this issue is confusing and helpful. It is confusing because Hamilton considers the common language (שָׂפָה אֶחָת) as the lingua franca of the then world, which did not obliterate individual dialects (לְשֹׁנֹת) of different ethnic groups, especially given the fact that Genesis 11 is a "dechronolization" of the progression of events.[4] Having made this comment—of course, in consultation with a good number of scholars[5]—Hamilton finds it difficult to deal with the narrator's information of Babel becoming the source of multiple human languages. Consequently, he circumvents this issue by saying, "It is unlikely that Gen 11:1–9 can contribute much, if anything, to the origin of languages."[6] In our opinion, this difficulty can be resolved if the language at Babel is accepted as the common denominator and cultural regulator.

Hamilton's other exegetical observations are helpful. In his interpretation of Genesis 10, Hamilton provides two useful clues concerning ethnicity and language: one, in the distribution of the human race, the word גּוֹיִם refers to an aggregate of disparate ethnic groups, but מִשְׁפָּחָה refers to a close-knit ethnic identity;[7] two, there is a pattern in the distribution of language and ethnicity of Noah's descendants—namely, those of Japheth, Ham, and Shem:

בְּאַרְצֹתָם לִלְשֹׁנוֹ לְמִשְׁפְּחֹתָם
("geography" [a], "language" [b], "ethno-political identity" [c]; v. 5)
לְמִשְׁפְּחֹתָם לִלְשֹׁנֹתָם בְּאַרְצֹתָם
("ethno-political identity" [c], "language" [b], "geography" [a]; v. 20)
לְמִשְׁפְּחֹתָם לִלְשֹׁנֹתָם בְּאַרְצֹתָם
("ethno-political identity" [c], "language" [b], "geography" [a]; v. 31).[8]

1987), 238.
4. Victor P. Hamilton, *The Book of Genesis: Chapters 1–17*, NICOT 1 (Grand Rapids, MI: Eerdmans, 1990), 350–51.
5. Hamilton, 350–51.
6. Hamilton, 358.
7. Hamilton, 334.
8. Hamilton, 346.

Interestingly, despite suggesting a pattern, Hamilton declines to determine its importance, especially after having discovered a chiastic arrangement (*abc, cba*) in the colophon in Genesis 10:5, 20.[9]

However, in our opinion, this structure projects the language as the overarching, constant cultural denominator. The language component remains saddled in the middle position (*b*), while the other two, the ethno-political identity and geography, alternate their locations. The narrator may not be relegating the latter two, but by extolling the cohesive attribute of language that binds them together in a given culture (Gen 10), he is directing his line of thought toward Babel (Gen 11) so as to present a perverted story of a language-defined monoculture of the human race.

That the narrator intends to do so is clear from how he ends the genealogy of Noah's descendants in Genesis 10 and how he begins the Babel story in Genesis 11. He eliminates the linguistic supremacy in Genesis 10:32 and thereby breaks the dominant formula of *abc, cba*, and *cba* employed until that point for describing the cultural composition of each ethnic group (מִשְׁפְּחֹת בְּנֵי־נֹחַ אֵלֶּה). 10:32 contains מִשְׁפְּחֹת (לְתוֹלְדֹתָם בְּגוֹיֵהֶם וּמֵאֵלֶּה נִפְרְדוּ הַגּוֹיִם בָּאָרֶץ אַחַר הַמַּבּוּל)—, the ethno-political identity, and בָּאָרֶץ, the geography, but it omits the language. However, the narrator quickly follows it up by making the language the sole identity marker of the Babel community in Genesis 11:1 (וַיְהִי כָל־הָאָרֶץ שָׂפָה אֶחָת וּדְבָרִים אֲחָדִים)—note here a heavy emphasis on language and the omission of the ethnic constitution. This literary inversion between Genesis 10:32 and 11:1 creates a chiastic relationship among the geography, ethno-political entity, and language and synchronizes the latter two, reconfirming a language-driven monoculture at Babel:

A—מִשְׁפְּחֹת
  B—בָּאָרֶץ
  B′—כָל־הָאָרֶץ
A′ —שָׂפָה אֶחָת וּדְבָרִים אֲחָדִים

---

9. Hamilton, 343.

This structure indicates that the same language is spoken by the worldwide clan. Furthermore, the larger chiastic relationship between the orders of the three components (*abc*) up until the opening of the Babel narrative (Gen 11:1) doubly strengthens the narrator's point wherein the language, in addition to being synonymous with the ethnicity of the people, becomes the governing entity (*abc, cba, cba, ab["putative" c]*) presented as follows:

A—בְּאַרְצֹתָם לְלְשֹׁנוֹ לְמִשְׁפְּחֹתָם ("geography" [a], "language" [b], "ethno-political identity" [c]; Gen 10:5)

  B—לְמִשְׁפְּחֹתָם לִלְשֹׁנֹתָם בְּאַרְצֹתָם ("ethno-political identity" [c], "language" [b], "geography" [a]; Gen 10:20)

  B′—לְמִשְׁפְּחֹתָם לִלְשֹׁנֹתָם בְּאַרְצֹתָם ("ethno-political identity" [c], "language" [b], "geography" [a]; Gen 10:31)

A′—כָל־הָאָרֶץ שָׂפָה אֶחָת וּדְבָרִים אֲחָדִים ("geography" [a], "language" [b], "————" ["putative" c]; Gen 11:1)

While the ethnicity of a people is quite prominent in Genesis 10, its absence in the Babel narrative (A′) is immaterial to the people's cultural identity. Perhaps this is because the Babel community is a homogenous group like the sons of God. As the sons of God are identified as being a common stock by virtue of their common act—who they marry (וַיִּקְחוּ; Gen 6:2)—and not their lineage, the uniform ethnicity at Babel is identified through its communal migration, because by now, the ethnicity is subsidiary to, or dissolved in, the apriority of one language.[10] With the language-defined monoculture at Babel explicated, we should now proceed to demonstrate the rationale for its rejection—namely, the subversion and prevention of divine speech.

---

10. Philip M. Sherman makes an identical remark on the synonymy between the language and nationality at Babel, although he does not offer a serious literary analysis. Philip M. Sherman, *Babel's Tower Translated: Genesis 11 and Ancient Jewish Interpretation*, Biblical Interpretation Series 117 (Leiden: Brill, 2013), 36.

1.2. The Monoculture-Subverting Divine Speech of the Creational Paradigm

The subversion of divine speech at Babel happens in an insidious manner involving stages of imitation and inversion. The language-centric monoculture first re-creates, or even appropriates, the divine speech. Phrases such as וַיֹּאמְרוּ אִישׁ אֶל־רֵעֵהוּ הָבָה נִלְבְּנָה (Gen 11:3), הָבָה נִבְנֶה־לָּנוּ עִיר (Gen 11:4), and וְנַעֲשֶׂה־לָּנוּ (Gen 11:4) echo Genesis 1:26, וַיֹּאמֶר אֱלֹהִים נַעֲשֶׂה אָדָם. The appropriation of divine speech is further translated into imitating a divine act. Yahweh culminates his creative work by working on the soil and making his own image (וַיִּיצֶר יְהוָה אֱלֹהִים אֶת־הָאָדָם עָפָר מִן־הָאֲדָמָה, Gen 2:7; בְּצַלְמֵנוּ כִּדְמוּתֵנוּ, Gen 1:26); similarly, the people at Babel work on the soil and make bricks in order to build a city that will project or reflect their own selves (נִלְבְּנָה לְבֵנִים וְנִשְׂרְפָה לִשְׂרֵפָה וַתְּהִי לָהֶם הַלְּבֵנָה לְאָבֶן, Gen 11:3; וְנַעֲשֶׂה־לָּנוּ שֵׁם, Gen 11:4). The parallelism between נִבְנֶה־לָּנוּ עִיר and וְנַעֲשֶׂה־לָּנוּ שֵׁם shows that the city is the people's name or an extension of themselves, just as humanity is God's image. The parallelism among נִבְנֶה־לָּנוּ עִיר, וְנַעֲשֶׂה־לָּנוּ שֵׁם, and נַעֲשֶׂה אָדָם בְּצַלְמֵנוּ suggests that there is a correspondence between what humanity means to God and what the city means to the people. In other words, this speech-act combination at Babel imitates the "fiat pattern" (speech act) of Genesis 1 and even impersonates divinity.[11] Yahweh speaks and the world comes into existence; likewise, the people speaking one language (speech) attempt to make (act) a city and a tower.

However, concomitantly, the speech-act combination at Babel (imitation and impersonation) also dissembles a sinister design to subvert the created order itself. The city and the heavenward tower therein intend to connect heaven and earth so as to cancel the spatial boundary between them, merging them into an inseparable, common

---

11. For more the fiat pattern, see Richard J. Middleton, *The Liberating Image: The Imago Dei in Genesis 1* (Grand Rapids, MI: Brazos, 2005), 61, 65, 68–69, 72, 281–83. Although my analysis differs from that of Sherman, he is correct in saying that the act of naming is a divine prerogative that the Babel community is applying to itself. Sherman, *Babel's Tower*, 51–52.

whole.[12] The divine speech act in Genesis 1 not only actualizes an orderly creation but also demarcates boundaries of different spheres and entities: the verb וַיַּבְדֵּל (to divide) is used twice to separate the light from the darkness and the heaven from the earth (וַיַּעַשׂ אֱלֹהִים אֶת־הָרָקִיעַ וַיַּבְדֵּל בֵּין הַמַּיִם . . . וַיִּקְרָא אֱלֹהִים לָרָקִיעַ שָׁמָיִם . . . וַיִּקְרָא אֱלֹהִים לַיַּבָּשָׁה אֶרֶץ; Gen 1:7–10).[13] All the building projects undertaken by humanity from then up until Babel are concerned with, and confined to, the earthly realm alone: Cain's city-building project is meant for an earthly inhabitation, although he names the city in order to promote his progeny (וַיְהִי בֹּנֶה עִיר וַיִּקְרָא שֵׁם הָעִיר כְּשֵׁם בְּנוֹ חֲנוֹךְ; Gen 4:17); the work of metallurgy performed by the Cainite generation was circumscribed to the earthly realm (יוּבָל הוּא הָיָה אֲבִי כָּל־תֹּפֵשׂ כִּנּוֹר וְעוּגָב; Gen 4:21); the building of Noah's ark is to preserve and perpetuate living creatures on earth (עֲשֵׂה לְךָ תֵּבַת עֲצֵי־גֹפֶר ; . . . . וּמִכָּל־הָחַי מִכָּל־בָּשָׂר שְׁנַיִם מִכֹּל תָּבִיא אֶל־הַתֵּבָה; קִנִּים; Gen 6:14, 19). Of course, human interference in the heavenly realm is a part of the creation mandate, but that pertains only to dominating winged creatures in the air (וּרְדוּ . . . . וּבְעוֹף הַשָּׁמַיִם; Gen 1:28). In fact, Jacob's dream at Bethel (Gen 28:10–17) suggests that it is only God (not humans) who demarcates the boundary between heaven and earth, possesses the authority to connect or dissolve them.[14]

---

12. Commentators normally speak of the tower in terms of its pompousness, people's safety, and human pride. For instance, see Hamilton, *Book of Genesis*, 353. However, it is much more that. According to Terence E. Fretheim, the tower recalls or resembles "the Babylonian *ziggurat*," which provided the connection and communication between heaven and earth. However, he refuses to concede that the tower in Gen 11 intends to crash into heaven and thus overthrow God; see Terence E. Fretheim, "The Book of Genesis: Introduction, Commentary, and Reflections," in *The New Interpreter's Bible*, vol. 1, ed. Leander E. Keck et al. (Nashville: Abingdon, 1994), 412. By contrast, Wenham comments that since the sky or heaven is God's abode, the Babel community builds a skyward tower to intrude heaven so as to intersect with God and be like him. Wenham, *Genesis 1–15*, 239. Wenham seems to be correct, but the effort to be like God begins with one language, not with the tower. As I have shown, the tower is an outcome of the speech-act combination.

13. Thus John W. Rogerson, "Genesis 1–11," in *Genesis and Exodus*, ed. John W. Rogerson, R. W. L. Moberly, and W. Johnstone (Sheffield, UK: Sheffield Academic, 2001), 79.

14. My observation is different from how Sherman analyzes it. See Sherman, *Babel's Tower*, 57–58.

Hence, the speech act at Babel seeks to overturn the speech act of the creation story (Gen 1), with its adverse implications for humanity. It is true, as Gordon J. Wenham comments, that the tower was very small from heaven's perspective, and Yahweh had to come down to see it;[15] however, as Yahweh himself says, the single language possesses the potential to actualize the conceived project (וַיֹּאמֶר יְהוָה הֵן עַם אֶחָד וְשָׂפָה אַחַת לְכֻלָּם וְזֶה הַחִלָּם לַעֲשׂוֹת וְעַתָּה לֹא־יִבָּצֵר מֵהֶם כֹּל אֲשֶׁר יָזְמוּ לַעֲשׂוֹת; Gen 11:6). Thus, the language-governed monoculture's attempt to merge the two demarcated spaces into a common whole means that humanity is exceeding its brief. The community at Babel is appropriating the divine sovereignty upon itself[16] instead of becoming God's functional vice-regent on earth (Gen 1: הַשָּׁמַיִם שָׁמַיִם לַיהוָה וְהָאָרֶץ נָתַן לִבְנֵי־אָדָם; cf. Ps 115:16).[17]

1.3. The Monoculture Preventing the Word/Speech-centric Divine Engagement with Humanity

The language-defined monoculture at Babel not only subverts the creational model of divine speech but also prevents divine intervention through the word. This can be established by comparing and contrasting the Babel story with the preceding events. That is to say, while the Babel story is similar to other events in terms of human rebellion, it is dissimilar to them in terms of the conspicuous absence of Yahweh's word-centric engagement with humanity.[18]

---

15. Wenham, *Genesis 1–15*, 240.

16. Here I disagree with Fretheim, who says that the building of the city and tower is an "under step," not an "overstep" of humanity because the people at Babel will endanger the development of the rest of creation and end up as underachievers. Fretheim, "Book of Genesis," 412. It is true that humanity at Babel is refusing to be imperiled by expanding itself into a dangerous world, but its security on earth becomes indestructible if humanity is able to join heaven and earth. Wenham makes an observation similar to mine; however, I have shown that this conclusion emerges from a different point. Wenham, *Genesis 1–15*, 242.

17. This is Middleton's central argument concerning the image of God. Middleton, *Liberating Image*.

18. My analysis in this section goes beyond the observation of Fretheim, who says that Yahweh's descent to Babel for a judicial purpose means his engagement with humanity, as Yahweh's presence on earth is inescapable.

Generally speaking, the monoculture of Babel accentuates the alienation of humanity from the divine (Yahweh), as the word מִקֶּדֶם ("from the east" or "eastward") suggests. As opposed to its purely spatial connotation in other places of Genesis (הַר הַקֶּדֶם, Gen 10:30; אֶל־אֶרֶץ קֶדֶם, Gen 25:6), the usage in Genesis 11:2 conveys a symbolic meaning of humanity further rebelling against Yahweh, which has its precedence in Adam and Eve's expulsion from Eden and Cain's wandering away from Yahweh's presence (וַיְגָרֶשׁ אֶת־הָאָדָם וַיַּשְׁכֵּן מִקֶּדֶם, Gen 3:24; וַיֵּשֶׁב בְּאֶרֶץ־נוֹד קִדְמַת־עֵדֶן, Gen 4:16).[19] Specifically, the Babel story replicates Genesis 3, where a common mode of communication overturns Genesis 1 and 2.[20] As the sequence indicates, Genesis 1 presents speech as an exclusive divine agent where God alone speaks, and Genesis 2 makes a divine allowance for human speech, which transpires among the equals of the same species (וַיִּקְרָא הָאָדָם שֵׁמוֹת, וַיֹּאמֶר הָאָדָם; Gen 2:20, 23). Note that here, only the sovereign speaks (וַיֹּאמֶר יְהוָה אֱלֹהִים לֹא־טוֹב; Gen 2:18), not vice versa: humanity does not speak to God, neither does animal speak to humanity. However, Genesis 3 breaks this pattern when a subordinate (serpent) universalizes the language and communicates with the woman (the ruler), and thereby it erases the boundary between other creatures and humanity (וְהַנָּחָשׁ הָיָה עָרוּם . . . וַיֹּאמֶר אֶל־הָאִשָּׁה; Gen 3:1). This common language even goes further to erase the distinction between God (the creator) and humanity (the created) so as to establish the sameness or oneness between them, with the possibility of humanity becoming like God (וַיֹּאמֶר הַנָּחָשׁ אֶל־הָאִשָּׁה . . . וִהְיִיתֶם כֵּאלֹהִים;

Fretheim, "Book of Genesis," 412. Fretheim's point on the divine presence is correct, but he misses out on the communicative aspect. In Genesis, Yahweh's presence on earth cannot be divorced from his word-centric communication even when the context is judicial. For instance, Yahweh engages himself in a lengthy conversation with Abraham before he destroys Sodom and Gomorrah (וַיֹּאמֶר יְהוָה . . . אֲרֲדָה־נָּא וְאֶרְאֶה . . . וַיִּגַּשׁ אַבְרָהָם וַיֹּאמַר; Gen 18:20, 21, 23).

19. Victor P. Hamilton restricts his remark on מִקֶּדֶם only to the geographical aspect. See Victor P. Hamilton, *Handbook on the Pentateuch* (Grand Rapids, MI: Baker, 1982), 80–81.

20. Rogerson remarks similarly, but only based on a curt observation that humanity is transgressing the boundary and aspiring for divinity. Rogerson, "Genesis 1–11," 91.

Gen 3:4–5). This is similar to the single language at Babel attempting to erase the division in the creational order so as to unify heaven and earth.

Despite the general and specific similarities between Babel and others, all the events of human rebellion up to Babel (Gen 11) do not prevent Yahweh from engaging with humanity through word-centric communications, although they may be negative or judgmental. For instance, Yahweh addresses all parties concerned directly even after humanity violates the divine command by eating the forbidden fruit. The two important verbs, וַיֹּאמֶר and וַיִּקְרָא, signifying Yahweh's speech at creation are repeated in Genesis 3 (vv. 9, 11, 13, 14, 16, 17); in Genesis 4, Yahweh speaks to an arrogant murderer, Cain (the verb וַיֹּאמֶר occurs in vv. 6, 9, 10, 15); and in Genesis 6–9, Yahweh speaks to Noah even when the whole earth is corrupt (the verb וַיֹּאמֶר occurs at different places in Gen 6–9 [6:13; 7:1; 8:17]). By contrast, as pointed out earlier, the speech-centric monoculture of Babel restrains Yahweh from speaking, which has been his standard form of engagement hitherto. The verb וַיֹּאמֶר in Genesis 11:6 is without an addressee; this is a self-deliberation, paralleling the people's self-motivating talk: וַיֹּאמְרוּ הָבָה נִבְנֶה, Genesis 11:4 = וַיֹּאמֶר, and הָבָה נֵרְדָה . . . יְהוָה, Genesis 11:6–7 (וַיֹּאמְרוּ = וַיֹּאמֶר יְהוָה; הָבָה = הָבָה, and נִבְנֶה = נֵרְדָה). Of course, one may say that Yahweh's self-deliberative statement in Genesis 11:6–7 echoes Genesis 1:26 and underscores a transaction of speech with humanity in some way, although it is negative—that is, while Yahweh's self-deliberative speech created humanity then, it is confusing humanity now. Such an assumption is weak because the self-deliberative statement of Genesis 1:26 immediately follows Yahweh's direct address to humanity (וַיֹּאמֶר אֱלֹהִים . . . וַיֹּאמֶר לָהֶם; Gen 1:28, 29). Again, insofar as the creational type of divine monologue in Genesis is concerned, Yahweh does get into this mode before and after destroying the humanity with the floodwater (וַיֹּאמֶר יְהוָה אֶמְחֶה אֶת־הָאָדָם אֲשֶׁר־בָּרָאתִי, Gen 6:7; וַיָּרַח יְהוָה אֶת־רֵיחַ הַנִּיחֹחַ וַיֹּאמֶר יְהוָה אֶל־לִבּוֹ, Gen 8:21), and yet both instances are followed respectively with Yahweh's speeches to Noah, the pivotal human character of the flood narrative (וַיֹּאמֶר אֱלֹהִים לְנֹחַ, Gen 6:13; וַיְבָרֶךְ אֱלֹהִים אֶת־נֹחַ וְאֶת־בָּנָיו וַיֹּאמֶר לָהֶם, Gen 9:1). This is evidently absent in Genesis II; here, the language-driven monoculture is pushing the dialoguing Yahweh out.

That Babel disrupts divine speech is clear not only from how it overturns the creational paradigm but also from how it does not fit with the redemptive paradigm. Up until Genesis II, Yahweh has engaged fallen humanity with a combination of judgmental speeches and magnanimous acts: Yahweh's condemning speech in Genesis 3 is followed up with his act of clothing the naked humanity (וַיַּעַשׂ יְהוָה אֱלֹהִים . . . וַיַּלְבִּשֵׁם; Gen 3:21); Yahweh's pronouncement of sentence for Cain is followed with his putting a sign of protection on Cain's body (וַיָּשֶׂם יְהוָה לְקַיִן אוֹת; Gen 4:15); and Yahweh's speech about destroying humanity is followed with his act of saving a remnant, which Noah accomplishes on God's behalf (וּמִכָּל־הָחַי מִכָּל־בָּשָׂר שְׁנַיִם מִכֹּל תָּבִיא; Gen 6:19), which culminates in Yahweh's act of covenant by way of giving the rainbow in the cloud (אֶת־קַשְׁתִּי נָתַתִּי בֶּעָנָן; Gen 9:13). However, at Babel, the redemptive pattern breaks. Here, Yahweh acts "punitively" or "correctively" without speaking to humanity.[21]

Finally, as opposed to Genesis I, other important verbs in Genesis II such as רָאָה and קָרָא (also בָּלַל) pejoratively influence the verb וַיֹּאמֶר (Yahweh's speech) and cumulatively undercut its connotation of divine communication at Babel: the verb רָאָה (to see) conveys positive divine assessment in the creation story, but it sounds condemning at Babel; the verb קָרָא (to call) in Genesis I conveys divine confirmation of creational existence, but in Genesis II, it suggests the human recognition of an abandoned entity; and the verb בָּלַל (to confuse) in the Babel story stands opposite to the verb בָּרָא in the creation narrative, strengthening the incompatibility between Genesis II and Genesis I.

To sum up, the narrator of Genesis rejects a global monoculture because its one language/speech-centered characteristic subverts God's (Yahweh's) language/speech as modeled in the creation. It wades into the area of divine speech-act performance. In Genesis I, Yahweh's work does not happen without his speech; in a similar

---

21. Also see Sherman, *Babel's Tower*, 53.

vein, the Babel community does not wish to undertake their ambitious construction project in a void or without speaking like him. But by speaking like God, the community ends up disengaging Yahweh's language/speech-centric communication with humanity. We shall now turn to the other part of our argument: the narrator's reason for promoting the "many."

2. The "Many" and the Space for Yahweh's Word/ Speech-centric Engagement (the Story of Hagar)

The stories of "many" cultures in Genesis are equally rife with human sinfulness, and hence, they fare no better than Babel. Nevertheless, from the narrator's viewpoint, their anti-Babel, multicultural context provides a platform for Yahweh to speak, as I will show in the representative story of Hagar.

2.1. Traces of Human Sinfulness and Babel in the Hagar Story

The story of Hagar begins with human sinfulness and traces of Babel. Although the sexual congress between her and Abraham seems to be legitimate (לְאַבְרָם אִישָׁהּ לוֹ לְאִשָּׁה), the narrator presents it as an illegitimate one. The usage of בֹּא־נָא ... וַיָּבֹא אֶל־הָגָר (Go in to my servant.... And he went in to Hagar; Gen 16:2, 4) is an echo of the illegitimate mixture between the sons of God and daughters of man (יָבֹאוּ בְּנֵי הָאֱלֹהִים אֶל־בְּנוֹת הָאָדָם; Gen 6:4).[22] By the standard of

---

22. Hamilton seems to be unsure of illegitimacy in the case of the sons of God precisely because they had sexual intercourse with their wives. Perhaps he makes this inference based on its licit (Gen 19:31; 38:8) and illicit (Gen 39:14) usages. Hamilton, *Book of Genesis*, 442. However, the issue of legitimacy is not decided by the usage of the verb בא alone but by the prohibitive exchange between humanity and divinity. A semantic comparison between בְּנֵי הָאֱלֹהִים and בְּנוֹת הָאָדָם throws up a conflict: while בְּנֵי and בְּנוֹת share a sociosemantic commonality, הָאֱלֹהִים and הָאָדָם must operate within a separated boundary. Abraham may be entitled to a concubine, but it will jeopardize his covenant with Yahweh (Gen 15). For a different but wider explanation condemning Abraham's act, see Gordon J. Wenham, *Genesis 16–50*, WBC 2 (Waco, TX: Word Books, 1987), 7.

Genesis 6, this is a fit case for divine retribution. Even more, the illegitimate transaction undermines the creational mandate and thus the divine word (וַיֹּאמֶר לָהֶם אֱלֹהִים פְּרוּ וּרְבוּ; Gen 1:28). Hence, in this context, Sarah's use of אִבָּנֶה ("I shall be builded"; Gen 16:2 NJPSV) echoes the Babel story (נִבְנֶה־לָּנוּ). Just as Babel subverts the divine word of the creational paradigm, the word of Sarah overthrows Yahweh's word, וְאֶעֶשְׂךָ לְגוֹי גָּדוֹל (Gen 12:2): note here the opposition between בנה (Sarah's wish for building) and עשׂה (Yahweh's word of creativity). Furthermore, Genesis 16 also echoes Babel in terms of challenging sovereignty. Humanity challenges the divine sovereignty at Babel, but Hagar treats the human/social authority with disdain in order to disequilibrate the hierarchy and elevate her status (וַתֵּרֶא כִּי הָרָתָה וַתֵּקַל גְּבִרְתָּהּ בְּעֵינֶיהָ; Gen 16:4). The verbs וַתֵּרֶא and לִרְאֹת have a similarly negative connotation in both the Babel and Hagar stories; while וּמִגְדָּל וְרֹאשׁוֹ attempts to dissolve the differences between heaven and earth, וַתֵּקַל גְּבִרְתָּהּ בְּעֵינֶיהָ disturbs the superior-subordinate equation. The trail of human sin and the trait of Babel in the Hagar narrative recur against the backdrop of a conversation/speech between Abraham and Sarah—וַתֹּאמֶר occurs twice (Gen 16:2, 5) and וַיֹּאמַר occurs once (Gen 16:6) in their conversation, just as וַיֹּאמְרוּ occurs twice in the Babel story (Gen 11:3, 4).

2.2. Yahweh's Word-centric Engagement in the Hagar Story within an Anti-Babel or "Many" Cultures Framework

Why does Yahweh engage with the people, particularly Hagar, through his word despite the story manifesting the vestige of Babel? As said already, this is because divine communication happens within an anti-Babel and procreational framework.

Unlike Babel, the Hagar story is undergirded first and foremost by the element of multiculturality or multiethnicity, as it characterizes and celebrates Hagar's identity. While the narrator avoids ethnic identities of Sarah and Abraham in spite of their exposure to cultural values of the land (מִקֵּץ עֶשֶׂר שָׁנִים לְשֶׁבֶת אַבְרָם בְּאֶרֶץ כְּנָעַן וַתִּתֵּן אֹתָהּ לְאַבְרָם אִישָׁהּ לוֹ לְאִשָּׁה in Gen 16:3; contrast this with לְאַבְרָם הָעִבְרִי in Gen 14:13), he does the opposite for Hagar. The narrator presents Hagar's ethnic identity in a chiastic structure:

A—status (maidservant; שִׁפְחָה)
   B—ethnic identity (מִצְרִית)
      C—name (וּשְׁמָהּ הָגָר)
      C′—name (אֶת־הָגָר)
   B′—ethnic identity (הַמִּצְרִית)
A′—status (maidservant; שִׁפְחָתָהּ)

Note that the ethnic identity in the second half of the structure is emphasized with much more definiteness (with -הַ). Interestingly, the narrator does not provide such a reinforced ethnocentric identity for Abraham's main servant (דַּמֶּשֶׂק אֱלִיעֶזֶר; Gen 15:2), who would have inherited Abraham's property in the event of Abraham's infertility.

Second, Yahweh's engagement with Hagar begins with an over-turning of the Babel setup. In the Babel story, the people find a plane at Shinar, but in the Hagar story, the deity finds Hagar in a desert on the road leading to Shur:

(Gen 11:2) וַיִּמְצְאוּ בִקְעָה בְּאֶרֶץ שִׁנְעָר

(Gen 16:7) וַיִּמְצָאָהּ מַלְאַךְ יְהוָה עַל־עֵין הַמַּיִם בַּמִּדְבָּר עַל־הָעַיִן בְּדֶרֶךְ שׁוּר

Here the opposition between וַיִּמְצְאוּ and וַיִּמְצָאָהּ מַלְאַךְ יְהוָה, בִקְעָה and בַּמִּדְבָּר, and בְּאֶרֶץ and בְּדֶרֶךְ and the wordplay between שִׁנְעָר and שׁוּר suggest that Yahweh can speak to Hagar (וַיֹּאמַר; Gen 16:8, 9, 11) only after the déjà vu of Babel is removed. Also importantly, the verb מצא in the Babel story connotes something like "to chance upon," but in the story of Hagar, it means the deity's deliberate and designed encounter.[23] This again eliminates the Babel connection before the angel of the Lord begins to converse.

Third, the word-centric divine intervention moves further to rectify Babel's challenge of the sovereign. This becomes clear from a parallel structure in Genesis 16:8–9:

---

23. Hamilton, *Book of Genesis*, 351, 451.

A—the divine query about Hagar's place of departure (וַיֹּאמַר הָגָר
שִׁפְחַת שָׂרַי אֵי־מִזֶּה בָאת)
B—the query continues about Hagar's destination (וְאָנָה תֵלֵכִי)
A′—Hagar confirms her departure (וַתֹּאמֶר מִפְּנֵי שָׂרַי גְּבִרְתִּי אָנֹכִי בֹּרַחַת)
B′—the divine counsel for Hagar's destination (וַיֹּאמֶר לָהּ מַלְאַךְ יְהוָה
שׁוּבִי אֶל־גְּבִרְתֵּךְ וְהִתְעַנִּי תַּחַת יָדֶיהָ)

The structured conversation between the angel of the Lord and Hagar redeems the relationship between the superior and the subordinate. In his query about Hagar's departure (A), Yahweh addresses Hagar as Sarah's maidservant (הָגָר שִׁפְחַת שָׂרַי), and Hagar acknowledges the same (שָׂרַי גְּבִרְתִּי).[24] Notably, a chiastic order in these words of both Yahweh and Hagar also confirms the latter's acceptance of Sarah's position: (a) maidservant—שִׁפְחַת (b) Sarah—שָׂרַי (b′) Sarah—שָׂרַי (a′) mistress—גְּבִרְתִּי. This reverses Hagar's earlier contemptuous conduct toward Sarah (וַתֵּקַל גְּבִרְתָּהּ בְּעֵינֶיהָ). However, the second divine query of Hagar's destination (B) is answered by the angel of the Lord himself (B′) because she evades it. Therefore, the angel of the Lord commands Hagar to make good her acknowledgment by returning to her mistress (שׁוּבִי אֶל־גְּבִרְתֵּךְ). Here the narrator's shift from וַיֵּשְׁבוּ (Gen 11:2) to שׁוּבִי is noticeable, which further buttresses his anti-Babel motif: while Yahweh overthrows the settling Babel that challenges divine sovereignty, he rejoins Hagar—the runaway, rebellious maidservant—with her social sovereign.

Fourth, the word-centric intervention employs the creational component in Yahweh's redemptive act. It is interesting, even intriguing, that the angel of the Lord pronounces the creational blessing for Hagar (וַיֹּאמֶר לָהּ מַלְאַךְ יְהוָה הַרְבָּה אַרְבֶּה אֶת־זַרְעֵךְ וְלֹא יִסָּפֵר מֵרֹב; Gen 16:10)—note that the word רבה repeats thrice in both the verb and noun forms.[25] This is interesting because the case of Hagar is about a lone female parent bearing an illegitimate child, which contravenes the endorsement of fruitfulness given to humanity through an approved

---

24. Wenham stops only with the divine reiteration of Hagar's status. Wenham, *Genesis 16–50*, 9.

25. Wenham also makes a similar point about the descendants of Hagar, but he connects it with the Abrahamic blessings. Wenham, 10.

relationship between man and woman (וַיֹּאמֶר לָהֶם אֱלֹהִים פְּרוּ וּרְבוּ; Gen 1:28). Procreation is not supposed to happen merely through any sexual activity, but only through marriage. Further, the angel of the Lord blesses the illegitimate child in Hagar's womb using a pattern of creational language—progressions of specifics by way of a climatic buildup:

A—Hagar's conception (הִנָּךְ הָרָה) = creation of light (וַיֹּאמֶר אֱלֹהִים יְהִי אוֹר; Gen 1:3)

B—delivery of a son (וְיֹלַדְתְּ בֵּן) = separation of light (וַיַּבְדֵּל אֱלֹהִים בֵּין הָאוֹר; Gen 1:4)

C—name of the son (וְקָרָאת שְׁמוֹ יִשְׁמָעֵאל) = naming of light (וַיִּקְרָא אֱלֹהִים לָאוֹר יוֹם; Gen 1:5)

X—God's concern for Hagar (כִּי־שָׁמַע יְהוָה אֶל־עָנְיֵךְ)

A—nature of the man, Ishmael (וְהוּא יִהְיֶה פֶּרֶא אָדָם)

B—Ishmael's universal animosity (יָדוֹ בַכֹּל וְיַד כֹּל בּוֹ)

C—Ishmael's hostility toward his brothers (וְעַל־פְּנֵי כָל־אֶחָיו יִשְׁכֹּן)

It might surprise the reader that the narrator's employment of a creational exemplar ends up producing both the inter- and intra-ethnic animosity vis-à-vis Ishmael.[26] However, there lies the narrator's viewpoint. According to him, multiethnic strife is much more palatable to Yahweh than Babel, which creates a monocultural coexistence, harmony, and oneness, because Yahweh, in any case, will find room to intervene in the former and rectify it by his word. Therefore, the story of Hagar closes with an anti-Babel frame, as Hagar's naming of the place suggests. The following contrast clarifies it:

(Gen 16:13, 14) וַתִּקְרָא שֵׁם־יְהוָה הַדֹּבֵר אֵלֶיהָ אַתָּה ... עַל־כֵּן קָרָא לַבְּאֵר בְּאֵר לַחַי רֹאִי

(Gen 11:9) עַל־כֵּן קָרָא שְׁמָהּ בָּבֶל כִּי־שָׁם בָּלַל

As this contrast shows, both Hagar and the Babel community name (קָרָא) the places, but with differences. While Hagar names the

---

26. For a detailed comment on Ishmael's habitation and hostile nature, see Hamilton, *Book of Genesis*, 454–55.

speaking Yahweh first[27] (שֶׁס־יְהוָה הַדֹּבֵר אֵלֶיהָ) and then the place; the Babel community only names the place where Yahweh is silent, though not inactive. It is critical to underline the shift between the beginning of Babel and the end of the story of Hagar. שָׂפָה אֶחָת וּדְבָרִים אֲחָדִים at Babel (Gen 11:1) subverts and prevents דְּבַר־יְהוָה, but Hagar, שִׁפְחָה מִצְרִית (Gen 16:1) proffers room for יְהוָה הַדֹּבֵר (16:13–14)—note the wordplay between דְּבָרִים and הַדֹּבֵר on the one hand and between שָׂפָה and שִׁפְחָה on the other. That the story of Hagar concludes with Yahweh's word-centric engagement (דבר) is important, because it shows that Yahweh's revelation, which primarily comes to Abraham (דְּבַר־יְהוָה; Gen 15:1, 4), is also available to a multiethnic, multilinguistic community in association with, or even independent of, Abraham.[28]

3. Why Not Mono, but Many Cultures?

This chapter began with a question as to why the narrator of Genesis rejects a global monoculture but retains the "many." And two representative texts—namely, Genesis 11 and 16 (the stories of Babel and Hagar, respectively)—are examined for this purpose. Our examination finds that both the monoculture and the "many" (the multiculture) are equally sinful. However, the narrator of Genesis rejects a global, language-defined monoculture because it subverts and prevents divine speech by imitating the divine speech act of the creational paradigm (Gen 1). The combination of one speech and the united act of building a city and the heavenward tower at Babel appears to present a legitimate expression and example of humanity bearing God's (Yahweh's) functional image, but underneath, it remains anticreational because it attempts to obliterate the established demarcation in the creational order. Thus, the speech-act combination of the monocultural Babel not only hijacks God's creative speech or his divinity and sovereignty but also seeks to stifle

---

27. This is not simply about Hagar as the lone person naming Yahweh, as commentators opine. See, for instance, Fretheim, "Book of *Genesis*," 454.

28. Hamilton opines that Hagar is "fascinated with the origin of revelation," although he does not engage in any literary analysis that we have presented. See Hamilton, *Book of Genesis*, 455.

his perpetual speech/word-centric engagement. Babel pressures God into monologue mode. This is a serious problem, since it disturbs the standard pattern of Yahweh's communication in Genesis up until then. In other words, the language-defined monoculture of Babel is both anticreational and antiredemptive. By contrast, the "many" is procreational and proredemptive. The "many" allows Yahweh's word-centric engagement with humanity because of its anti-Babel/ multicultural and procreational paradigm, although it manifests the traits of Babel. The story of Hagar shows that Yahweh's initiative to intervene in a multicultural context brings creational redemption to the fore and elicits an apt response from Hagar, a representative of multiethnicity, toward the divine word (revelation). In so doing, the Hagar story brings the nations within the ambit of Abrahamic blessing. This is a reason why the narrator of Genesis remains interested in the stories of the "many."

Bibliography

Bagg, Ariel M. "Palestine under Assyrian Rule: A New Look at the Assyrian Imperial Policy in the West." *JAOS* 133, no. 1 (2013): 119–144.

Bassett, F. W. "Noah's Nakedness and the Curse on Canaan: A Case of Incest?" *VT* 21, no. 2 (1971): 232–237.

Fretheim, Terence. "The Book of Genesis: Introduction, Commentary, and Reflections." In *The New Interpreter's Bible*, vol. 1, edited by Leander E. Keck, Walter Brueggemann, Walter C. Kaiser, and Terence E. Fretheim, 321–674. Nashville: Abingdon, 1994.

Hamilton, Victor P. *The Book of Genesis: Chapters 1–17*. NICOT 1. Grand Rapids, MI: Eerdmans, 1990.

———. *Handbook on the Pentateuch*. Grand Rapids, MI: Baker, 1982.

Huntington, Samuel P. *The Clash of Civilizations*. New York: Touchstone, 1997.

Middleton, Richard J. *The Liberating Image: The Imago Dei in Genesis 1*. Grand Rapids, MI: Brazos, 2005.

Parpola, Simo. "National and Ethnic Identity in the Neo-Assyrian Empire and Assyrian Empire Identity in Post Empire." *JAAS* 18, no. 2 (2004): 5–22.

Rogerson, John W. "Genesis 1–11." In *Genesis and Exodus*, edited by John W. Rogerson, R. W. L. Moberly, and W. Johnstone, 36–99. Sheffield, UK: Sheffield Academic, 2001.

Sherman, Philip M. *Babel's Tower Translated: Genesis 11 and Ancient Jewish Interpretation*. Biblical Interpretation Series 117. Leiden: Brill, 2013.

Wenham, Gordon J. *Genesis 1–15*. WBC 1. Waco, TX: Word Books, 1987.

———. *Genesis 16–50*. WBC 2. Waco, TX: Word Books, 1987.

3

"The God of the Nations" (Rom 3:29)

A Pharisee's Confession?

ANDREW B. SPURGEON

"God—is he God only for the Jews or for the nations also?" asked Paul (Rom 3:29a).[1] Without waiting for an answer, he said, "Yes, he is also the God of the Nations" (Rom 3:29b). If this question and answer were from a contemporary missiologist or missionary, it wouldn't surprise us. However, these were from a Pharisee, the choicest protégé of Gamaliel—one who cherished the uniqueness of circumcision, law, and the exclusivity of YHWH and the Jews from the surrounding nations.

Since childhood, Paul would have seen a warning sign in the temple court forbidding the nations from crossing a designated area of the temple on pain of death.[2] He would have referred to the nations as "sinners," since they didn't have the law and circumcision (Gal 2:15). He would have thought Jews were God's elect and the others were not. Jews were pure; the nations were impure. Jews were God's people; others weren't. If Jews had a command concerning the nations, it was to separate themselves from the surrounding nations so they wouldn't follow them to worship other gods.

---

1. All Scripture references in this chapter are my translations unless indicated otherwise.

2. Craig S. Keener, *The IVP Bible Background Commentary: New Testament*, 2nd ed. (Downers Grove, IL: IVP Academic, 2014), 393.

Historically, however, was YHWH the God of the Jews alone? In other words, was Abraham *a Jew* when God called him? Even before him, were Adam and Eve Jews? Noah, Enoch, Methuselah, or Melchizedek—were they all Jews with whom God fellowshipped? Absolutely not! They were all non-Jews, *people of nations*, and God was their God. Judaism, then, follows God's calling and salvation but does not precede it. He was always the God of the people of many nations.

Forgetting the past, then, some intertestamental Jews sought an exclusive faith. In their zeal for the traditions of their fathers, they forgot the inclusivity of the Jewish faith. So was Paul—committed to the exclusivity or purity of Judaism. He narrated his pride associated with his race (ascribed honor): "Circumcised on the eighth-day, from Israel race, of the tribe of Benjamin, and a Hebrew speaker among the Hebrews" (Phil 3:5). In addition, he had acquired honors that added to his exclusivity: "A Pharisee, trained in the study of the law, one who persecuted the church because of [his] zeal" (Phil 3:5–6; my translation), and he was one who was "advancing among [his] contemporaries because of [his] extreme zeal for the traditions of [his] fathers" (Gal 1:14). That "extreme zeal" was to preserve the uniqueness and exclusivity of Judaism. Jews were God's people. YHWH was their God.

Paul's encounter with the Jewish Messiah who commissioned him to preach the gospel to the nations, however, changed Paul's theology. He understood that the God of the Jews had always been *the* God of the nations. Paul then rewrote his theology, saying, "Abraham, the Gentile, received circumcision as a sign—a seal of approval of his righteousness that is by faith. He is therefore the father of all who believe, including the uncircumcised or Gentiles" (Rom 4:11). The relationship to God was always based on faith and not on one's ethnicity or exclusivity. Abraham, the father of the Jews, was a non-Jew while he believed in God. God was, after all, the God of the nations.

Even the law, another uniqueness of Judaism, came 430 years after Abraham's faith in God (Gal 3:17).[3] So it too couldn't have influenced

---

3. "All Jews learned the precepts of Torah from their very birth and were prepared to die for them if necessary." Josephus, *C. Ap.* 1.8.42, trans. H. St. J. Thackeray, LCL (London: Loeb, 1997).

Abraham's faith, covenant, or blessings. Faith and righteousness proceeded by centuries the markers or badges of Judaism—circumcision and the law. So Paul asked, "God—is he God only for the Jews or for the nations also?" And by divine inspiration, concluded, "Yes, he is also the God of the nations."

So how was he *the* God of the nations?

First, he was the God of all nations because he was the creator of all people. This was Paul's first argument in Romans: "God's incomprehensible attributes—power and divinity—are visibly seen since the creation of the universe. Therefore, people have no excuse to say that they don't know God" (Rom 1:20). Creation itself reveals God to people. As such, he is their God. Yet the people refused to give him glory or thank him for his provisions (Rom 1:21). So he handed them over to the passions of their desires, and they worshipped gods they themselves made. He was/is the God of all nations because he had created everyone and everything.

Second, he was the God of all nations because he was a fair judge of all people. Whereas people judged partially—that is, judging others while they themselves failed to observe the law that they imposed on others—God judged impartially. Paul wrote, "God repays to each one according to his or her own works. To those who patiently and with good work seek glory, honor and immortality, he will give eternal life. To those with strife and disbelief of truth pursue unrighteousness, he gives anger and wrath" (Rom 2:6–8). What they sought by their faithful actions, God offered. If, with hard labor, they sought immortality, he provided longevity of life and fame. If they pursued unrighteousness, he offered just results. Not only was he fair in what he offered; he equally distributed these fair judgments to the Jews and the nations. Paul wrote, "There is no partiality with God. Those who sin in the absence of the law perish without having the law; those who sin while having the law, they'll receive judgment based upon the law" (Rom 2:11–12). Since God judged Jews who possessed the law by the law and nations apart from the law (since they did not have the law), he was a fair and universal judge, the God of all nations.

Third, he was the God of all nations because he offered a righteousness (rightness) that was not based on the law, a righteousness (i.e., "being set right") that was apart from the law. If his rightness or his offer of rightness were based on the Law of Moses, only those who had the law could obey the law and receive it. But God remained right and universally faithful by offering a faith-centered rightness on the merits of the Lord Jesus's atonement (Rom 3:21–26). The early church wrestled with this problem: Were they to circumcise the nations that believed in Christ and command them to obey the law? The elders and apostles met in Jerusalem, discussed, and concluded that neither they nor the Holy Spirit wanted to burden the nations with any laws except to flee idolatry, adultery, murder, and degradation of life (Acts 15:28–29). By offering a righteousness that was apart from the law, God proved he was *the* God of all nations.

To everyone who accepted Jesus as Lord, regardless of their race, God offered his blessings without partiality. Peter and his friends witnessed that at Cornelius's house, where Peter confessed, "Now, I accept this truth: God is not partial. But, people from every nation who fear him and do what is right is acceptable to him" (Acts 10:34–35). As he said that, the Holy Spirit came on all those who heard his message (Acts 10:44). And the Jewish believers who had come with Peter were astonished that the gift of the Holy Spirit had been poured out even on the nations (Acts 10:45). That was only the beginning. God gave the nations the privilege of calling him "Abba, Father" (Rom 8:15; Gal 4:6) just as Jews had in the past (Matt 5:16, 45, 48; 6:1, 4, 6, 8–9, 14–15; Mark 14:36). He called them as "holy" people just as Jews were (Rom 1:7; 1 Cor 1:2) and saw them as his new dwelling place, the temple of God (1 Cor 6:19).

So Paul asked the Romans, "God—is he God only for the Jews or for the nations also?" and concluded, "Yes, he is also the God of the nations." The same is true now: God isn't exclusively the God of the Christians. He is still the God of the nations, even when they don't acknowledge him as such or give him thanks. "He is the God of the nations."

1. Contemporary Biases

Was Paul's bias unique? Is contemporary Christianity free of such exclusive thinking? I am afraid not. The following are some examples of our own biases.

We, for example, assume Asian or African theologies are not *pure* theologies as are the Western theologies. Asians and Africans corrupt the orthodox theologies, we assume. Are we regressing back to a mindset where missionaries thought natives were "incapable of understanding Christian doctrine in depth, [and] would spread heresies"[4] and so keep the formation of theology to the traditional scholars? I am not advocating a divide or separation between hemispheres or continents, neither am I advocating for a new and novel post-*whatever*, minority-based, and minority-sensitive hermeneutic. I am, however, calling for Christians of all nations to value one another and to write biblical theologies in collaboration with one another. "God— is he God only for the Jews or for the nations also? Yes, he is also the God of the nations."

A second bias is the assumption that the gospel has uniform expressions of "worship." In India, worshippers take off their slippers or shoes when entering a church building. In Singapore, worshippers (including the physically challenged) stand when the music begins, thinking that's the only way to serve God.[5] Where do these uniform expressions come from? "Bow your heads and close your eyes." "Stand in honor of God and his word." Don't misunderstand me, these expressions aren't inherently wrong. However, when churches practice such uniform expressions and expect others to follow them, they give a false assurance of piety. Paul writes, "Such actions, indeed, seem to have wisdom and self-imposed piety, false humility, and harsh treatment of the body. But they are of no value in controlling one's passions of flesh" (Col 2:23). Instead of helping us attain true spirituality, such expressions alienate us from those around us. They

---

4. Marilyn French, *From Eve to Dawn: A History of Women in the World*, vol. 2 (New York: Feminist, 2008), 207.

5. A new expression in Singapore is "spiritual retreat." Unless one takes a day off work and goes on a "spiritual retreat," they are somehow less spiritual.

give the impression, conscientiously or unconsciously, that we belong to the "in-group" and know the secret codes of Christianity, whereas others are in the "out-group" and don't understand true spirituality. These uniform expressions become like circumcision and law, badges that separate us from the world. "God—is he God only for the Jews or for the nations also? Yes, he is also the God of the nations."

A third bias is the polarization between sacred and secular. In every religion, priests and sages receive special recognitions, privileges, attire, and status. However, the Lord Jesus changed that status quo when he girded his waist and washed the disciples' feet. He, the master, was their servant. As such, Paul, a devoted Jew and a Pharisee, worked as a tanner in Corinth, something his former pharisaical life would have forbidden him—that is, touching the skin of a dead animal. Later, he instructed the men in Corinth not to have any ornaments on their heads (a hat, toga, or headgear) that separated them from the rest of the community and gave the impression that they were priests.[6] Christians have one high priest, the Lord Jesus Christ (1 Tim 2:5; Heb 8:6; 9:15; 12:24). Forgetting these lessons, modern Christianity exalts the leaders with robes, hats, places of honor, and titles, thus creating an artificial divide between sacred and secular. If we genuinely believe in the priesthood of all believers, then none of us should seek exaltation. Instead, we'll see ourselves as farmers, masons, servants, and stewards in God's field and house while serving his children faithfully (1 Cor 4).

So how do we remove these subtle hints of exclusivity and embrace the inclusivity of the gospel? We act upon the premise "One gospel, many cultures."

But what does that mean?

---

6. For priests covering their heads, see Cynthia L. Thompson, "Hairstyles, Head-Coverings, and St Paul: Portraits from Roman Corinth," *Biblical Archaeologist* 51, no. 2 (June 1988): 99–115.

2. One Gospel, Many Cultures

First, we hold on to a clear understanding of the gospel. We are familiar with the four spiritual laws and the evangelism explosion—even
the "God has a wonderful plan for your life" and "Would you like to
go to heaven?" methods and statements. Nothing is wrong with these
methods of evangelism if they achieve the intended goal of drawing
the hearers to the Lord Jesus Christ. Paul, however, summarized his
gospel in thirteen words: "Remember Jesus Christ, risen from death,
from David's seed, this is my gospel" (2 Tim 2:8). Basically, the gospel is about Jesus Christ, his lineage to King David, and his resurrection from the dead. Paul expands this in Romans 1:1–4. There he
proclaims a *royal* decree: King David has a son, Jesus Christ, who is
raised from the dead and continues to reign as the king (Christ, Messiah). Anyone who wholeheartedly believes this message of Jesus's
kingship and submits to him receives God's approval and declara-
tion of rightness and is saved. Paul said to the Romans, "When you
confess with your mouth 'Jesus is Lord' and believe in your heart
'God raised him from death,' you will be saved" (Rom 10:9). When
the centurion in Philippi asked Paul, "What must I do to be saved?"
Paul said, "Believe in the Lord Jesus, and you will be saved, also
your family" (Acts 16:30–31). The gospel, in simple terms, is people
putting their trust in one Lord, Jesus the Messiah, for their salvation. E. Stanley Jones, a missionary to India, said it beautifully: "If
we present Christianity as a rival to other religions, it will fail. Our
position should be: There are many religions. There is but one gospel. We are not setting a religion over against other religions, but a
gospel over against human need, which is the same everywhere. The
greatest service we can give to anyone in East or West is to introduce
him [or her] to the moral and spiritual power found in Christ. India
needs everything. We humbly offer the best we have. The best we
have is Christ."[7] Any gospel we proclaim that omits Jesus Christ, his
rule as the Lord and king, his resurrection, or trusting/believing in
him is not a gospel at all.

---

7. E. Stanley Jones, "Report on the New India," *Christian Century* 64 (1947): 556.

Second, we need a clear understanding of culture. G. Hofstede defines culture as "the collective programming of the mind which distinguishes the members of one group from another."[8] J. Mulholland sets three premises: culture has a set of shared and enduring meanings, values, and beliefs; it orients a group's behavior; and it distinguishes one group from another.[9] Helen Spencer-Oatey gives twelve key characteristics of culture.[10] A friend of mine succinctly summarized culture as how "sinful people learn to live together in peace."

Cultural practices are not simply neutral. What one people group thinks of as culturally neutral can be culturally positive, negative, religious, or even idolatrous to another people group. *Namaskara*, putting hands together to greet one another, for example, appears to be a "neutral" cultural practice in India and Thailand. But not all agree. Sadhguru writes, "So namaskaram is not just a cultural aspect. There is a science behind it. If you are doing your *sadhana* [spiritual exercise], every time you bring your palms together, there is a crackle of energy—a *boom* is happening. On the level of your life energy, there is a giving, or you are making yourself into an offering to the other person."[11] When a monotheist hears Sadhguru's expla-

---

8. G. Hofstede, *Culture's Consequences: International Differences in Work-Related Values* (London: Sage, 1980), 21.

9. J. Mulholland, *The Language of Negotiation* (London: Routledge, 1991).

10. The key characteristics of culture are as follows: (1) culture is manifested at different layers of depth; (2) culture affects behavior and interpretations of behavior; (3) culture can be differentiated from both universal human nature and unique individual personality (Hofstede's chart); (4) culture influences biological processes (i.e., eating, coughing); (5) culture is associated with social groups; (6) culture is both an individual construct and a social construct; (7) culture is always both socially and psychologically distributed in a group, and so the delineation of a culture's features will always be fuzzy; (8) culture has both universal (etic) and distinctive (emic) elements; (9) culture is learned; (10) culture is subject to gradual change; (11) the various parts of a culture are all, to some degree, interrelated; and (12) culture is a descriptive not an evaluative concept. Helen Spencer-Oatey, "What Is Culture? A Compilation of Quotations," GlobalPAD Core Concepts, 2012, https://globalpeopleconsulting.com/what-is-culture.

11. Sadhguru, "Meaning of Namaskar or Namaskaram—I Bow to the Divinity in You," Isha Foundation, accessed December 12, 2021, https://isha.sadhguru .org/my/en/wisdom/article/namaskar-meaning.

nation of *namaskara* (i.e., "I am worshipping another every time I do *namaskara*"), then they find *namaskara* objectionable. So how can we make the one gospel applicable to many cultures?

The answer lies in (1) examining a cultural practice; (2) categorizing it into a-religious, irreligious, and religious; and (3) surrendering the irreligious and religious practices to the Lord Jesus but practicing the a-religious cultural practices. Some cultural practices are easy to separate into a-religious, irreligious, and religious practices. For example, removing one's slippers to enter a person's house is an a-religious practice, offering a pig on a Jewish altar is an irreligious action, and offering one-tenth to God is a religious act of obedience. However, such categorizing isn't always easy, but it is necessary for us to be culturally relevant. I'll illustrate with four examples.

2.1. Bindis and Culture

The first illustration is the mark on the foreheads of Indians. Although to a visitor, all marks might look the same, to the Hindu Indians, there are four different marks—bindi, *sindoor*, *tilaka*, and *vibhuti*—with various meanings. A bindi (lit. a drop, dot, or small particle) placed on one's forehead (often with a powder, paste, or jewelry) has two meanings. First, it is decorative, and Indian women wear it for beauty or as an expression of happiness. Traditionally, the red color represents love and prosperity. When it is merely a decoration, it is a-religious. Second, some wear bindi with a religious connotation. When it is between the eyebrows, it can represent the sixth chakra (energy point), the seat of concealed wisdom, or the "third eye," the abode of the Brahma. A *sindoor* is a red powder mark on the hairline of a married woman. It is a sign of someone's married state in north and northeast India. As such, it is a cultural and a-religious mark. A *tilaka* (or *kumkuma*), however, is a religious mark on the forehead or body (e.g., neck, upper arm, chest, or torso) of a devotee, male or female, that signifies his or her devotion to a deity. These marks change with each deity. The worshippers of Vishnu, for example, use sandalwood paste and make a long straight line starting from just below the hairline to the tip of the nose and insert an elongated *U* in the middle. A *tilaka* is thus a religious symbol.

Vibhuti, white ash made from wood burned in the sacred fire in the temple, too has two distinct functions. First, after worship in a temple, the priests smear it on the foreheads of the worshippers to mark the worshippers' piety. Second, some use *vibhuti* to represent their caste: the Brahmins wear white chalk marks signifying purity, and the Kshatriya wear red marks signifying the valor of their warrior race. In this case, *vibhuti* functions as a "boundary marker," separating one caste from another, which some consider moral/immoral and others do not. So how does an Indian Christian maintain one gospel among these many cultures?

In the early days, leaders taught Indian Christians not to use any marks on their foreheads. By listening to the former theologians, Indian Christians alienated themselves from Indian society. Perhaps it would be wise for Indian Christians to classify these marks into irreligious, religious, and a-religious first and then choose to keep a-religious marks. None of these marks are irreligious. However, a *tilaka* is a religious mark identifying a worshipper's deity. As such, a Christian should not wear a *tilaka* of a god/goddess. A bindi, however, has both religious and a-religious significance. As an a-religious sign, it represents love or prosperity. I suggest that Indian ladies may wear bindi as a cultural and fashion statement, provided it is not between their eyebrows. A *sindoor* is purely a cultural marker indicating a woman's married state. As such, it is culturally appropriate to wear a *sindoor* on one's forehead. *Vibhuti* can represent a worshipper's piety to a god. As such, it is a religious mark. But it can also represent a person's caste. As a religious mark, it should not be worn, but as an a-religious caste mark, it may be worn (whether caste is moral or immoral, I'll discuss next). Paul, who vehemently opposed circumcising the nations, obeyed James's instruction and paid for the ritual purity of four young men in Jerusalem (Acts 21:17–26). Similarly, evaluating cultural practices and choosing to keep a-religious practices of one's culture will not alienate Christians from the culture they are in and will confirm that we truly believe the message "Yes, he is also the God of the nations."

2.2. Caste and Culture

The second illustration is the caste system of India. *Manusmriti,* a Hindu sacred text, segregates people into priests (Brahmins), warriors (Kshatriyas), merchants (Vaishya), and workers (Sudras). Those who do not belong to these castes find their place in Scheduled Tribes (Adivasi) or Scheduled Castes (Dalits). Caste (*jati*), unfortunately, is based on a people group's color (*varna*), and a person is born into a caste. Color racism exists worldwide. Most societies shun racism based on the color of one's skin, at least officially. The constitution of India, however, upholds caste divisions.[12]

Earlier Christians taught Indian Christians to abandon the caste system, thinking of it as an evil practice. They, however, did not realize how caste affects one's family, income, and livelihood. Vani K. Borooah, Amaresh Dubey, and Sriya Iyer explain,

> In response to the burden of social stigma and economic backwardness borne by persons belonging to some of India's castes, the Constitution of India allows for special provisions for members of these castes.... These special provisions have taken two main forms: action against adverse discrimination towards persons from the SC [Scheduled Caste] and the ST [Scheduled Tribe]; and compensatory discrimination in favor of persons from the SC and the ST. Compensatory discrimination has taken the form of guaranteeing seats in national and state legislatures and in the village *panchayats* [judgment courts], places in educational institutes, and the reservation of a certain proportion of government jobs for the SC [Scheduled Caste] and the ST [Scheduled Tribe].[13]

---

12. This is evidenced by laws that reclassified the Scheduled Caste. See "Cabinet Approves Amendments in Constitution (Scheduled Castes) Order, 1950," *Sify News,* February 1, 2017, http://www.sify.com/news/cabinet-approves -amendments-in-constitution-scheduled-castes-orders-news-national -rcbnL5fajbeee.html.
13. Vani K. Borooah, Amaresh Dubey, and Sriya Iyer, "The Effectiveness of Jobs Reservation: Caste, Religion and Economic Status in India," *Development and Change* 38, no. 3 (2007): 423–24.

The Indian constitution incorporates caste distinctions to provide "compensatory discrimination" for those in disadvantaged groups (like "Affirmative Action" in the West or "Reservation" in Nepal). When Christians ask new believers from a low caste to forsake their caste, Christians are asking them to forgo their places in the educational system, job market, and politics. Christians who receive regular foreign income do not understand a poor person's dilemma. Should they forsake the caste identity and privileges by becoming a Christian? Is God not the God of Scheduled Caste? Is caste a "religious cultural phenomenon" that needs to be submitted to the Lord Jesus?

Paul said to the Corinthians, "Although I am free, I enslave myself to everyone to win many people" (1 Cor 9:19). Paul, a free Roman citizen, chose slavery for the advancement of the gospel. Indian Christians, although casteless in Christ, can tolerate the caste system and use its positive aspects for the advancement of the gospel. But how?

First, Indian Christians can allow converts from the low castes to remain in their caste so that they can retain their jobs and privileges. Studies have shown that the provision in the Indian constitution has resulted in a 5 percent increase "in regular salaried and wage employment" among these groups.[14] Caste is functional, at least, in providing jobs for the poor.

Second, Indian Christians who retain their caste identity can enter India's legal (*panchayats*) and political systems and defend Christianity. Charan Banerjee (1847–1902), a Hindu convert from Bengal, joined the Indian National Congress in 1885 and defended Bengali Christians as Indians. He wrote, "In having become Christians, we have not ceased to be Hindus [Indians]. We are Hindu [Indian] Christians. . . . We have embraced Christianity but we have not discarded our nationality."[15] Christians, by retaining their caste identities, can enter India's legal and political arena and defend Christianity as an Indian faith.

---

14. Borooah, Dubey, and Iyer, 443.
15. Kaj Baagø, *A History of the National Christian Council of India, 1914–1964* (Nagpur, India: National Christian Council, 1967), 67.

Third, Indian Christians themselves should not commit caste discrimination but fight against the evils of the caste system. Paul, who subjected himself to slavery for the advancement of the gospel, wrote to the Corinthians, "If you are able to procure your freedom, do so" (1 Cor 7:21). Similarly, he pleaded with his friend, Philemon, for the freedom of Onesimus, a slave (Phlm 8–16). While utilizing the positive aspects of the caste system for the betterment of the poor, Indian Christians should not practice its evils. Indian Christians should be caste opportunists—those who use the constitutional privileges of the caste system to uplift the poor and further the gospel. At the same time, they should also fight against social inequalities and the abuse of the low caste and oppressed.

2.3. Polytheism and Culture

The third illustration is polytheism. Circa 700 BCE, a Hindu student, Yajnavalkya, asked his teacher, Aruni, how many gods were in Hinduism. Aruni replied, "Three hundred and three and three thousand and three." Unsatisfied with the answer, Yajnavalkya pressed Aruni further. The teacher concluded by saying, "There is only one 'God,' the *BRAHMAN*, or all."[16] This statement summarizes Hinduism: it is a monotheistic polytheism. A Hindu believes in one Brahman (god) who appears in many forms. Suhag Shukla, the founder of the Hindu American Foundation, says the number-one myth about Hinduism is saying that Hindus worship 330 million gods. She writes, "There is one supreme God that cannot be fully known or understood. Hindus are encouraged to relate to God in the way that suits them best, like worshiping many deities who are believed to be manifestations of God. . . . That's why Hinduism is often thought of as polytheistic. It is not."[17]

Similarly, Indians do not consider themselves to be idol worshippers or idolaters. To a Hindu Indian, idols represent gods, but the

---

16. Constance A. Jones and James D. Ryan, *Encyclopedia of Hinduism*, Encyclopedia of World Religions (New York: Facts on File, 2007), 507.

17. Moni Basu, "9 Myths about Hinduism—Debunked," *CNN Belief Blog*, April 25, 2014, http://religion.blogs.cnn.com/2014/04/25/9-myths-about-hinduism-debunked/comment-page-1/.

idols are not gods. Gandhi, for example, said, "No Hindu considers an image to be God."[18] An idol is a *murti*—a "solid body" representing a spirit god. A *linga* (genitalia) does not represent a phallus, immorality, fertility, or infertility; it represents the deity Shiva.[19] Hindus, then, worship one god through various avatars (manifestations) and *murtis*. Since each avatar has a specific responsibility, a Hindu worshipper addresses various avatars multiple times a day in the form of *pujas*.[20]

Historically, we Christians have shunned the worship of Hindus as polytheistic and alienated ourselves from them. But is that the only way to relate to the Hindus? If so, how will we communicate, "Yes, he is also the God of the Indians?"

First, Indian Christians should not advance the oft-repeated claim that Hindus worship millions of gods. This may anger the Hindus and hinder the advancement of the gospel. Paul, in Athens, said, "People of Athens, I see you are very religious in every way" (Acts 17:22). Paul did not condemn the Athenians as polytheists, although they worshipped twelve main deities. He exalted them as "very religious" (lit. "having many gods") and introduced YHWH to them (Acts 17:23). Indians, like the Athenians, are a very religious people. A Hindu performs fourteen to sixteen steps of *puja* daily to multiple gods and goddesses. How can we call them "irreligious"? They are "very religious." Indian Christians need to present the gospel within the context of such piety and without insulting Hindus by calling them polytheists, irreligious, or idolaters.

Second, Indian Christians need to believe in the existence of other gods and lords. Paul wrote, "Just as people say there are gods in heaven and on earth—there are many gods and lords. But for us, there is but one God, the Father, . . . and one Lord, Jesus Christ" (1 Cor 8:5–6). Paul, without denying the existence of other gods, affirmed that, for Christians, there was only one God and one Lord. Similarly, Indian Christians can affirm that there are other deities

18. Charles R. Andrews, *Mahatma Gandhi: His Life and Ideas* (Delhi: Jaico, 2005), 12.

19. Anantanand Rambachan, "Seeing the Divine in All Forms: The Culmination of Hindu Worship," *Dialogue & Alliance* 4, no. 1 (1990): 6.

20. Rambachan, 9.

(benevolent or destructive) behind Hindu avatars. As such, those gods and lords have a strong hold on their worshippers. Presenting the gospel (Jesus as Lord and king) is a spiritual battle to those who already have other lords or gods. So Christians must approach the people with gentleness but with fear of the invisible divinities and demons behind their worship. Paul said, "We do not wrestle against flesh and blood, but against rulers, authorities, powers of darkness, and spiritual forces of evil in the heavens" (Eph 6:12). God alone can free a person from the hold of another god or lord. And once God opens a person's eyes, they will worship the one true God and the Lord Jesus Christ (1 Cor 8:6).

Indian Christians need to find a middle ground between synchronistic theology and Christian militancy. Synchronistic theology teaches that a Hindu can worship Adonai in addition to their other gods and goddesses; Christian militancy judges those who disagree with orthodoxy as heretics. A middle ground focuses on the message of Jesus Christ alone and presents it to the culture gently and with sensitivity. As E. Stanley Jones says, "We humbly offer the best we have. The best we have is Christ."[21]

2.4. *Prasada* and Culture

The fourth illustration is eating *prasada*, "a deity's grace bestowed on worshippers." Hindu worshippers bring fruit, milk, and coconuts and offer them to their gods. After the gods have had their fill and blessed them, the priests return the deity's grace (*prasada*) to the worshippers. Accepting the *prasada* concludes the worship.[22] The worshippers eat the *prasada* in the presence of the gods or take them home to share with their families and neighbors. But early missionaries, without understanding Indian culture, taught Indian Christians to avoid *prasada*. As a result, Indian Christians have refused to eat *prasada* from their relatives and neighbors, thus isolating themselves from the Indian community and drawing the criticism, "Christianity is a foreign religion."

21. Jones, "Report," 556.
22. Rambachan, "Seeing the Divine," 9.

But is eating *prasada* against the Christian faith? Indian Christians need to reevaluate the Bible's teachings on food offered to idols. Paul addressed that topic in 1 Corinthians 8–10. Although he prohibited a Christian from entering a temple to eat food offered to a god, since it might lead a weak Christian to idolatry (1 Cor 8:1–10:24), he permitted Christians in Corinth to eat any food offered in the market, even food that had been offered to a god before it was sold in the market (1 Cor 10:25–26). Similarly, he instructed them to boldly eat any food offered by their non-Christian neighbors without asking any questions (1 Cor 10:27–31). Paul's guiding principle was that "the earth and its produce—all belong to the Lord" (1 Cor 10:26). "If I eat the meal with thankfulness," he said, "why am I denounced for something I thank God for?" (1 Cor 10:30).[23] These passages help Indian Christians understand how to respond to *prasada* offered to them by Hindu family members or neighbors.

First, Indian Christians should not actively seek *prasada* or enter other gods' temples to eat food offered to gods. Some radical Indian Christians have been known to enter Sikh and Hindu temples to eat free food, *prasada*. Their actions confuse the Hindus—while they claim that they worship a jealous God who abhors idolaters, they seek *prasada*. Instead of confusing the Hindus, Indian Christians should follow Paul's example: "If what I eat causes anyone to fall into sin, I will never eat meat again, so that I will not cause them to fall" (1 Cor 8:13). Going hungry is better than free food in a temple.

Second, when neighbors offer *prasada*, Indian Christians should accept it. If the Hindu neighbor waits for them to eat it, they should eat the *prasada* with thanksgiving (1 Cor 10:26, 30). If the neighbor isn't waiting to see if one eats it, one may discard it. Christians should operate on the principle that whether they eat or drink or whatever they do, they do it all for the glory of God (1 Cor 10:31). If by eating *prasada* they lead someone to idolatry, they should not eat it; their eating will not glorify God. If by eating *prasada* they draw someone

---

23. For a detailed study, see Andrew B. Spurgeon, *Twin Cultures Separated by Centuries: An Indian Reading of First Corinthians* (Carlisle, UK: Langham Global Library, 2016), 149–90.

to Christ, they should eat it; that kind gesture of accepting a gift from a nonbeliever will glorify God.

Third, when children under the guidance of their parents become believers, Christians must encourage them to honor their parents and eat the *prasada* they offer, while in their hearts, they acknowledge the Lord Jesus as the provider of the food and thank him for it. In the past, Christians have driven wedges between children and parents by instructing the children to refuse *prasada* from their parents or relatives. Instead, if the Christians will instruct the children to obey their parents and eat *prasada* by thanking the Lord Jesus for his provision, they might draw the parents to faith through their children's submissive actions. Of course, the children can stop eating *prasada* if the parents don't demand them to eat or when they grow up and have left the parents' home.

3. Summary

Havilah Dharamraj and Angukali V. Rotokha beautifully illustrate how we, Indian Christians, are confused about our identity:

> The *Panchatantra* tells the story of Chandarava the jackal. In his search for food he strayed into the city. Beset by dogs, he fled into a dyer's courtyard and hastily leaped into a vat of indigo dye. Since his new *avatar* defied identification as any known beast, the blue jackal was elevated to kingship over the animals of the forest. He proclaimed himself to be Kukudruma, the heaven-sent. One day, the howling of a pack of passing jackals fell on his indigo ears. Instinctively, he raised his head and howled a response. His cloak of anonymity fell, and so did he. Without pressing the parallels too far, it can be suggested that the Indian Christian is, metaphorically speaking, a blue jackal, in that he is unsure who he is—Chandarava or Kukudruma, or both.[24]

---

24. Havilah Dharamraj and Angukali V. Rotokha, "History, History Books and the Blue Jackal," in *Indian and Christian: Changing Identities in Modern India, Papers from the First SAIACS Annual Consultation*, ed. Cornelis Bennema and Paul Joshua Bhakiaraj (Bangalore: SAIACS, 2011), 14.

Dharamraj and Rotokha are correct. While we speak against caste discrimination in India, we succumb to it when we seek spouses for our children. Those who apply for college admissions state their caste, hoping to receive a seat reserved for that caste. We fear the evil eye and bad omens and seek auspicious days, just like our non-Christian neighbors. At the same time, we offer a *Christian* culture to Indians and expect them to stop going to movies, playing cards on Sundays, and drinking alcohol. We have set our boundary markers and expect Indians to abandon their culture and mold to our culture. In this way, we offer a non-Indian Christianity and corrupt the gospel of Jesus Christ.

How can God be the God of Indians? We find the a-religious cultural uniqueness and hold on to it while we exalt the Lord Jesus above everything else. We also find the irreligious cultural practices, such as bribing, and shun them. And we do not participate in the religious practices of others, such as entering a temple to eat *prasada*.

Sundar Singh, a Sikh convert to Christianity a century ago, cautioned, "Indians do need the water of life, but not in a European cup. They should sit down on the floor in church; they should take off their shoes instead of their turbans. Indian music should be sung. Long informal addresses should take the place of sermons."[25] Paul would ask us to present God as the God of all nations. That includes the message that God loves each culture's unique a-religious practices. Embracing them wholeheartedly and presenting the pure gospel will send the message, "Yes, he is God of all nations." And yes, Christians truly believe in "one gospel but many cultures."

Going back to the three biases I mentioned, first, we must value indigenized theologies that are *relevant* but *exegetically sound*. Earlier Indian theologians like A. J. Appasamy and P. Chenchiah tried to promote Indigenous theologies but failed because they weren't sound exegetes of the Scripture or culture. Indigenous theology isn't substituting Indian words into Western theologies. True Indigenous theology is finding an accurate, dynamic equivalent in places

---

25. Burnett Hillman Streeter and Aiyadurai Jesudasen Appasamy, *The Sadhu: A Study in Mysticism and Practical Religion* (London: Macmillan, 1921), 228.

where the original doesn't communicate. Imagine me explaining cricket to an American by saying, "It's just like baseball except the cricket players run back and forth between the wickets, whereas baseball players run around the diamond." Cricket and baseball aren't dynamic equivalents except for the fact that both sports use a bat and a ball (although they are different in appearance and composition). A dynamic equivalent is comparing first-class matches with limited overs cricket or Twenty20 cricket. Similarly, referring to God as Brahman or incarnations as avatars aren't dynamic equivalents. If we want true indigenization, we need another set of equivalencies that are exegetically sound both to the Scriptures and to our culture. Second, instead of imposing a uniform mode of service or worship, we should venture into nontraditional modes of services, tailor-made to fit our situations. An example would be hosting a worship service in a coffee shop at two in the morning for those who get off work from call centers. Third, we drop all forms of artificial divide between the sacred and secular. Every Christian (not only the leaders, ministers, and missionaries) can take the gospel to their workplace and school and present it to their colleagues and classmates. All become missional Christians engaged in God's work in the world. Seminaries and Bible colleges, instead of training professionals with degrees that compete with the world, biblically equip the "equippers of the saints."[26]

"One gospel, many cultures" simply means we retain the *purity* of the gospel in the *plurality* of cultures. Each culture is unique and has religious, irreligious, and a-religious cultural expressions. Those a-religious practices that do not corrupt the gospel, we keep. Those religious and irreligious practices that taint the gospel, we omit. But we never judge one culture by another culture. When we exalt one culture over another or one expression of "worship" over another, we fall into the same trap of thinking exclusively. We are

---

26. Darrell L. Guder, "The Implications of a Missional Hermeneutic for Theological Education," in *Reading the Bible Missionally*, ed. Michael W. Goheen, Gospel and Our Culture Series, ed. John R. Franke (Grand Rapids, MI: Eerdmans, 2016), 285–98.

called to maintain the *purity* of the gospel in the *plurality* of cultures. "One gospel, many cultures." One God for all nations.

Bibliography

Andrews, Charles R. *Mahatma Gandhi: His Life and Ideas*. Delhi: Jaico, 2005.

Baagø, Kaj. *A History of the National Christian Council of India, 1914–1964*. Nagpur, India: National Christian Council, 1967.

Basu, Moni. "9 Myths about Hinduism—Debunked." *CNN Belief Blog*, April 25, 2014. http://religion.blogs.cnn.com/2014/04/25/9-myths-about -hinduism-debunked/comment-page-1/.

Borooah, Vani K., Amaresh Dubey, and Sriya Iyer. "The Effectiveness of Jobs Reservation: Caste, Religion and Economic Status in India." *Development and Change* 38, no. 3 (2007): 423–445.

Dharamraj, Havilah, and Angukali V. Rotokha. "History, History Books and the Blue Jackal." In *Indian and Christian: Changing Identities in Modern India, Papers from the First SAIACS Annual Consultation*, edited by Cornelis Bennema and Paul Joshua Bhakiaraj, 14–37. Bangalore: SAIACS, 2011.

French, Marilyn. *From Eve to Dawn: A History of Women in the World*. Vol. 2. New York: Feminist, 2008.

Guder, Darrell L. "The Implications of a Missional Hermeneutic for Theological Education." In *Reading the Bible Missionally*, edited by Michael W. Goheen, 285–298. Gospel and Our Culture Series. Edited by John R. Franke. Grand Rapids, MI: Eerdmans, 2016.

Hofstede, G. *Culture's Consequences: International Differences in Work-Related Values*. London: Sage, 1980.

Jones, Constance A., and James D. Ryan. *Encyclopedia of Hinduism*. Encyclopedia of World Religions. New York: Facts on File, 2007.

Jones, E. Stanley. "Report on the New India." *Christian Century* 64 (1947): 555–556.

Josephus. Translated by Henry St. J. Thackeray et al. 10 vols. LCL. Cambridge, MA: Harvard University Press, 1926–1925.

Keener, Craig S. *The IVP Bible Background Commentary: New Testament*. 2nd ed. Downers Grove, IL: IVP Academic, 2014.

Mulholland, J. *The Language of Negotiation*. London: Routledge, 1991.

Rambachan, Anantanand. "Seeing the Divine in All Forms: The Culmination of Hindu Worship." *Dialogue & Alliance* 4, no. 1 (1990): 5–12.

Sadhguru. "Meaning of Namaskar or Namaskaram—I Bow to the Divinity in You." Isha Foundation. Accessed December 12, 2021. https://isha.sadhguru.org/my/en/wisdom/article/namaskar-meaning.

Spencer-Oatey, Helen. "What Is Culture? A Compilation of Quotations." GlobalPAD Core Concepts, 2012. https://globalpeopleconsulting.com/what-is-culture.

Spurgeon, Andrew B. *Twin Cultures Separated by Centuries: An Indian Reading of First Corinthians*. Carlisle, UK: Langham Global Library, 2016.

Streeter, Burnett Hillman, and Aiyadurai Jesudasen Appasamy. *The Sadhu: A Study in Mysticism and Practical Religion*. London: Macmillan, 1921.

Thompson, Cynthia L. "Hairstyles, Head-Coverings, and St Paul: Portraits from Roman Corinth." *Biblical Archaeologist* 51, no. 2 (June 1988): 99–115.

4

Bindis, Castes, and Festivals

The Epistle to the Galatians and Its Relevance
for Cultural Contextualization in India

ERIC R. MONTGOMERY

When Roberto de Nobili arrived in Goa on the western shore of India on May 20, 1605, the Jesuit mission had been underway for more than sixty years. During that time, the Jesuits had significant success in converting Indians to Christianity in many regions of southern India. However, the mission to the city of Madurai in southern Tamil Nadu had not produced substantial converts. In 1606, de Nobili traveled to Madurai in order to assess the situation. He determined that Hindus in Madurai rejected Christianity because they saw it as an impure, foreign religion.

With this in mind, de Nobili developed a new mission strategy. He moved out of the Jesuit residence in Madurai and lived in a hut located in the Brahmin (high caste) quarter of the city. De Nobili adopted the dress of a sannyasi (religious ascetic), placed sandalwood paste on his forehead to identify himself as a guru or teacher, and ate only vegetarian meals. He became proficient in Tamil and Sanskrit languages, studied the Hindu religious texts, and told his Brahmin neighbors that he had come to preach a new spiritual law. Through these efforts, de Nobili succeeded in converting many Brahmins and people of other castes to Christianity.

Unlike other Jesuit missionaries, de Nobili allowed his converts to continue their social/religious customs. He permitted Brahmin converts to continue wearing the *yagnopavitam* (sacred thread) and *kudumi* (tuft of hair) that marked them as Brahmins.[1] De Nobili allowed converts to retain their Tamil names and did not restrict them from celebrating the Tamil religious festival of Pongal. He also did not try to bridge the chasm between castes. De Nobili recognized that Indians of different castes would not worship together, and it would not be acceptable for a single missionary to minister to both high- and low-caste Hindus. So de Nobili established churches exclusively for high-caste Hindu converts. He also trained one group of Jesuits to minister to Brahmins and other high-caste Indians, and he trained a second group of missionaries to minister to the lower castes.

De Nobili's approach was not without controversy. In 1610, he was called before an inquisition at Goa in order to defend his lifestyle and methods. The controversy surrounding de Nobili and his novel approach continued for more than a decade. Finally, on January 31, 1623, Pope Gregory XV issued the constitution *Romanæ Sedis Antistes* in favor of de Nobili. The constitution permitted Hindu converts to retain certain cultural practices, such as the sacred thread, hair tuft, use of sandalwood paste on the forehead, and Hindu bathing rituals. But the constitution also exhorted converts to overcome their caste divisions.

The debate about contextualization is not a new one, as de Nobili's story illustrates. When Protestant missionaries entered the field en masse in the nineteenth century, they wrestled with many of the same questions (a good case in point is Hudson Taylor's mission in China). The last half century has witnessed an increased interest in cultural contextualization with the advent of globalization and needed reflection upon the errors of colonialism. During this time, scholars and missiologists have often looked to passages like Acts 17:16–34 and 1 Corinthians 9:19–23 to understand Paul's cultural accommodation or to derive a biblical model for contextualizing the gospel message.[2] However, there are other texts in the New Testa-

---

1. The *yagnopavitam* is a thread of three cotton strands draped from the left shoulder diagonally across the chest.
2. See, for example, J. Daryl Charles, "Engaging the (Neo)Pagan Mind: Paul's Encounter with Athenian Culture as a Model for Cultural Apologetics (Acts

ment that can aid in this endeavor.[3] In particular, Paul's letter to the Galatians has much to offer.[4]

The aim of this chapter is twofold. The first goal is to examine how Paul interacted with the native culture(s) of his Galatian audience and how he constructed a new cultural identity for them. The second objective is to apply Paul's construction of culture in his letter to the Galatians to three test cases that are relevant for Christians in the Indian context. Each test case is based on a question that is commonly debated among Indian Christians: (1) Is it appropriate for Christians to wear a bindi? (2) How should Christians deal with caste divisions? and (3) Can Christians participate in Indian festivals and holy days?

I. Paul and Culture in Galatians

When Paul wrote his epistle to the Galatian churches, he was cognizant of three different cultures. First, Paul had in the forefront of his mind his own Jewish culture.[5] Paul's letter is filled with references to Jewish religion and history, and of course, a central theme

---

17:16–34)," *Trinity Journal* 16, no. 1 (1995): 47–62; Margaret M. Mitchell, "Pauline Accommodation and 'Condescension' (συγκατάβασις): 1 Cor 9:19–23 and the History of Influence," in *Paul beyond the Judaism/Hellenism Divide*, ed. Troels Engberg-Pedersen (Louisville, KY: Westminster John Knox, 2001), 197–214; Dean Flemming, "Contextualizing the Gospel in Athens: Paul's Areopagus Address as a Paradigm for Missionary Communication," *Missiology* 30, no. 2 (2002): 199–214; and Terry L. Wilder, "A Biblical Theology of Missions and Contextualization," *Southwestern Journal of Theology* 55, no. 1 (2012): 3–17.

3. Dean Flemming, *Contextualization in the New Testament: Patterns for Theology and Mission* (Downers Grove, IL: InterVarsity, 2005).

4. Jennifer Slater O. P., *Christian Identity Characteristics in Paul's Letter to the Members of the Jesus Movement in Galatians: Creating Diastratic Unity in a Diastratic Divergent South African Society* (Bloomington, IN: AuthorHouse, 2012); Aliou Cissé Niang, *Faith and Freedom in Galatia and Senegal: The Apostle Paul, Colonists and Sending Gods*, Biblical Interpretation Series 97 (Leiden: Brill, 2009).

5. Admittedly, it is overly simplistic to speak of a singular, monolithic Jewish culture in the first-century Mediterranean world. Perhaps it is possible to speak of certain practices and beliefs that most Jews held in common (a so-called common Judaism), but scholars have increasingly emphasized the diversity within first-century Judaism.

of Paul's letter is circumcision. Paul's opponents were persuading the Galatian Christians to adopt certain Jewish religious practices, which Paul vehemently argued against.[6] Second, either consciously or unconsciously, Paul was aware of the broader Greco-Roman culture in which both he and his addressees were immersed.[7] Paul wrote to the Galatians in Greek, although Greek may not have been the mother tongue for either him or his recipients. Paul also made use of Greek and Roman concepts in his letter, such as Roman legal adoption, slavery, the Hellenistic philosophical concept of the corrupt flesh, and the roles of a *paidagōgos* (Gal 3:24–25), *epitropos*, and *oikonomos* (Gal 4:2).[8]

Third, Paul was aware of the Galatians' own culture.[9] The Galatians were part of the broader Anatolian culture, but they also had

6. The identity of the opponents is highly debated. Whether Paul's opponents were Judaizers, pneumatic antinomians, gnostics, or syncretists, it is clear they were compelling the Galatian Christians to adopt certain Jewish practices like circumcision. For the different views of the identity of the opponents, see Joseph B. Tyson, "Paul's Opponents in Galatia," *NovT* 10, no. 4 (1969): 241–54; George Howard, *Paul: Crisis in Galatia; A Study in Early Christian Theology*, 2nd ed. (Cambridge: Cambridge University Press, 1990), xiii–xxxiii, 1–19; and Walt Russell, "Who Were Paul's Opponents in Galatia?," *BibSac* 147 (1990): 329–50.

7. Again, the idea of a singular, homogenous Greco-Roman culture is a vast oversimplification. For an overview of the ethnic and cultural diversity of the first-century Mediterranean world, and especially Asia Minor, see J. Daniel Hays, "Paul and the Multi-ethnic First-Century World: Ethnicity and Christian Identity," in *Paul as Missionary: Identity, Activity, Theology, and Practice*, ed. Trevor J. Burke and Brian S. Rosner, Library of New Testament Studies 420 (London: T&T Clark, 2011), 76–87.

8. For Roman legal adoption, see Francis Lyall, "Roman Law in the Writings of Paul: Adoption," *JBL* 88, no. 4 (1969): 458–66. A *paidagōgos* was a household slave who functioned as the attendant or tutor for a school-aged child. See Norman H. Young, "*Paidagogos*: The Social Setting of a Pauline Metaphor," *NovT* 29, no. 2 (1987): 150–76. The terms *epitropos* and *oikonomos* were used in Roman law for guardians who were appointed to administer the affairs of a minor child. See John K. Goodrich, "Guardians, Not Taskmasters: The Cultural Resonances of Paul's Metaphor in Galatians 4.1–2," *JSNT* 32, no. 3 (2010): 251–84.

9. Surveys of Galatian history and culture can be found in Stephen Mitchell, *Anatolia: Land, Men, and Gods in Asia Minor*, vol. 1, *The Celts and the Impact of Roman Rule* (Oxford: Clarendon, 1993); Gareth Darbyshire, Stephen Mitchell, and Levent Vardar, "The Galatian Settlement in Asia Minor," *Anatolian Studies* 50

their own unique history. In the early third century BCE (sometime in the 270s), Celtic tribal groups from Europe immigrated to the area of central Anatolia and settled around the cities of Gordion, Ancyra, and Tavium. These Celtic immigrants brought their own distinctive culture and language to the region. Over time, between the third century BCE and the first century CE, the Galatians gradually assimilated much of the surrounding Anatolian and Hellenistic cultures. But the Galatians also imprinted aspects of their Celtic culture on their Anatolian neighbors. Karl Strobel refers to this as a process of "mutual acculturation."[10]

That Paul had in mind, at least to some degree, the Galatians' native culture is evident at several points in his letter.[11] In Galatians 4:8, he refers to the gods that the Galatians formerly worshipped. The Galatians venerated a wide array of deities, but the principal ones included Zeus; the Phrygian mother goddess, Cybele; and the moon god, Men. Later, in Galatians 5:12, Paul alludes to the practice of self-emasculation, which was part of the sacred rites for priests of Cybele.[12] More subtle cultural references may be found elsewhere in the letter. For example, Stephen Finlan has argued that the curse-transfer imagery in Galatians 3:13 is based on two cultural backgrounds: the scapegoat tradition of Judaism and curse-transmission rituals common in Galatian culture.[13]

(2000): 75–97; and Karl Strobel, "The Galatians in the Roman Empire: Historical Tradition and Ethnic Identity in Hellenistic and Roman Asia Minor," in *Ethnic Constructs in Antiquity: The Role of Power and Tradition*, ed. Ton Derks and Nico Roymans, Amsterdam Archaeological Studies 13 (Amsterdam: Amsterdam University Press, 2009), 117–44.

10. Strobel, "Galatians in the Roman Empire," 127.
11. The degree of Celtic cultural influence on Paul's audience depends on whether Paul was writing to the north Galatians or south Galatians. The Galatians of Celtic lineage were predominantly located in the north. In either case, Paul's letter indicates that his audience had at least some familiarity with Celtic Galatian culture.
12. Cybele was originally a Phrygian deity that was adopted into the Galatian religious system as early at the third century BCE. Strobel, "Galatians in the Roman Empire," 131.
13. Stephen Finlan, *The Background and Contents of Paul's Cultic Atonement Metaphors*, Academia Biblica 19 (Leiden: Brill, 2004), 101–11.

Although Paul was aware of three different cultures in his correspondence with the Galatians, he did not allow his addressees to conform entirely to any one of these cultures. Paul argued adamantly that the Galatian Christians should not become Jewish. He vehemently rejected his opponents who were compelling the Galatians to adopt Jewish circumcision, and it is clear from Galatians 2:14 that he did not favor the non-Jewish believers adopting Jewish purity and dietary practices. Likewise, Paul did not allow the Galatians to remain as full members of the larger Greco-Roman culture. He certainly did not approve of idolatry, the emperor cult, or the moral values (especially the sexual ethics) of the broader Greco-Roman society.

While Paul did not permit the Galatian Christians to become Jewish or conform entirely to the Greco-Roman culture, he also did not allow them to remain completely Galatian. There are a number of subtle indications in Paul's letter that he sought to separate the Galatian Christians from their native religious culture. For example, in Galatians 3:1, Paul asks, "O foolish Galatians! Who has bewitched [ebaskanen] you?"[14] The word baskainō was used commonly in Greek texts for witchcraft and magic, especially the evil eye.[15] When Paul asked his rhetorical question in Galatians 3:1, he was not only disparaging his opponents for misguiding the Galatians; he was also disparaging the practices associated with the term baskainō.[16] By using this word, Paul was casting scorn upon superstitious magic practices like the evil eye—practices that would have been common in Galatian popular culture. Paul did not want his opponents to "bewitch" the Galatian Christians, nor did he want the Galatians to be engaged in superstitious magic practices.

---

14. New Testament quotations are taken from the English Standard Version unless otherwise indicated.

15. Hans Dieter Betz, Galatians, Hermeneia (Philadelphia: Fortress, 1979), 131.

16. Scholars have debated whether Paul's opponents were literally enticing the Galatians with magic or whether Paul's language is merely rhetorical. The answer to this question is not pertinent for the present study, since in either case, Paul viewed baskainō as something negative.

Using a similar rhetorical strategy, Paul disparaged the native Galatian practice of emasculation in Galatians 5:12. Here, Paul sarcastically declares, "I wish those who unsettle you would emasculate [apokopsontai] themselves" (Gal 5:12). As many commentators have observed, Paul's invective in 5:12 is a not-so-veiled reference to the Galli, the priests of Cybele, who voluntarily submitted themselves to castration.[17] As with baskainō in Galatians 3:1, Paul's intentional use of terminology is meant to portray a native Galatian religious/cultural custom (in this case, emasculation) as an undesirable act.[18]

A third example can be seen in Galatians 4:8, where Paul makes an assertion that many people today would consider politically incorrect. He says, "Formerly, when you did not know God, you were enslaved to those that by nature are not gods" (Gal 4:8). Here, Paul bluntly tells the Galatians that the deities they formerly worshipped are, in reality, false gods. By making this statement, Paul sought to separate the Galatians from their native religious heritage.

It is clear that Paul did not want the Galatian Christians to conform entirely to the cultural practices of the Greeks, Romans, Jews, or even their own Galatian culture. Rather, as we will see, Paul sought to construct a new culture, a distinctly Christian culture, that was meant to be the primary identity for the Galatian Christians. However, in doing so, Paul did not abolish the Galatians' native cultural identity. Rather, he relativized it and subsumed it under their new identity in Christ.[19]

---

17. Betz, Galatians, 270; Martinus C. de Boer, Galatians: A Commentary, New Testament Library (Louisville, KY: Westminster John Knox, 2011), 325–26.

18. J. Cornelis de Vos, "'I Wish Those Who Unsettle You Would Mutilate Themselves!' (Gal 5:12): Circumcision and Emasculation in the Letter to the Galatians," in Jewish Cultural Encounters in the Ancient Mediterranean and Near Eastern World, ed. Mladen Popović, Myles Schoonover, and Marijn Vandenberghe, JSJSup 178 (Leiden: Brill, 2017), 201–17.

19. A similar argument has been made by other scholars, including Ruth Anne Reese and Steven Ybarrola, "Racial and Ethnic Identity: Social Scientific and Biblical Perspectives in Dialogue," Asbury Journal 65, no. 1 (2010): 65–82; and Bruce Hansen, All of You Are One: The Social Vision of Galatians 3.28, 1 Corinthians 12.13 and Colossians 3.11 (London: T&T Clark, 2010).

There are a number of indications throughout Paul's letter that he sought to establish a new cultural identity for the Galatians. He describes this new culture as having its own value system (e.g., Gal 5:13–6:10), patron deity (Jesus), religious rituals (e.g., baptism), and social customs (e.g., eating together).[20] Like many ancient people groups, the Galatian Christians wore distinctive clothing: they were clothed with Christ (Gal 3:27). They also had their own identity markers: they possessed God's spirit and they bore the fruits of that spirit. The Galatian Christians met in their own *ekklēsiai* just as Jews met in synagogues and other groups met in their respective voluntary associations.[21] Perhaps most importantly, the Galatians had their own cultural narrative and worldview.[22] They were spiritual descendants and heirs of the patriarch Abraham (Gal 3:29), and they looked forward to a time in the future when they would inherit their own kingdom—the kingdom of God (Gal 5:21).

In Galatians 4, Paul tells his audience that they have been adopted into their new cultural identity. They were formerly slaves (Gal 4:8–9), but they had been redeemed (Gal 4:5) and adopted into a new family (Gal 4:5–7). The fact that Paul's letter is filled with kinship terminology suggests that the metaphor of family is important for Paul's argument and the Galatians' self-identity.[23] The Galatian Christians are now part of a new "household of faith" (Gal 6:10). They have a

---

20. For the value system, see Philip F. Esler, "Group Boundaries and Intergroup Conflict in Galatians: A New Reading of Galatians 5:13–6:10," in *Ethnicity and the Bible*, ed. Mark G. Brett (Leiden: Brill, 1996), 215–40. In terms of eating together, presumably, the Galatian Christians celebrated the Lord's Supper together, although this is not explicitly mentioned in Paul's letter.

21. On the formation of ethnically based voluntary associations in the Roman world, see K. Verboven, "Resident Aliens and Translocal Merchant *Collegia* in the Roman Empire," in *Frontiers in the Roman World: Proceedings of the Ninth Workshop of the International Network Impact of Empire (Durham, 16–19 April 2009)*, ed. Olivier Hekster and Ted Kaizer (Leiden: Brill, 2011), 335–48.

22. Atsuhiro Asano, *Community-Identity Construction in Galatians: Exegetical, Social-Anthropological and Socio-historical Studies*, JSNTSup 285 (London: T&T Clark, 2005), 149–79.

23. On Paul's use of kinship and household terminology for the construction of social identity, see David G. Horrell, "From ἀδελφοί to οἶκος θεοῦ: Social Transformation in Pauline Christianity," *JBL* 120, no. 2 (2001): 293–311.

new paterfamilias, God (Gal 4:6), and a multitude of brothers (and sisters) who were also adopted into the family.[24] The Galatian Christians are coheirs with the paterfamilias's own natural son (Gal 4:1–7; cf. Rom 8:17) and are entitled to all of the rights and privileges of their new family as natural children. As with any Roman legal adoption, the integration of the Galatian Christians into their new family meant that they had gained a new cultural identity, and their old identity receded into the background.[25]

Near the end of his letter, Paul makes several references to the Christians' new identity. In Galatians 6:14–15, he writes, "But far be it from me to boast except in the cross of our Lord Jesus Christ, by which the world has been crucified to me, and I to the world. For neither circumcision counts for anything, nor uncircumcision, but a new creation." In these verses, Paul makes two astonishing claims. First, he says that he has died to the world. Paul makes a very similar statement in Galatians 2:20, where he says, "I have been crucified with Christ. It is no longer I who live, but Christ who lives in me." In both passages, Paul asserts that whatever he was before Christ (i.e., his former life and old identity; cf. Gal 1:13) has died. Second, in Galatians 6:15, Paul dismisses circumcision and uncircumcision as things of the world that have no value. What does have value is a "new creation"—that is, a new life in the spirit.[26] The old identity markers (i.e., circumcision and uncircumcision) have been rendered irrelevant because there is a new identity in Christ.

In Galatians 6:16, Paul goes on to say, "And as for all who walk by this rule, peace and mercy be upon them, and upon the Israel of God." There is much debate among scholars as to whether "Israel of God" refers to ethnic Jews (or Jewish Christians) or to all Christians, both Jews and gentiles.[27] If Paul used the phrase to refer to

---

24. Trevor J. Burke, *Adopted into God's Family: Exploring a Pauline Metaphor*, New Studies in Biblical Theology 22 (Downers Grove, IL: InterVarsity, 2006), 83–89.
25. Lyall, "Roman Law," 466.
26. Moyer V. Hubbard, *New Creation in Paul's Letters and Thought*, SNTSMS 119 (Cambridge: Cambridge University Press, 2004), 188–232.
27. For a survey of views, see Ole Jakob Filtvedt, "'God's Israel' in Galatians 6.16: An Overview and Assessment of the Key Arguments," *CBR* 15, no. 1 (2016): 123–40.

all Christians, as seems likely,[28] then he was placing the Galatian Christians within the history of God's people, Israel. They had been grafted into Israel (cf. Rom 11:17–24), but not Israel as a geopolitical entity or a distinct ethnic community. For Paul, the Israel to which the Galatians belonged was a heavenly, spiritual Israel (Gal 4:21–31). Their citizenship was now in heaven, in the "Jerusalem above" (Gal 4:26; cf. Phil 3:20; Eph 2:6; Col 3:1–3).

The Galatian Christians had become members of a new *ethnos*.[29] They were not merely members of a new religion but rather a new race or people group with its own cultural distinctives. This should not be surprising, since scholars have often observed that the early Christians portrayed their community as an *ethnos* distinct from other *ethnoi*.[30] As mentioned previously, the Galatian Christians (and Christians more generally) possessed a unifying ethnic history that identified them as descendants of Abraham and heirs of the promises God made to him (Gal 3:29). They were united together by their kinship as brothers and sisters who had been adopted into the family of God.

As a distinctive *ethnos*, Christians also had their own *nomos*, or set of cultural customs. In the Hellenistic worldview, every *ethnos* had its own *nomos*. The Jews had the *torah* (Greek: *nomos*) of Moses that governed their way of life. Likewise, Christians had their own *nomos*, the *nomos tou Christou*—the "law of Christ." In Galatians 6:2, Paul directs the Galatian Christians to "bear one another's burdens, and so fulfill the law of Christ" (cf. 1 Cor 9:21). Slightly earlier, in Galatians

28. Gregory K. Beale, "Peace and Mercy upon the Israel of God: The Old Testament Background of Galatians 6,16b," *Bib* 80, no. 2 (1999): 204–23; Andreas J. Köstenberger, "The Identity of the ΊΣΡΑΗΛ ΤΟΥ ΘΕΟΥ (Israel of God) in Galatians 6:16," *Faith and Mission* 19, no. 1 (2001): 1–16; Thomas R. Schreiner, *Galatians*, Zondervan Exegetical Commentary on the New Testament (Grand Rapids, MI: Zondervan, 2010), 381–83.
29. Hays, "Paul and the Multi-ethnic," 84–86.
30. Denise Kimber Buell, "Rethinking the Relevance of Race for Early Christian Self-Definition," *HTR* 94, no. 4 (2001): 449–76; Denise Kimber Buell, *Why This New Race: Ethnic Reasoning in Early Christianity* (New York: Columbia University Press, 2005); Samuel Vollenweider, "Are Christians a New 'People'? Detecting Ethnicity and Cultural Friction in Paul's Letters and Early Christianity," *Early Christianity* 8, no. 3 (2017): 293–308.

5:14, Paul informs the believers that "the whole law is fulfilled in one word: 'You shall love your neighbor as yourself.'" Thus, love for others is viewed as a summation of the law of Christ. The law of Christ is not a list of commandments; rather, it is a uniquely Christian way of life lived in imitation of Jesus's own self-sacrificial love.[31]

Up to this point, I have focused on the new cultural identity Paul constructed for the Galatian Christians. However, it is important to recognize that Paul did not abolish the concept of ethnicity, nor did he erase the ethnic distinctives of his audience.[32] In many ways, the Galatians remained part of their native culture. They probably ate the same foods, spoke the same language(s), observed many of the same social customs, and utilized most of the same material culture as they had always done. Certainly, they had to give up aspects of their native cultural identity, particularly their religious culture and possibly some patterns of behavior, but by and large, they were still culturally Galatian in their day-to-day lives.

In Galatians 3:28, Paul remarks, "There is neither Jew nor Greek, there is neither slave nor free, there is no male and female, for you are all one in Christ Jesus." This verse has often been taken as evidence that Paul sought to erase ethnic, social, and gender differences, but Paul's statement needs to be understood within the larger context of his letter.[33] In Galatians 2:14–15, Paul undoubtedly describes both Peter and himself as Jewish. Furthermore, we know from Paul's other letters that Paul still thought in categories of Jew and non-Jew (Rom 1–2; 11:1–24), male and female (1 Cor 7:1–16; 11:2–16), and slave and free (1 Cor 7:21–24; Phlm). Paul's statement in Galatians 3:28 is not meant to erase all cultural distinctions and create a Christian *ethnos* that is uniform and homogenous. Rather, Paul relativized the earthly ethnic and cultural identities of his recipients and subsumed them

31. Richard B. Hays, "Christology and Ethics in Galatians: The Law of Christ," *CBQ* 49, no. 2 (1987): 268–90; Heikki Räisänen, *Paul and the Law*, 2nd ed., WUNT 29 (Tübingen, Germany: Mohr Siebeck, 1987), 80–82.
32. Charles H. Cosgrove, "Did Paul Value Ethnicity?," *CBQ* 68, no. 2 (2006): 268–90.
33. For example, Daniel Boyarin, *A Radical Jew: Paul and the Politics of Identity* (Berkeley: University of California Press, 1994).

under the larger and more significant identity of being "in Christ."[34] In Christ, all believers become unified and equal while living out the reality of their ethnic, social, and gender differences.[35]

Before turning to the case studies, there are three relevant observations that should be made about Paul's construction of culture in his letter to the Galatians. First, it is worth noting that the new *ethnos* Paul constructed was not sui generis. In the process of writing his letter to the Galatians, Paul freely borrowed ideas and concepts from the surrounding cultures. Paul employed metaphors from the Hellenistic world like justification (a legal metaphor), redemption (a commercial metaphor), and adoption (a social metaphor). He also utilized Hellenistic ethical terminology and rhetorical methods as part of his letter.[36] Paul was not a cultural snob. Quite the contrary. The apostle felt entirely free to use whatever was available from the surrounding cultures in order to communicate his message as long as it was in conformity with his fundamental principles.

Second, the culture Paul constructed was high on values and low on norms.[37] While Paul valued Christians eating meals together (Gal

---

34. John M. G. Barclay, "'Neither Jew nor Greek': Multiculturalism and the New Perspective on Paul," in *Ethnicity and the Bible*, ed. Mark G. Brett (Leiden: Brill, 1996), 211–12; William S. Campbell, "Religion, Identity and Ethnicity: The Contribution of Paul the Apostle," *Journal of Beliefs and Values* 29, no. 2 (2008): 139–50; Hansen, *All of You*, 67–106.

35. In a sense, Paul's vision of the Christian *ethnos* was similar to the social reality of the Roman world. In the Roman Empire, there were many Roman citizens who were not ethnically Roman or even Italian. These people were Greek, Jewish, Egyptian, Spanish, and Anatolian, but they were united by their Romanness.

36. Betz, *Galatians*, 14–25, 286; Andrew Chester, "The Relevance of Jewish Inscriptions for New Testament Ethics," in *Early Christian Ethics in Interaction with Jewish and Greco-Roman Contexts*, ed. Jan Willem van Henten and Joseph Verheyden, Studies in Theology and Religion 17 (Leiden: Brill, 2013), 133–35; Craig S. Keener, "A Comparison of the Fruit of the Spirit in Galatians 5:22–23 with Ancient Thought on Ethics and Emotion," in *The Language and Literature of the New Testament: Essays in Honor of Stanley E. Porter's 60th Birthday*, ed. Lois K. Fuller Dow, Craig A. Evans, and Andrew W. Pitts, Biblical Interpretation Series 150 (Leiden: Brill, 2016), 574–98.

37. Values are generally defined as the principles a society deems to be good, right, or ethical, while norms are the specific rules that determine how one should behave in a certain situation. See Jon Elster, "Norms," in *The Oxford*

2:11–14), he did not specify norms about what kind of meal should be eaten, where it should be eaten, or how it should be eaten. Paul valued Christians assembling together as a community or association, but he did not prescribe a particular location, frequency, the kinds of activities to be engaged in, or the leadership structure for such assemblies. Paul clearly valued Christians caring for the poor (Gal 2:10) and serving one another (Gal 5:13), but he never specified how such care and service should be rendered. Even the fruits of the Spirit listed by Paul in Galatians 5:22–23 are only general principles, not specific directives. This suggests that Paul was content to let each community of believers determine the exact social norms that would embody these values.

Third, the Christian culture Paul constructed had aspects of tightness and looseness. Cultures are "tight" in areas where they exhibit strong and binding social norms, whereas they are "loose" in areas where norms are relaxed and flexible.[38] For example, first-century Jews were culturally tight when it came to exclusive Yahweh worship, but they were loose with regard to the use of magic.[39] Most Jews were apparently tight when it came to avoiding the consumption of pork, but there seems to have been looseness about whether one could prepare and eat Roman dishes.[40] Paul's constructed culture was tight in areas related to community, ethics/morality, Jesus

---

Handbook of Analytical Sociology, ed. Peter Hedström and Peter Bearman (Oxford: Oxford University Press, 2009), 195–217; Karl-Dieter Opp, "Norms," in International Encyclopedia of the Social & Behavioral Sciences, 2nd ed., vol. 17, ed. James D. Wright (Amsterdam: Elsevier, 2015), 5–10; and Helmut Thome, "Values, Sociology Of," in International Encyclopedia of the Social & Behavioral Sciences, 2nd ed., vol. 25, ed. James D. Wright (Amsterdam: Elsevier, 2015), 47–53.

38. Michele J. Gelfand, Lisa Hisae Nishii, and Jana L. Raver, "On the Nature and Importance of Cultural Tightness-Looseness," Journal of Applied Psychology 91, no. 6 (2006): 1225–44. The terms tightness and looseness are often applied to cultures as a whole, but the terminology can also be applied to aspects of a single culture.

39. See, for example, Gideon Bohak, Ancient Jewish Magic: A History (Cambridge: Cambridge University Press, 2008), 70–142.

40. Andrea Berlin, "Jewish Life before the Revolt: The Archaeological Evidence," JSJ 36, no. 4 (2005): 417–70, esp. 420–34.

devotion, and his gospel message of faith, but he was loose in many areas concerned with daily life. For example, Paul was apparently loose regarding what kinds of employment a Christian could undertake or whether it was permissible to join the military or attend the theater. This suggests that Paul expected unity in the areas of tightness, but he left ample room for differences among Christians in the areas of looseness.

2. Test Case #1: Bindis

To a Westerner, the most obvious identification marker of a Hindu (particularly a Hindu woman) is a bindi, a dot placed on the forehead between the eyebrows. Traditionally, the bindi symbolized the presence of a mystical third eye, which is the focal point of energy and wisdom. For many people in modern Indian culture, the traditional, mythological meaning of the bindi has receded into the background, and the bindi has taken on other primary significances such as a symbol of general religious devotion, a decoration for cosmetic beauty or fashion, or a sign that a woman is married and will bring prosperity to her husband. In some circles, the bindi is even worn as a symbol of feminine empowerment and resistance to traditional roles imposed on women by the male-dominated culture.[41] That said, for most Indians, the bindi remains an object of religious devotion and superstition. The bindi is normally applied in the morning as part of a *puja* (a ritual or act of worship), and most Indian women view the bindi as a magical token that protects their husbands' lives and well-being.

It is not uncommon for some Indian Christians to also wear a bindi. Bindi wearing is more prevalent among people who converted to Christianity out of Hinduism, especially if the convert is an older female. Wearing a bindi is more acceptable among certain denominations, particularly Roman Catholics, but is strongly discouraged

---

41. Mary Grace Antony, "On the Spot: Seeking Acceptance and Expressing Resistance through the Bindi," *Journal of International and Intercultural Communication* 3, no. 4 (2010): 346–68.

in most Evangelical Protestant denominations. Evangelical Protestants in India often accuse Roman Catholics of being too syncretistic in matters like bindi wearing.[42] Thus, there is significant controversy among Christians regarding the use of bindis.[43]

Based on what we know from Galatians, what would Paul say about Christians wearing a bindi? Certainly, Paul would object to the use of a bindi in connection with Hindu worship. Presumably, though, most Indian Christians who continue to wear a bindi do not do so out of devotion to Hindu gods. But many Christians still view the bindi superstitiously as a magical token that brings blessings and provides protection against evil and misfortune. Since Paul disparaged superstitious magic practices like the evil eye in Galatians 3:1, it is likely that he would reprimand Christians who continue to wear a bindi for its magical protection.

It is important to point out that many Christian women continue to wear a bindi so that they are socially acceptable. In general, Indians assume that a woman who does not wear a bindi is either a widow or inauspicious.[44] Thus, some Christian women who stop wearing a bindi can find themselves ostracized and excluded from weddings, festivals, and other social events. What would Paul say to these women who use a bindi for social rather than religious purposes?

Paul would probably not issue a general prohibition against bindi wearing just because the bindi has a religious significance for people in the surrounding culture. In the Greco-Roman world, there were a number of ethnic dress items that had religious associations, but Paul never condemned such clothing in his letters. An interesting case in point is the Phrygian cap, which may have been worn by

---

42. Anita Yadala Suneson, "Indian Protestants and Their Religious Others: Views of Religious Diversity among Christians in Bangalore" (PhD diss., Uppsala University, 2019), 169–70.

43. Ole Kirchheiner has studied this controversy among Nepali Christians. See Ole Kirchheiner, "The Challenge of Tika between Christian and Traditional Nepalis," *Nepali Christian Journal* 5 (2017): 95–116. I am not aware of a similar study conducted on Indian Christians.

44. In India, widows are generally considered to be cursed. They are viewed as an evil omen that will bring misfortune to those around them.

some of Paul's Galatian readers.[45] The Phrygian cap was a conical cloth hat that had a peak that bends over frontward. The cap was typically connected with people of eastern origin.[46] Like the bindi, the Phrygian cap also had a religious, mythological association. Attis, the consort of the goddess Cybele; the moon god, Men; and the god Mithras were all commonly depicted as wearing a Phrygian cap. Yet in spite of its religious associations, it seems unlikely that Paul would have prohibited the Galatians from wearing a Phrygian cap as part of their customary ethnic dress. Such a prohibition would be contrary to Paul's emphasis on internal spirituality and his avoidance of prescribing specific external practices.[47]

If we supplement Paul's letter to the Galatians with information from his other letters, then a nuanced answer emerges. In 1 Corinthians 9:19–21, Paul writes, "For though I am free from all, I have made

---

45. We do not have positive evidence that any of the Galatian Christians wore a Phrygian cap, but it is certainly possible that such was the case. The hat was quite popular in the broader Anatolian region, and it was fashionable even as far away as Thrace and Dacia. The Phrygian cap was also closely associated with traditional Galatian religious culture, particularly the worship of Cybele. The Galli (the self-emasculated priests of Cybele) often wore the Phrygian cap in imitation of Attis. This evidence, while admittedly circumstantial, suggests that some of the Galatian Christians might have adopted the Phrygian cap as part of their local cultural identity.

46. Richard A. Gergel, "Costume as Geographic Indicator: Barbarians and Prisoners on Cuirassed Statue Breastplates," in *The World of Roman Costume*, ed. Judith Lynn Sebasta and Larissa Bonfante (Madison: University of Wisconsin Press, 2001), 191–209; Tuna Şare Ağtürk, "Headdress Fashions and Their Social Significance in Ancient Western Anatolia: The Seventh through Fourth Centuries BCE," *Anatolia* 40 (2014): 66–67.

47. Paul's indifference to the Phrygian cap (assuming that some of the Galatians actually wore it) is noteworthy because it is likely that some of Paul's fellow Jews would not have tolerated it. The author of 2 Macc mentioned the "Greek hat" (*petasos*) as one of the despicable practices that the high priest Jason introduced to the people of Jerusalem (2 Macc 4:12). The *petasos* was a wide-brimmed sun hat that did not have a particular religious association, but the author of 2 Macc deemed it to be unsuitable for Jews simply because of its strong connection with Hellenistic culture. See Daniel R. Schwartz, *2 Maccabees*, Commentaries on Early Jewish Literature (Berlin: de Gruyter, 2008), 223–24. If some Jews objected to the *petasos*, then almost certainly they would have disallowed the Phrygian cap.

myself a servant to all, that I might win more of them. To the Jews I became as a Jew, in order to win Jews. To those under the law I became as one under the law (though not being myself under the law) that I might win those under the law. To those outside the law I became as one outside the law (not being outside the law of God but under the law of Christ) that I might win those outside the law." Here, Paul states that he is willing to adopt the cultural norms and practices of his various audiences in order to win them to Christ. If we apply this logic to bindi wearing, then Paul might permit Indian Christians to wear a bindi so that they can maintain good relationships with their Hindu family, friends, and neighbors, with the ultimate goal of bringing them to faith in Christ. It is important to point out that Paul would not be condoning bindi wearing purely for the sake of social acceptance. Rather, Paul would be permitting bindis for the sake of overcoming a social barrier so that Indian Christians can bring their Hindu relatives and neighbors to faith in Christ.

Paul might also tell Indian Christians to avoid wearing a bindi around other Christians, especially those who are recent converts or weak in their faith. In Romans 14, Paul discusses the controversial issue of eating meat sacrificed to idols, and he tells the Roman believers that they have the freedom to eat or not eat. However, he warns them to avoid using their freedom in a way that would cause weaker believers to stumble (Rom 14:13–15, 20–21). In the same regard, Paul would likely tell Indian Christians to avoid wearing a bindi around other Christians because it might cause their fellow believers to become upset and judgmental (cf. Rom 14:15), or it might cause them to start wearing a bindi against their own conviction (cf. Rom 14:23).

It is evident from the foregoing discussion that Paul's response to bindi wearing would be complex and multifaceted. His response would vary from person to person, depending on each one's reason for wearing a bindi. Paul certainly would object to the religious and superstitious use of bindis, although Paul probably would not issue a universal prohibition against bindis. Like the Phrygian cap, the bindi is viewed both religiously and as part of the culture's normal dress. Thus, Paul would allow Christians to wear a bindi for the sake of relating to and evangelizing their Hindu neighbors, but he would advise them to avoid wearing a bindi around other Christians who might stumble.

3. Test Case #2: Caste Divisions

Roberto de Nobili recognized that one of the greatest barriers to the gospel in India is caste divisions. The Hindu caste system divides society into a grand hierarchy, assigning each person to a group, and each group serves a particular function within the social system. In its most basic reduction, the caste system divides people into four *varnas*, or classes: Brahmins (the priestly class), Kshatriyas (the ruling class), Vaishyas (the merchant and artisan class), and the Sudras (the laboring class). Implicitly, there is a fifth class: Dalits (those who are outside the *varna* classification or those who are untouchable).

Alongside the *varna* system is another system of division called *jati*. *Jatis* are small, localized communities of people centered on a particular profession, language, clan/tribe, or religion/deity. The members of a *jati* are born into the community, and such communities are often strictly endogamous. Although the members of different *jatis* will coexist within a larger social setting, such as a town or village, the members of one *jati* are typically introverted when it comes to socializing, religious practice, sharing food, and other socially intimate customs. Each *jati* is governed by certain social norms and practices that all members are expected to follow. Thus, one's *jati* is a primary identity marker for Hindus.

The fundamental problem with the caste system is that it creates systemic discrimination and social division. Members of one caste will not worship together with members of another caste. They will not share food together, occupy the same space, or be baptized in the same water. Unlike other kinds of social identity markers, such as nationality or language, there is an objective value associated with each caste. In the caste system, some castes are objectively "higher" than others.

What would Paul say about caste divisions? Previously, I argued that Paul did not nullify ethnic, social, or gender distinctions, but he relativized and subsumed such differences under the unifying and equalizing identity of being "in Christ" (Gal 3:28). Paul did not demand that Jews give up their Jewish culture or that the Galatians give up their Galatian culture, except for those aspects that are contrary to the gospel. However, while Paul allowed cultural differences and identities to remain, such worldly identities are rendered irrelevant and valueless (cf. Gal 5:6; 6:15) because of the supreme value of the new identity in Christ.

Paul's body metaphor in 1 Corinthians 12:12–31 is helpful here. Paul allowed an eye to remain an eye and a hand to remain a hand, but he did not allow the eye to think that it is better than the hand or to separate itself from the hand (1 Cor 12:21). Each body part remains distinct, but it is united together with the other body parts in mutual care, respect, and dependency. In Paul's view, each body part exists for the well-being of the body as a whole, not for itself.

Based on this, it seems that Paul would offer a nuanced answer to the question of caste divisions. Paul would not object to the members of a caste adhering to their own culturally distinct practices, such as their particular mode of employment, manner of dress, or style of cooking. However, Paul would oppose the caste system as an *ideological system*. An integral part of the Indian caste system is the valuation placed upon others, which results in feelings of superiority/ inferiority, favoritism, divisiveness, discrimination, and oppression. This ideology is fundamentally opposed to Paul's gospel. Paul would expect Indian Christians to see their primary identity as being "in Christ" (i.e., as Christians), thus abrogating the value and relevance of caste identity. Paul would allow Christians to observe the cultural practices of their particular caste (so long as they are not immoral or idolatrous), but he would demand that believers transcend all cultural differences and demonstrate unity and Christlike love and affection for all others.

4. Test Case #3: Festivals

India is a society rich in festivals and holy days. In modern times, there are prominent nationwide celebrations like Diwali (the Festival of Lights) and Holi (the Festival of Colors) as well as regional or local holy days like Pongal, a popular harvest festival in the state of Tamil Nadu. All of the traditional Indian festivals and holy days are linked to the mythology of Hinduism. Festivals usually celebrate a particular event from a god's life, such as his victory over another god in battle or a great miracle that the god performed. In addition, many Indians participate in holy day rituals for superstitious reasons. They believe that by performing certain ritual acts, they will gain good fortune and prosperity and ward off evil.

Since the days of Roberto de Nobili, missionaries have debated whether Christians should celebrate these Hindu festivals. Four hundred years after de Nobili, there is still no common consensus among Christians in India. Anecdotal evidence indicates that Roman Catholics are more likely than Protestants to celebrate these festivals, although opinions differ based on denomination, locality, demographics, and other factors.

Based on Paul's letter to the Galatians, what would he say regarding Christians observing such festivals? An answer to this vexing question might be found in Galatians 4:8–11, where Paul writes, "Formerly, when you did not know God, you were enslaved to those that by nature are not gods. But now that you have come to know God, or rather to be known by God, how can you turn back again to the weak and worthless elementary principles of the world, whose slaves you want to be once more? You observe days and months and seasons and years! I am afraid I may have labored over you in vain."

Many commentators interpret Galatians 4:10 to mean that the Galatian Christians were being led astray to observe the Jewish cultic calendar. While this is the more prevalent interpretation, a number of scholars have argued that Galatians 4:10 refers to the cultic festivals and holy days that were native to the Galatians, either Roman, Greek, Anatolian, or Celtic.[48] If the later interpretation is

---

48. Betz, *Galatians*, 218; Troy Martin, "Pagan and Judeo-Christian Time-Keeping Schemes in Gal 4.10 and Col 2.16," *NTS* 42, no. 1 (1996): 105–19; J. Louis Martyn, *Galatians: A New Translation with Introduction and Commentary*, Anchor Bible Commentary (New York: Doubleday, 1997), 414–18; Justin K. Hardin, *Galatians and the Imperial Cult: A Critical Analysis of the First-Century Social Context of Paul's Letter*, WUNT, vol. 2, no. 237 (Tübingen, Germany: Mohr

correct, then Paul saw the Galatians' own native holy days as "weak and worthless elementary principles" that would lead the Galatians back into spiritual slavery. Like the gods-that-are-not-gods in Galatians 4:8, the Galatians' traditional calendrical observations were powerless to bring them into a proper relationship with God (cf. Gal 4:4–7).

Thus, to answer the preceding question, Paul would probably give Christians in India the same message. He would object to the observance of holy days for religious or superstitious reasons. However, as in the previous two test cases, the answer is complicated. Paul's objection assumes that the worshippers view holy day observance as either a religious ritual or a magical/superstitious act that grants supernatural power to the performer. However, in twenty-first-century India, as in the Western world, many people (especially young people) do not view their native holy days as religious or superstitious rituals.

What would Paul say to a Christian family in modern India that celebrates Pongal nonreligiously? It is difficult to know, but I suspect that Paul would consider it as being similar to bindi wearing. He would probably condone holy day observance for the sake of overcoming social barriers so that Indian Christians can share the gospel with their Hindu relatives and neighbors. However, he would also tell them to avoid observing holy days around other Christians because it might cause their fellow believers to stumble.

5. Galatians and Cultural Contextualization

Paul's Galatian readers lived in a highly complex, multicultural world. To varying degrees, their lives were shaped by the surrounding Roman social structure, the pervasiveness of Hellenism, the rich medley of local cultures (Celtic, Phrygian, etc.), and the influence of Judaism. When the Galatians became followers of Christ, they also

---

Siebeck, 2008), 116–47; Christina Harker, *The Colonizers' Idols: Paul, Galatia, and Empire in New Testament Studies*, WUNT, vol. 2, no. 460 (Tübingen, Germany: Mohr Siebeck, 2018).

took on a new cultural identity. They were adopted into a new family and became part of a new *ethnos* with its own cultural distinctives. They now followed a supreme law of mutual love, and they conducted themselves according to the spirit of God.

Yet the Galatian Christians did not cease to be Galatian. They did not simply swap one cultural identity for another, nor did they completely relinquish their native culture and become absorbed into a uniform, homogenous Christian community. Certainly, they had to abandon certain aspects of their native culture that conflicted with their new identity in Christ, particularly their former religious practices and some patterns of behavior. However, in many ways, their identity as Galatians was maintained, although it was relativized and subsumed under their identity in Christ.

Paul's letter to the Galatians has much to teach us about the contextualization of the gospel, especially in our own complex, globalized, multicultural world. Paul's construction of culture allowed for a wide range of variation among Christians within set parameters. As noted previously, Paul's letter emphasizes values over norms. This permits a great deal of variability in how Christians enact certain values. It is also important to observe the areas in which Paul constructs cultural tightness and looseness in his letter. While the areas of tightness should be strictly maintained, the areas of looseness give space for flexibility and even loving and respectful disagreement within the Christian community.

In addition, Paul's letter can offer valuable insight into specific questions that face various Christian communities around the globe. In this study, I examined three test cases that are pertinent to the Indian context. In all three cases, Paul's letter to the Galatians is able to provide some clues as to how the apostle might address these issues if he was present with us today. As we have seen, in each case, Paul's answer would be nuanced and complex (as we might expect from the apostle). Certainly, it is not possible for Paul's letter to the Galatians, nor even the entire New Testament, to answer every question related to contextualization. However, there are probably more answers than we might suspect if we pay careful attention to the text and apply some well-reasoned speculation.

There is no doubt that the questions and controversies surrounding culture and the gospel will continue far into the future. In the four hundred years since Roberto de Nobili's pioneering work, scholars and missiologists have unquestionably produced more heat than light. However, perhaps if we listen to the apostles and exercise mutual love ourselves, then we can find a way forward.

Bibliography

Ağtürk, Tuna Şare. "Headdress Fashions and Their Social Significance in Ancient Western Anatolia: The Seventh through Fourth Centuries BCE." *Anatolia* 40 (2014): 66–67.

Antony, Mary Grace. "On the Spot: Seeking Acceptance and Expressing Resistance through the Bindi." *Journal of International and Intercultural Communication* 3, no. 4 (2010): 346–368.

Asano, Atsuhiro. *Community-Identity Construction in Galatians: Exegetical, Social-Anthropological and Socio-historical Studies.* JSNTSup 285. London: T&T Clark, 2005.

Barclay, John M. G. "'Neither Jew nor Greek': Multiculturalism and the New Perspective on Paul." In *Ethnicity and the Bible*, edited by Mark G. Brett, 211–212. Leiden: Brill, 1996.

Beale, Gregory K. "Peace and Mercy upon the Israel of God: The Old Testament Background of Galatians 6,16b." *Bib* 80, no. 2 (1999): 204–223.

Berlin, Andrea. "Jewish Life before the Revolt: The Archaeological Evidence." *JSJ* 36, no. 4 (2005): 417–470.

Betz, Hans Dieter. *Galatians.* Hermeneia. Philadelphia: Fortress, 1979.

Bohak, Gideon. *Ancient Jewish Magic: A History.* Cambridge: Cambridge University Press, 2008.

Boyarin, Daniel. *A Radical Jew: Paul and the Politics of Identity.* Berkeley: University of California Press, 1994.

Buell, Denise Kimber. "Rethinking the Relevance of Race for Early Christian Self-Definition." *HTR* 94, no. 4 (2001): 449–476.

———. *Why This New Race: Ethnic Reasoning in Early Christianity.* New York: Columbia University Press, 2005.

Burke, Trevor J. *Adopted into God's Family: Exploring a Pauline Metaphor.* New Studies in Biblical Theology 22. Downers Grove, IL: InterVarsity, 2006.

Campbell, William S. "Religion, Identity and Ethnicity: The Contribution of Paul the Apostle." *Journal of Beliefs and Values* 29, no. 2 (2008): 139–150.

Charles, J. Daryl. "Engaging the (Neo)Pagan Mind: Paul's Encounter with Athenian Culture as a Model for Cultural Apologetics (Acts 17:16–34)." *Trinity Journal* 16, no. 1 (1995): 47–62.

Chester, Andrew. "The Relevance of Jewish Inscriptions for New Testament Ethics." In *Early Christian Ethics in Interaction with Jewish and Greco-Roman Contexts*, edited by Jan Willem van Henten and Joseph Verheyden, 107–146. Studies in Theology and Religion 17. Leiden: Brill, 2013.

Cosgrove, Charles H. "Did Paul Value Ethnicity?" *CBQ* 68, no. 2 (2006): 268–290.

Darbyshire, Gareth, Stephen Mitchell, and Levent Vardar. "The Galatian Settlement in Asia Minor." *Anatolian Studies* 50 (2000): 75–97.

de Boer, Martinus C. *Galatians: A Commentary.* New Testament Library. Louisville, KY: Westminster John Knox, 2011.

de Vos, J. Cornelis. "'I Wish Those Who Unsettle You Would Mutilate Themselves!' (Gal 5:12): Circumcision and Emasculation in the Letter to the Galatians." In *Jewish Cultural Encounters in the Ancient Mediterranean and Near Eastern World*, edited by Mladen Popović, Myles Schoonover, and Marijn Vandenberghe, 201–217. JSJSup 178. Leiden: Brill, 2017.

Elster, Jon. "Norms." In *The Oxford Handbook of Analytical Sociology*, edited by Peter Hedström and Peter Bearman, 195–217. Oxford: Oxford University Press, 2009.

Esler, Philip F. "Group Boundaries and Intergroup Conflict in Galatians: A New Reading of Galatians 5:13–6:10." In *Ethnicity and the Bible*, edited by Mark G. Brett, 215–240. Leiden: Brill, 1996.

Filtvedt, Ole Jakob. "'God's Israel' in Galatians 6.16: An Overview and Assessment of the Key Arguments." *CBR* 15, no. 1 (2016): 123–140.

Finlan, Stephen. *The Background and Contents of Paul's Cultic Atonement Metaphors.* Academia Biblica 19. Leiden: Brill, 2004.

Flemming, Dean. *Contextualization in the New Testament: Patterns for Theology and Mission.* Downers Grove, IL: InterVarsity, 2005.

———. "Contextualizing the Gospel in Athens: Paul's Areopagus Address as a Paradigm for Missionary Communication." *Missiology* 30, no. 2 (2002): 199–214.

Gelfand, Michele J., Lisa Hisae Nishii, and Jana L. Raver. "On the Nature and Importance of Cultural Tightness-Looseness." *Journal of Applied Psychology* 91, no. 6 (2006): 1225–1244.

Gergel, Richard A. "Costume as Geographic Indicator: Barbarians and Prisoners on Cuirassed Statue Breastplates." In *The World of Roman Costume*, edited by Judith Lynn Sebasta and Larissa Bonfante, 191–209. Madison: University of Wisconsin Press, 2001.

Goodrich, John K. "Guardians, Not Taskmasters: The Cultural Resonances of Paul's Metaphor in Galatians 4.1–2." *JSNT* 32, no. 3 (2010): 251–284.

Hansen, Bruce. *All of You Are One: The Social Vision of Galatians 3.28, 1 Corinthians 12.13 and Colossians 3.11.* London: T&T Clark, 2010.

Hardin, Justin K. *Galatians and the Imperial Cult: A Critical Analysis of the First-Century Social Context of Paul's Letter.* WUNT, vol. 2, no. 237. Tübingen, Germany: Mohr Siebeck, 2008.

Harker, Christina. *The Colonizers' Idols: Paul, Galatia, and Empire in New Testament Studies.* WUNT, vol. 2, no. 460. Tübingen, Germany: Mohr Siebeck, 2018.

Hays, J. Daniel. "Paul and the Multi-ethnic First-Century World: Ethnicity and Christian Identity." In *Paul as Missionary: Identity, Activity, Theology, and Practice*, edited by Trevor J. Burke and Brian S. Rosner, 76–87. Library of New Testament Studies 420. London: T&T Clark, 2011.

Hays, Richard B. "Christology and Ethics in Galatians: The Law of Christ." *CBQ* 49, no. 2 (1987): 268–290.

Horrell, David G. "From ἀδελφοί to οἶκος θεοῦ: Social Transformation in Pauline Christianity." *JBL* 120, no. 2 (2001): 293–311.

Howard, George. *Paul: Crisis in Galatia; A Study in Early Christian Theology.* 2nd ed. Cambridge: Cambridge University Press, 1990.

Hubbard, Moyer V. *New Creation in Paul's Letters and Thought.* SNTSMS 119. Cambridge: Cambridge University Press, 2004.

Keener, Craig S. "A Comparison of the Fruit of the Spirit in Galatians 5:22–23 with Ancient Thought on Ethics and Emotion." In *The Language and Literature of the New Testament: Essays in Honor of Stanley E. Porter's 60th Birthday*, edited by Lois K. Fuller Dow, Craig A. Evans, and Andrew W. Pitts, 574–598. Biblical Interpretation Series 150. Leiden: Brill, 2016.

Kirchheiner, Ole. "The Challenge of Tika between Christian and Traditional Nepalis." *Nepali Christian Journal* 5 (2017): 95–116.

Köstenberger, Andreas J. "The Identity of the 'ΙΣΡΑΗΛ ΤΟΥ ΘΕΟΥ (Israel of God) in Galatians 6:16." *Faith and Mission* 19, no. 1 (2001): 1–16.

Lyall, Francis. "Roman Law in the Writings of Paul: Adoption." *JBL* 88, no. 4 (1969): 458–466.

Martin, Troy. "Pagan and Judeo-Christian Time-Keeping Schemes in Gal 4.10 and Col 2.16." *NTS* 42, no. 1 (1996): 105–119.

Martyn, J. Louis. *Galatians: A New Translation with Introduction and Commentary*. Anchor Bible Commentary. New York: Doubleday, 1997.

Mitchell, Margaret M. "Pauline Accommodation and 'Condescension' (συγκατάβασις): 1 Cor 9:19–23 and the History of Influence." In *Paul beyond the Judaism/Hellenism Divide*, edited by Troels Engberg-Pedersen, 197–214. Louisville, KY: Westminster John Knox, 2001.

Mitchell, Stephen. *Anatolia: Land, Men, and Gods in Asia Minor*. Vol. 1, *The Celts and the Impact of Roman Rule*. Oxford: Clarendon, 1993.

Niang, Aliou Cissé. *Faith and Freedom in Galatia and Senegal: The Apostle Paul, Colonists and Sending Gods*. Biblical Interpretation Series 97. Leiden: Brill, 2009.

Opp, Karl-Dieter. "Norms." In *International Encyclopedia of the Social & Behavioral Sciences*, 2nd ed., vol. 17, edited by James D. Wright, 5–10. Amsterdam: Elsevier, 2015.

Räisänen, Heikki. *Paul and the Law*. 2nd ed. WUNT 29. Tübingen, Germany: Mohr Siebeck, 1987.

Reese, Ruth Anne, and Steven Ybarrola. "Racial and Ethnic Identity: Social Scientific and Biblical Perspectives in Dialogue." *Asbury Journal* 65, no. 1 (2010): 65–82.

Russell, Walt. "Who Were Paul's Opponents in Galatia?" *BibSac* 147 (1990): 329–350.

Schreiner, Thomas R. *Galatians*. Zondervan Exegetical Commentary on the New Testament. Grand Rapids, MI: Zondervan, 2010.

Schwartz, Daniel R. *2 Maccabees*. Commentaries on Early Jewish Literature. Berlin: de Gruyter, 2008.

Slater O. P., Jennifer. *Christian Identity Characteristics in Paul's Letter to the Members of the Jesus Movement in Galatians: Creating Diastratic Unity in a Diastratic Divergent South African Society*. Bloomington, IN: AuthorHouse, 2012.

Strobel, Karl. "The Galatians in the Roman Empire: Historical Tradition and Ethnic Identity in Hellenistic and Roman Asia Minor." In *Ethnic Constructs in Antiquity: The Role of Power and Tradition*, edited by Ton Derks and Nico Roymans, 117–144. Amsterdam Archaeological Studies 13. Amsterdam: Amsterdam University Press, 2009.

Suneson, Anita Yadala. "Indian Protestants and Their Religious Others: Views of Religious Diversity among Christians in Bangalore." PhD diss., Uppsala University, 2019.

Thome, Helmut. "Values, Sociology Of." In *International Encyclopedia of the Social & Behavioral Sciences*, 2nd ed., vol. 25, edited by James D. Wright, 45–53. Amsterdam: Elsevier, 2015.

Tyson, Joseph B. "Paul's Opponents in Galatia." *NovT* 10, no. 4 (1969): 241–254.

Verboven, K. "Resident Aliens and Translocal Merchant *Collegia* in the Roman Empire." In *Frontiers in the Roman World: Proceedings of the Ninth Workshop of the International Network Impact of Empire (Durham, 16–19 April 2009)*, edited by Olivier Hekster and Ted Kaizer, 335–348. Leiden: Brill, 2011.

Vollenweider, Samuel. "Are Christians a New 'People'? Detecting Ethnicity and Cultural Friction in Paul's Letters and Early Christianity." *Early Christianity* 8, no. 3 (2017): 293–308.

Wilder, Terry L. "A Biblical Theology of Missions and Contextualization." *Southwestern Journal of Theology* 55, no. 1 (2012): 3–17.

Young, Norman H. "*Paidagogos*: The Social Setting of a Pauline Metaphor." *NovT* 29, no. 2 (1987): 150–176.

5

Paul, Culture, and Sexual Immorality in 1 Corinthians 5 and 6

ARREN BENNET LAWRENCE

In his first epistle to the Corinthians, Paul addressed several problems of the Corinthian church. In chapters 5 and 6, he addressed three issues, of which two of them are related to sexual immorality. In chapter 5, he wrote against incest, which was practiced by one man, while in chapter 6, he addressed sexual immorality, particularly prostitution. Paul uses culture as the basis for his arguments in 1 Corinthians 5. However, he exhorts against one of the common cultural practices of his time, prostitution, in chapter 6.

In 1 Corinthians 5:1, Paul states that one of the church believers in Corinth was involved in incest, a kind that was not even found among the pagans. Paul's argument is this: as this kind of incest—that is, a man having sex with his father's wife (1 Cor 5:1)—is not even found among the pagans, the church should excommunicate him (5:2, 13). Here, Paul uses a common cultural practice as one of his arguments against incest.

However, when Paul exhorts against prostitution (1 Cor 6:12–20), he argues against one of the common cultural practices of his time. As we will see, prostitution was quite common. A careful analysis is needed to understand the rationale behind Paul's use of culture in chapter 5 of 1 Corinthians and his argument against culture in chapter 6. Before going into the details of Paul's rationale behind his usage and his argument against certain cultural practices, it is important to understand his exhortation in 1 Corinthians 5:1–13 and 6:12–20. In this inquiry, Paul's use of culture will be identified and examined. In the next section, the rationale behind his usage of culture and exhortation against culture in 1 Corinthians 5 and 6 will be analyzed.

1. Pauline Pro-cultural Argument in 1 Corinthians 5:1–13

First Corinthians 5 tackles the issue of incest in the Corinthian church. Paul says, "It is actually reported that there is sexual immorality among you, and of a kind that is not tolerated even among pagans, for a man has his father's wife" (1 Cor 5:1). A man has his "father's wife." This man could be called Mr. MFW (Man who has his Father's Wife). It is not clear whether Mr. MFW had seduced his father's divorced wife (stepmother) or had a consensual relationship with his stepmother after his father's death.[1] The latter is more plausible, as a son would not have the liberty to sleep with his father's wife when his father was alive, according to the social context of the Greco-Roman World.[2] Another important detail that one must observe in 1 Corinthians 5:1 is that this kind of sexual immorality was not even tolerated among the pagans. Paul conveys this cultural argument at the beginning of the exhortation itself (1 Cor 5:1). This shows that the cultural argument is observably one of the strongest in Paul's rhetoric to persuade the church against Mr. MFW.

1.1. The Church Should Excommunicate the Incestuous Man

In 1 Corinthians 5:1–2, Paul's argument is this: even in the pagan culture, this kind of sexual immorality is not tolerated. Leon Morris says, "Even those who were notoriously lax in sexual matters

---

1. Leon Morris, *The First Epistle of Paul to the Corinthians*, TNTC (Leicester, UK: InterVarsity, 1983), 86.
2. Morris, 86.

reprobated such a union as this."[3] Craig S. Keener notes that the pagan "culture [of the Corinthians] repudiated such behavior."[4]

In 1 Corinthians 5:1–13, Paul accuses the Corinthian church of accommodating a man who has his father's wife (5:1). *Epenthesate* (mourned) is usually used to indicate the mourning of the dead.[5] The church should have reacted to this situation as though they had lost a member of the church. Instead of mourning, they seemed to be boasting about Mr. MFW (1 Cor 5:2). It is possible that he was one of the influential men in the city or even "a patron" of the house church in Corinth.[6] If he was a socially prominent person or a patron, then it would have been culturally inappropriate for the believers to criticize him. It would have been unacceptable culturally for a group that was lower in the social strata to castigate someone from the higher social class.[7] Therefore, there are many social and cultural dynamics at play in the church's accommodation of Mr. MFW. Paul repeats the idea of the removal of the man from the church many times in this passage (1 Cor 5:1–13).[8] This becomes the primary adjuration for Paul. Moreover, the subargument in 1 Corinthians 5:1–2 is this: as this kind of sin is not even found among the pagans, the church should excommunicate Mr. MFW.

In 1 Corinthians 5:3–5, Paul asserts his apostolic authority to admonish the congregation to excommunicate the man from the church. Even though Paul was far away from the church, the believers should not assume that he does not have any authority in chastening the church members. Though he was absent from the church, he was present with them in spirit. Moreover, Paul had already pronounced judgment on the man who did such a thing (1 Cor 5:3).

3. Morris, 86.
4. Craig S. Keener, *1–2 Corinthians*, NCBC (Cambridge: Cambridge University Press, 2005), 49.
5. Morris, *First Epistle*, 86.
6. Keener, *1–2 Corinthians*, 49.
7. Anthony Thiselton, *The First Epistle to the Corinthians*, NIGTC (Grand Rapids, MI: Eerdmans, 2000), 83.
8. In 1 Cor 5, Paul says this openly with words such as "Remove the wicked man from among yourselves" (1 Cor 5:13 EHV). In other places, he implicates the same idea using other words (1 Cor 5:5, 7, 9, 11).

Probably he is referring here to his previous letter to the Corinthian church (1 Cor 5:9; see later). When the church is gathered together, Paul's spirit is also present, along with the power of Lord Jesus (1 Cor 5:4). Therefore, the church must execute Paul's judgment pronounced in 0.5 Corinthians (a letter written before 1 Corinthians). In 1 Corinthians 5:5, Paul says that the church should "deliver this man to Satan" to emphasize his main argument that they should excommunicate him.[9] The man being placed outside the church implies that he is located outside the realm of God's grace and in the realm of Satan's control.[10]

Similarly, in 1 Corinthians 5:6–9, Paul brings forth the analogy of separating leavened dough from the unleavened lump to keep the unleavened lump unadulterated. For Paul, by excommunicating the man, the other members of the church would be kept chaste and holy.[11] If Mr. MFW was an influential man and if he was adored by the youth and others, they might follow his lifestyle, which would cause serious complications for the holiness of the community. Cicero in *Philippicae* 8.5.15 says that Mark Antony must be executed, as it is better to amputate an infected part of the body rather than permit the whole body to be infected. Similarly, for Paul, the church should excommunicate the man, as one would "cleanse out the old leaven" to preserve the rest as the "new lump" and "unleavened . . . for Christ" (1 Cor 5:6–9). Therefore, in 1 Corinthians 5:6–9, Paul employs this analogy to admonish them to expel the man.

Likewise, in 1 Corinthians 5:9–13, Paul harnesses an argument from his previous letter and clarifies the things he wrote to reaffirm his position on the excommunication of the man. In a letter composed before 1 Corinthians (0.5 Corinthians?), Paul urged the Corinthian believers "not to associate with sexually immoral people" (1 Cor 5:9). Even after the reception of the letter, the Corinthian believers have not expelled Mr. MFW. Therefore, Paul elucidates on

---

9. Paul uses the same language for excommunication in 1 Tim 1:20.

10. Morris, *First Epistle*, 88; Thiselton, *First Epistle*, 86; F. W. Grosheide, *The First Epistle to the Corinthians*, NICNT (Grand Rapids, MI: Eerdmans, 1979), 124.

11. Morris, *First Epistle*, 89; Keener, *1–2 Corinthians*, 50–51; Alan F. Johnson, *1 Corinthians*, IVPNTC (Leicester, UK: InterVarsity, 2004), 91.

his previous ambiguous exhortation, in 1 Corinthians 5:10–13, to reiterate that this man must be excommunicated from the church.[12]

Paul employs four subarguments in imploring the Corinthian believers to excommunicate Mr. MFW. They are as follows: (1) it was against the culture (1 Cor 5:1–2), (2) he was present with them in the spirit (5:3–5), (3) it would secure the others in the church (5:6–8), and (4) he had already written in the previous letter (5:9–13). The first argument is the focus of the first part of this chapter. Why did Paul use this as the first argument to strengthen his case for the excommunication of the immoral brother?

1.2. Incest in the Greco-Roman World

Keener notes, "Rome often allowed communities of resident aliens, including synagogues, to judge their own members for violations of their own law (cf. Acts 18:15)."[13] Similarly, Paul anticipates the church to function like the synagogue in executing the judgment of excommunication. For this, Paul employs the cultural argument at the beginning of the passage itself (1 Cor 5:1). As this kind of sin is not even tolerated in the pagan culture, the Christians should not accommodate this man in the church. This cultural argument is intriguing. Greco-Roman writers wrote against incest frequently. The Roman jurist Gaius (130–80 CE) mentions that "it is illegal to marry a father's or mother's sister . . . nor can I marry her who was at one time my mother-in-law or stepmother" (*Institutes* I. 63). It was then illegal according to Roman law to marry one's stepmother. Though this was the case in the second century CE, there is no reason to doubt that this practice was tolerated in the first century CE.

In *Pro Cluentio* (69 BCE), Cicero points out how "unbelievable" it is that a lady called Sania married her son-in-law, Aulus Aurius Melinus, who was the brother-in-law of Cluentis, the daughter of Sania, and a client of Cicero (*Pro Cluentio* 5.27). For Cicero, a mother-in-law

---

12. Paul clarifies in 1 Cor 5:10 that he did not ask the Corinthian believers to be separated ("not to associate with") from the sexually immoral of the world—that is, the outsiders. But he exhorted them to not to associate with the sexually immoral brother—that is, the Christian believer (1 Cor 5:11).

13. Keener, *1–2 Corinthians*, 50.

marrying the son-in-law was implausible, as it was reported by Gaius in the second century CE. This is what Cicero says: "Oh, the incredible wickedness of the woman, and, with the exception of this one single instance, unheard of since the world began! Oh, the unbridled and unrestrained lust! Oh, the extraordinary audacity of her conduct!" (*Pro Cluentio* 5.15).[14] Poet Catullus from the first century BCE articulates that neither all the fresh water nor all the seawater could cleanse the sins of Gallius, who slept with his mother and sister: "What is he doing, Gallius, who has an itch with mother and sister and stays up all night with tunics cast aside? What is he doing, who does not allow his uncle to be a husband? Do you know the weight of crime he undertakes? He undertakes, O Gallius, so much as neither furthest Tethys nor Oceanus, father of nymphs, can cleanse: for there is no crime which can go further, not even if with lowered head he swallowed himself" (Catullus 88).[15]

In Euripides's *Hippolytus* (480–406 BCE), Theseus appeals to Poseidon, his father (one of the chief gods of the Greek pantheon) to strike his son Hippolytus and slaughter him before the end of the day because he slept with his wife (i.e., the stepmother of Hippolytus; 885–90). Theseus declares that through this incestuous deed, Hippolytus "has shamed the holy eye of Zeus" (chief god of the Greek pantheon). For Euripides, this kind of incestuous relation is such a shame that it is punishable by a swift death.[16] Diodorus Siculus in *Bibliotheca Historica* inscribes the story of Poseidon, who was married to Halia and had six sons and a daughter (55.4). Later, when these sons were brought to madness by the works of Aphrodite, "they slept with their mother against her will" (55.6). When Poseidon learned about this incestuous behavior, he killed his own sons and buried them "because of their shameful deed" (55.7). Though they

---

14. Here is the original: *O mulieris scelus incredible et praeter hanc unum in omni vita inauditum! O libidinem effrenatam et indomitam! O audaciam singularem!*

15. Neither all the freshwater (Tethys) nor all the seawater (Oceanus) could wash his sins away. Tethys is the goddess of fresh water, and Oceanus is the god of the sea.

16. Craig S. Keener, "Adultery," in *Dictionary of New Testament Background: The IVP Bible Dictionary Series*, ed. Craig A. Evans and Stanley E. Porter (Leicester, UK: InterVarsity, 2000), 14.

did this act because of the madness caused by Aphrodite, they were reprimanded by Poseidon, their father, instantaneously. Sleeping with the father's wife brought forth instantaneous death in many ancient epics.

In *Love Romances*, Parthenius writes about Periander of Corinth, who slept with his own mother without his knowledge. In the night, Periander could not identify the woman who came and slept with him because it was dark and she did not speak. After several nights, he was intrigued to see the woman. One day, he placed a light in the room. When the woman arrived, and when she was about to lie on the bed, he lit the light and identified the woman as his own mother. From then, on he became a madman who was afflicted "in brain and heart" (17.1–7). Similarly, one of the classic stories of a son sleeping with his mother is that of Oedipus.[17] In Homer, in the earliest form of the story, Oedipus did not commit this act in ignorance (*Odyssey* 11.271–280). However, later tragedy writers accentuated this act as one of ignorance to reduce his guilt (Euripides, *Phoen.* 869–71; Sophocles, *Oed. Col.* 525–28; *Oed. Try.* 1237–79). Because of this dishonorable act, Oedipus suffered losing his eyes, and he too became a madman.

Some forms of incestuous relationships were acceptable in some Greco-Roman cultures. In Greek mythology, Aeolus permitted his sons to get married to his daughters (Parthenius, *Love Romances* 2.2; Homer, *Odys.* 10.7). In Athens, men could marry their half sisters (Achilles Tatius, *Leuc.* 1.3.1–2; Cornelius Nepos, *Pref.* 4). Egyptian men could wed their full sisters (Pans. 1.7.1; papyri in Lewis, 43–44). Even some assumed that the Persians permitted their sons to get married to their mothers (Sextus Empiricus, *Pyr.* 1.152; Philo, *Spec. Leg.* 3.3 13). Appian reports that a Seleucid king permitted his stepson to marry his wife (Appian, *Rom. Hist.* 11.10.61). However, Keener says, "Romans rejected all marriages with siblings, and Greeks rejected all except with paternal half-sisters (Didorus Siculus, *Bib. Hist.* 10.31.1)."[18] Through the literary evidence presented from the Greco-Roman

---

17. Epictetus, *Disc.* 1.24.16; Martial, *Epigr.* 10.4.1; Herodian, *Hist.* 4.9.3; Justin Martyr, *Apol.* I.27.

18. Keener, "Adultery," 14.

world, it is apparent that a son marrying his mother or stepmother was not commonly tolerated. Culturally, this incestuous practice was frowned upon if not considered illegal. Therefore, Paul employs this cultural practice as one of the key arguments in exhorting the excommunication of Mr. MFW. Paul's presentation of this cultural practice as an argument is remarkable because in the next chapter, 1 Corinthians 6:12–20, he speaks against another culturally prevalent sexual practice that was widely conventional in the Greco-Roman culture, prostitution. While Paul went along with the culture in the aspect of incest in 1 Corinthians 5:1–13, he pens against it in 6:12–20.[19]

2. Paul's View of Prostitution in 1 Corinthians 6:12–20

After adjuring the believers to excommunicate the incestuous man, Paul admonishes them against judicial lawsuits in 1 Corinthians 6:1–11. In 1 Corinthians 6:12–20, he appeals against the practice of prostitution and sexual immorality among the believers. He opens the section by saying, "'All things are lawful for me,' but not all things are helpful. 'All things are lawful for me,' but I will not be dominated by anything" (1 Cor 6:12). Probably, Paul is reciting the slogans of the Corinthians, which were possibly mentioned by Paul earlier.[20] His statement "You are not under the law" (Gal 5:18) could have been taken to the extreme by some Corinthian believers to justify their licentiousness. Paul states that though he has the liberty to do every-thing, he will not be mastered by prostitution and sexual immorality (1 Cor 6:12). In addition, his use of words such as *food* and *stomach* in 1 Corinthians 6:13 possibly counters some Corinthians' arguments that as God created food for the stomach and the stomach for the food, sexual organs (or the body) are created for sexual immoral-ity (sexual pleasures). Paul counters them and says, "The body is not meant for sexual immorality, but for the Lord" (1 Cor 6:13). The believers should not assume that the body is going to be destroyed

---

19. Paul's rationale behind using the cultural argument will be dealt with in sec-tion 3 of this chapter.
20. Thiselton, *First Epistle*, 93.

with the world.[21] For Paul, the body will be raised by the Lord, by his power (1 Cor 6:14). Therefore, the Corinthian believers should not use their bodies for sexual immorality with harlots.

In 1 Corinthians 6:12–20, Paul does not employ cultural argument for his persuasion the way he did in 5:1–13. Here, he contends against prostitution, a common cultural practice (see the following section). In this persuasion, Paul harnesses various arguments. In 1 Corinthians 6:12–14, he argues against the wrong perceptions of some Corinthian believers about prostitution and their bodies. In 1 Corinthians 6:15–18, Paul articulates that a person also brings Christ into prostitution by engaging in prostitution with a harlot. In some philosophical views such as Platonism, material things are not considered real, and therefore, a person can do anything with the body.[22] Knowledge and soul are considered eternal, and thus, anything done to the body is not considered detrimental.[23] However, for Paul, as the body is already a member of Christ (1 Cor 6:15), a believer engaging in prostitution brings Christ into prostitution. As a Christian, the believer is already a member of Christ. And by being with a prostitute, he becomes one with her (1 Cor 6:16). Therefore, in engaging in sexual immorality with a prostitute, the believer is committing a grave sin as he brings Christ into prostitution.[24] Therefore, Paul implores believers to flee from prostitution (1 Cor 6:18).

In 1 Corinthians 6:18–20, Paul brings his argument from 6:12–14 about sinning against one's own body to a climax. The believer should "flee from sexual immorality" because "every other sin a person commits is outside the body, but the sexually immoral person sins against his own body" (1 Cor 6:18). Paul intensifies this argument by showing two more things: (1) the body of a believer is not just a material thing but the temple of the Holy Spirit (1 Cor 6:19), and (2) this body is not one's own, as God bought the person with a price (6:20). Through the blood of Jesus Christ, God purchased the

---

21. As the followers of Plato assumed.
22. Frederick Copleston, *History of Philosophy: Greece and Rome*, vol. 1 (New York: Image, 1993), 160–61.
23. Copleston, 142–62.
24. Thiselton, *First Epistle*, 468.

believer. Therefore, the believer is not his own. Consequently, he must glorify God through his body by fleeing from sexual immorality with a harlot. With this series of arguments, Paul went against the conventional cultural practice of prostitution, stating that it goes against the teaching of the Word. Paul strongly opposed prostitution by pointing out the several reasons why prostitution is not to be practiced by Corinthian believers (1 Cor 6:12–20). However, prostitution was quite prevalent in the Greco-Roman world of Paul's time.

2.1. Prostitution and Culture in the Greco-Roman World

Adultery was seemingly quite common among the gentiles in the Greco-Roman world of Paul (Seneca, *Dial.* 12.16.3; Plutarch, *Brid.* 46; *Mor.* 144E–F; Juvenal, *Sat.* 4.1–20; Aulus Gellius, *Noc. Att.* 5.11.2). Suetonius (69–122 CE), in *On Benefits*, says, "Men now-a-days no longer secretly but openly outrage the wives of others, and allow to others access their wives" (1.9.4). He continues in 3.16.3 and exaggerates the promiscuous behavior of women of his time by saying that only an ugly woman would settle for two lovers per day. For Suetonius, regular women would have one man "for each hour of the day" (3.16.4). His exaggerations show the prevalence of sexual immorality in the society. This would have also fashioned the cultural practices of the day.

It must also be said that adultery was considered a shameful act by many (Diodorus Siculus, *Bib. Hist.* 12.21.2; Seneca, *Dial.* 2.18.2; Plutarch, *Reg. Imp. Apophth. Mor.* 179E; Epictetus, *Disc.* 2.4; 2.10.18; 2.18.15; Euripides, *Hippol.* 403–18). In addition, prostitution was considered shameful even though it was legal in Roman law (Diodorus Siculus, *Bib. Hist.* 12.21.2; Artemidorus, *Oneir.* 1.78; Aulus Gellius, *Noc. Att.* 9.5.8; 15.12.2–3; Dio Chrysostom, *Or.* 7.133). Roman law describes a prostitute as "any woman who openly makes money selling her body" (*Digest* 23.2.43, pr. 1). Robert Knapp opines, "The law did not punish prostitution. It was legal and a prostitute could not be prosecuted for her profession. Sexual relations with a [prostitute] did not constitute adultery, nor could an unmarried [prostitute] be a party to adultery, much less be guilty of adultery herself. *Stuprum* (illegal intercourse) was the term for sexual relations with an unmarried girl/woman (or widow), or boy/man, but it was inapplicable to sexual relations with [prostitutes]."[25] As prostitution produced a substantial amount of tax revenue to the empire, it was tolerated.[26] One receipt from Egypt identifies the money received from prostitutes as tax money. It says, "Pasemis, to Senpsenmonthes, daughter of Pasemis, greetings. I have received from you for the tax on prostitutes at Memnonia for the first year of Nero, the Emperor, four drachmas. Dated the fifteenth day of the month of Pharmouthi" (*O. Berl Inv.* 25474/Nelson). Sometimes, the officials also gave permission for practicing prostitution for one day. One document from Egypt says, "Pelaias and Sokraton, tax collectors, to the prostitute Thinabdella, greetings. We give you permission to have sex with whomever you might wish in this place on the day given below. Year 19, the 3rd day of the month Phaophi. [Signed] Sokraton, Simon's son" (*WO* 1157/ Nelson). This demonstrates the state-sanctioned practice of prostitution in the Greco-Roman world. Thomas A. J. McGinn points out that even the state benefited considerably from the prostitution industry (which was legalized by Emperor Caligula).[27] Suetonius states, "On the proceeds of the prostitutes at a rate equivalent to the cost of one trick; and it was added to this section of the law, that those who had practiced prostitution or pimping in the past owed the tax to the treasury, and even married persons were not exempt" (*Life of Gaius* 40). In fact, another account says that Caligula himself ran a brothel in his palace. Suetonius says, "And lest any type of plunder go untried, in his palace he set up a number of small rooms just like in a brothel and decorated them sumptuously. He had married women and freeborn stand in the cells, again just like in a brothel. Then he sent heralds around to the markets and places of public business to invite young and old to indulge their lusts. He had money available

---

25. Robert Knapp, *Invisible Romans: Prostitutes, Outlaws, Slaves, Gladiators and Others* (London: Profile, 2011), 205. The words in brackets have been changed to avoid derogatory terms.
26. Keener, "Adultery," 11; Keener, *1–2 Corinthians*, 59.
27. Thomas A. J. McGinn, *The Economy of Prostitution in the Roman World: A Study of Social History and the Brothels* (Ann Arbor: University of Michigan Press, 2004), 76.

to offer at interest to those who came—and men at the ready who openly wrote down their names, as contributing to Caesar's income" (*Life of Gaius*, 41).

Though prostitution was considered shameful, it was tolerated and accepted by most. Marcus Argentarius's epigram describes a pimp named Psyllus who would bring prostitutes to banquets, which helped dissuade young men from adultery (*Grk. Anth.* 7.403). He says, "Psyllus, who used to take to the pleasant banquets of the young men the venal ladies that they desired, that hunter of weak girls, who earned a disgraceful wage by dealing in human flesh, lies here. But do not cast stones at his tomb, wayfarer, nor bid another do so. He is dead and buried. Spare him, not because he was content to gain his living so, but because as keeper of common women he dissuaded young men from adultery." Prostitution was then considered a positive thing, at least by a few, as it helped men avoid adultery. Consequently, adultery was considered worse than prostitution. In this sense, prostitution was more acceptable than adultery. In addition, prostitution was not considered immoral. Knapp says, "So as far as is known, authorities did not care about the moral aspect of prostitution—after all, intercourse with a whore did not break any laws, or even any moral strictures as far as the man was concerned, since it did not constitute adultery."[28] Plautus, in his *Curculio*, shows a character declaring that there is no stigma or a negative legal repercussion in prostitution, which is contrary to the social and legal risks of adultery. As he enters the brothel, the character says, "No one says 'no,' or stops you buying what is openly for sale, if you have the money. No one prohibits anyone from going along the public road. Make love to whomever you want—just be sure you don't wander off it onto private tracks—I mean, stay away from married women, widows, virgins, young men, and boys of good family" (32–37). Similarly, Artemidorus states, "But having sex with a woman working as a prostitute in a brothel signifies only minor disgrace and very little expense" (*Dreams* 1.78).

---

28. Knapp, *Invisible Romans*, 205.

McGinn says that the practice of prostitution was done explicitly in the Roman Empire.[29] It was found everywhere in the empire. It was not done in a hidden alley or in the dark corners of the city. The Romans preferred to run prostitution rackets out in the open so as to keep the venal sex workers as foils to the respectable women of the family (materfamilias/matrons).[30] These sex workers in some ways added more value to the respectable women, according to McGinn. Though it appears like a crude justification of prostitution, it also shows the prevalence of prostitution in the empire. The interesting fact is that prostitution was not a secret business but a common one that was practiced even in the significant parts of the city.[31]

Prostitution was found in the city in the brothels, which were connected to *cauponae*—that is, inns and taverns.[32] *Satyricon* depicts a brothel when it describes how Encolpius has lost track of his friend Ascyltos on his way back to the inn he was staying in. Encolpius asks an old woman who was selling vegetables how to get to the inn. The clever lady tricks him and takes him into a brothel, where he also finds his friend:

> I noticed some men and naked women walking cautiously about among placards of price. Too late, too late I realized that I had been taken into a whorehouse . . . I began to run through the brothel to another part, when just at the entrance Ascyltos met me . . . I hailed him with a laugh, and asked him what he was doing in such an unpleasant spot. He mopped himself with his hands and said, "If you only knew what has happened to me." "What is it?" I said. "Well," he said, on the point of fainting, "I was wandering all over the town without finding where I had left my lodgings, when a respectable person came up to me and very kindly offered to direct me. He took me round a number of dark turnings and brought me out here, and then began to offer me money and solicit me. A whore demanded a fiver for a cubby, and he was already pawing me. The worst would

29. McGinn, *Economy of Prostitution*, 4.
30. McGinn, 4.
31. McGinn, 4.
32. McGinn, 15.

have happened if I had not been stronger than he." (Titus Petronius, *Satyricon* 7)

Both Encolpius and Ascyltos were tricked to go to a brothel by people who would have gotten a commission for bringing more people to the brothel. This again portrays the prevalence of prostitution. McGinn states that in Roman cities such as Pompeii, "generally speaking, inns, lodging houses, taverns, and restaurants of all kinds were associated with the practice of prostitution, often, though not exclusively."[33] Ulpian says, "Octavenus nevertheless most correctly states that even the woman who gives herself openly for free ought to be counted among the prostitutes. . . . We moreover call the women 'madams' who offer women for hire, even if they carry on this commerce under another name. If anyone running a <u>tavern</u> has women for hire (and many are accustomed to have female prostitutes under the guise of having <u>tavern maids</u>), then she also is properly called a 'madam'" (*On the Edict*, in *Digest* 23.2.43. pr. 1–3 and 7–9).

The establishments that offer lodging along with food and drinks with sexual pleasures were *tabernae, meritoria, cauponae, stabula, deversoria,* and *synoecia,* while *popinae* and *thermopolia* were primarily places for eating and drinking.[34] The places of prostitution also used slang such as *ganeum, ganea,* and *gurgustium,* which all meant "low dive" to indicate prostitution. McGinn says, "The practice of prostitution in inns and taverns was so common as to be taken for granted, as a famous graffito burlesquing the settlement of a hotel bill suggests. Among the charges, the writer lists one for (the service of) a 'girl' (*puella*), which, since no separate charge is given, evidently embraces the cost of a room."[35]

In addition, prostitution was also found in baths (*balneum*). Ammianus Marcellinus says that in the baths, "if they [the bathers] suddenly learn that a previously unknown prostitute has appeared, or some whore of the common herd, or an old harlot whose body is up for cheap, they rush forward jostling, pawing the newcomer, and

---

33. McGinn, 15–16.
34. McGinn, 16.
35. McGinn, 18.

praising her with outrageously exaggerated flattery like Egyptians laid on their Cleopatra" (*History* 28.4.9).

On one of the walls of a bath in Pompeii, it is inscribed, "Whoever sits here, read this above all: if you want to have sex, look for Attis—you can have her for a denarius" (*CIL* 4.1751). Prostitution was also found at circuses and at special events such as banquets, parties, fairs, and public shows.[36] Moreover, prostitution was also found near the sacred places. Temples were popular hangout places for prostitutes.[37] Plautus articulates prostitutes gathering at the Temple of Venus in this way: "The altar area is mobbed right now. Surely you don't want to hang around there among those prostitutes on display, playthings of millers, and the rest of the harlots—miserable, dirt-smeared, filthy little slave-lings, stinking of the whorehouse and their profession, of the chair and bare bench they sit on to solicit, creatures no free man ever touched, not to mention married, five-dollar prostitutes of the vilest little slaves" (*Little Carthaginian* 265–70).

Furthermore, some prostitutes worked from home as well, as is possibly reflected in the House of the Vettii at Pompeii. In one of the rooms at the back of this house were found explicit pictures similar to those found in the brothel.[38] There is also a graffito in front of this house that states, "Eutychis, a Greek girl with sweet ways, 2 asses" (*CIL* 4.4592).

The prices charged for sex with the prostitutes in brothels ranged from 1 as to 32 asses (10 asses is 1 denarius; i.e., one day's labor).[39] A common price for a prostitute could be a quarter of a denarius.[40] A graffiti from Pompeii says, "Optata, household slave, yours for 2 Asses" (*CIL* 4.5105) and "I'm yours for 2 asses" (*CIL* 4.5372).[41]

---

36. McGinn, 22–27.
37. Knapp, *Invisible Romans*, 218.
38. Knapp, 213.
39. One as is one-tenth of a denarius, a day's wage for a skilled laborer. Knapp, *Invisible Romans*, 221. However, some consider one as one-sixteenth of a denarius. McGinn, *Economy of Prostitution*, 42.
40. Knapp, *Invisible Romans*, 221.
41. With two asses, one could buy one's daily bread or a decent cup of wine or a chunk of cheese. See Knapp, 221.

Another graffiti on the wall of the Pompeiian brothel says, "On this spot Harpocras spent a denarius for a good sex with Drauca" (*CIL* 4.2193). Depending on the beauty and the class of the girl, the price was determined.[42] McGinn says, "Slave owners and aggressive pimps probably compelled the vast majority of slave and free prostitutes to work and to work and a great deal for little reward. For those few women who were not otherwise coerced into entering the profession, economic constraints, above all the depressed job market for women, might have made prostitution seem more remunerative than was actually the case. The supply must have been at all times full."[43]

This again displays the prevalence of prostitution in the Roman world from the point of view of economics. Though larger coins such as sesterces (2½ asses) and denarius (about 10 asses) were accessible, people in prostitution usually quoted their price in asses. The possible reason for this could be the availability of prostitution at such low prices and also possibly to lure customers from all walks of life. Knapp says, "Ordinary people carried their money in this coin . . . and so [prostitutes] naturally priced their services in this coin."[44] The availability of sexual services for low rates indicates the common practice of prostitution in Roman antiquity. The presence of a similar trend could be assumed in Roman Corinth as well.

Sometimes, children were traded to pimps to be bred for prostitution (Quintilian, *IO* 7.1.55; Seneca, *Ep.* 101.14–15). Most of the prostitutes were slaves, so procuring possible prostitutes for trade would not have been that difficult.[45] Many abandoned children, male and female, were also adopted and groomed for prostitution.[46] Knapp states, "Prostitutes were, quite literally, everywhere."[47] In Pompeii alone, it is estimated that 1 percent of the entire population could

---

42. McGinn, *Economy of Prostitution*, 54.
43. McGinn, 73.
44. Knapp, *Invisible Romans*, 221.
45. McGinn, *Economy of Prostitution*, 56.
46. McGinn, 56.
47. Knapp, *Invisible Romans*, 211.

have been prostitutes.[48] Knapp says that "the combination of strong demand, a relatively low health risk, and an absence of alternative ways for women to make money pushed many into prostitution."[49] As women could not work in many industries, and since the industries in which they were allowed to work, such as weaving or wet-nursing, did not employ all women, prostitution seemingly was "very appealing to a person of marketable age and/or desperate condition."[50] Even with the lowest documented pay for one customer (2 asses), a prostitute could earn about 10 or 20 asses per day with five to ten customers per day.[51] This is way more than what a woman could earn in any other occupation. This is even about twice as much as what a well-paid male worker could earn.[52] Knapp says, "Walking down the street of any town, you would have seen the whores standing around the forum, beckoning you from a doorway, or soliciting you leaving the theater. They were a familiar and popular aspect of the lives of ordinary folk."[53] McGinn articulates that in the Roman world, "prostitution was, on any estimate, wide spread."[54] He adds, "For the male customer, venal sex was both widely available and relatively inexpensive."[55]

2.2. Prostitution in Corinth

Prostitution was considered so common in Corinth that it was customary to describe an immoral person with the name of Corinth. Aristophanes (450–385 BCE) used the term *korinthiazomai*, "act like a Corinthian," to mean a sexually immoral person or a harlot (*Fragm.* 354). Plays were written with the title *Korinthiastes* (the whoremonger) by Philetaerus (fourth century BCE) and Poliochus (Athenaeus, *Deiphosophistae* 313, 559a). Even Plato used the term *Korinthia kore*, "a Corinthian maid," to identify a harlot (*Resp.* 3.404d).

---

48. Knapp, 211.
49. Knapp, 211.
50. Knapp, 208.
51. Knapp, 222.
52. Knapp, 222.
53. Knapp, 225.
54. McGinn, *Economy of Prostitution*, 72.
55. McGinn, 73.

Strabo, the Greek historian, mentions one thousand temple prostitutes present in the Aphrodite temple in Corinth. It is considered
an infamous depiction of Corinth and its sexual immorality.[56] He
says,

> The Temple of Aphrodite became so wealthy that it acquired more
> than a thousand temple-slaves (hierodoulous), courtesans (het-
> airas) whom both men and women dedicated to the goddess. Con-
> sequently, because of these women the city became crowded with
> people and grew rich. For ship-captains carelessly squandered their
> money there; hence the saying, "Not for every man is the trip to
> Corinth!" Moreover, a certain courtesan is remembered as having
> said to a woman who reproached her that she did not like to work
> or come into contact with wool, "Yet, such as I am, I have already in
> a short time brought down three masts" [i.e., debauched three ship
> captains]. (*Geogr.* 8.6.20)

Strabo's depiction could have been an exaggeration. Moreover, it
could have depicted the situation of the old Corinth (before 145 BCE,
which was destroyed by the Romans), as there was no big Aphrodite
temple found in the excavations that could have accommodated one
thousand courtesans.[57] Nevertheless, Corinth should have had its
red-light district, as were found in other seaport towns of the Roman
world.[58] Furthermore, Corinth could have revived the customs of the
old Corinth to host many prostitutes.[59] In 464 BCE, Pindar writes
about Xenophon's dedication of one hundred sacred prostitutes to
the Aphrodite temple in Corinth because she helped him win in the
Olympic Games. Pindar says,

> Young girls, who welcome many strangers, handmaidens

---

56. Jerome Murphy-O'Connor, *St. Paul's Corinth: Texts and Archaeology* (Collegeville, MN: Liturgical, 2002), 56.
57. Murphy-O'Connor, 56; Knapp, *Invisible Romans*, 204.
58. Joseph A. Fitzmyer, *First Corinthians*, AYB (New Haven, CT: Anchor Yale Bible,
2008), 35.
59. Keener, "Adultery," 12.

Of persuasion in wealthy Corinth . . .
Mistress of Cyprus [Aphrodite], here to your grove
Xenophon has brought a hundred-bodied herd of grazing girls,
Rejoicing in his fulfilled vows. (Pindar fr. 122 S)

Similarly, if nine others dedicated the same number of sacred prostitutes to the temple, Strabo's number could be made realistic. If ninety people dedicated ten sacred prostitutes over a period of time or if nine hundred others dedicated one sacred prostitute each, the number mentioned by Strabo could be achieved as well. Though these are just predictions, these accounts show the prevalence of the practice of prostitution in Corinth.

Though Corinth may not have had one thousand prostitutes in Paul's time, it nevertheless offered "erotic pleasures," as Aristeides writes (*Poseidon* 23). Herodotus pens about Aphrodite temples and women practicing prostitution (*Hist.* 1.199). Herodotus, too, reports the existence of sacred prostitution with respect to the worship of Aphrodite, though among Babylonians, not among Corinthians: "Every woman who lives in that country must once in her lifetime go to the temple of Aphrodite and sit there and be lain with by a strange man. . . . When once a woman has taken her seat there, she may not go home again until one of the strangers throws a piece of silver into her lap and lies with her, outside the temple. . . . Once she has lain with him, she has fulfilled her obligation to the goddess and gets gone to her home" (Herodotus, *Hist.* 1.199).[60] Athenaeus of Naucratis identifies prostitution in Corinth in this way:

Now I am going to recite for your benefit, Cynulcus, a kind of Ionian speech, "spinning it out far," as Aeschylus's Agamemnon would say, on the subject of prostitutes; I will begin with the beautiful city of Corinth, since you have referred with insults to my residence there

---

60. Alternately, Knapp says, "Despite a few references that seem to indicate the existence of sacred, temple prostitution in the Romano-Grecian world, a recent very careful and encompassing study has shown conclusively that it existed neither at Corinth (the prime candidate) nor any place else." Knapp, *Invisible Romans*, 204.

as a sophist. It is an ancient custom in Corinth, as Chamaeleon of Heracleia records in his book On Pindar, whenever the city prays to Aphrodite in matters of grave importance, to invite as many prostitutes as possible to join in their petitions, and these women add their supplications to the goddess and later are present at the sacrifices. When, accordingly, the Persian invaded Greece, as Theopompus records, likewise Timaeus in the seventh book, the Corinthian prostitutes entered the temple of Aphrodite and prayed for the salvation of the Greeks. Hence also, when the Corinthians dedicated in honour of the goddess the tablet which is preserved even to this day, recording separately the names of the prostitutes who had made supplication on that occasion and were later present at the sacrifices. . . .

But that the prostitutes also celebrate their own festival of Aphrodite at Corinth is shown by Alexis in The Girl in Love: "The city celebrated a festival of Aphrodite for the prostitutes, but it is a different one from that held separately for freeborn women. On these days it is customary for the prostitutes to revel, and it is quite in the mode for them to get drunk here in our company." (*Deiphosophistae* 13:573c–574c)

In fact, one of the famous harlots of the Greco-Roman world hailed from Corinth. Lais was considered a high-class prostitute known to the Greek world.[61] She was so famous that Emperor Hadrian put the picture of her famous tomb in Corinth in the coin that he minted. One epitaphic poem, written by Antipater of Sidon about Lais, says,

I contain her who in Love's company luxuriated in gold and purple, more delicate than tender Cypris, Lais, citizen of sea-girt Corinth, Brighter than the white waters of Peirene, that mortal Cytherea, who had more notable suitors than the daughter of Tyndareus,[62] all plucking her mercenary favors. Her very tomb smells of sweet-scented saffron, her bones are still moist with fragrant ointment and

---

61. Donald Engels, *Roman Corinth: An Alternative Model for the Classical City* (Chicago: University of Chicago Press, 1990), 98.
62. Helen of Troy.

her anointed locks still breathe a perfume as frankincense. For her, Aphrodite tore her lovely cheeks, and sobbing Love groaned and wailed. Had she not made her bed the public slave of gain Greece would have fought for her as for Helen. (*Epigrams* 7.218)

Apart from the famous prostitutes, archeological evidence from the Asclepius temple displays the clay votive offerings of human genitals presented to Asclepius for healing. The many genital clay figurines show evidence of widespread venereal diseases.[63] Gordon D. Fee says, "Sexual sin [in Corinth] undoubtedly was in abundance."[64]

As shown previously, prostitution in Corinth should be considered as a prevalent practice in the time of Paul. In addition, the frequent travels of the merchants to the city could have made the sex trade in Corinth flourish further.[65] Corinth was placed in a strategic location—between two cities. It was situated on the isthmus separating the Aegean Sea from the Gulf of Corinth and the Ionian Sea. Strabo states that "Corinth is called wealthy due to its commerce, since it is located on the Isthmus and is the master of two harbors, one of which leads directly to Asia and the other to Italy. . . . The exchange of merchandise from both distant countries is made easier by the city's location. And, just as in early times, the seas around Sicily are not easy to navigate" (*Geo.* 8.6.20).

Corinth was located in a strategic place for Mediterranean trade, as traveling south of Corinth in the rough sea was not advisable, and it took more than six days to cross the unpredictable sea. Ships coming from the east, then, would stop Cenchrea and unload the goods and pass through Corinth and embark at Lechaion on their way to Rome and Spain. This made Corinth a prominent city with a mixture of cultures and worldviews. This also aided the flourishing of prostitution and sexual promiscuity in the name of hospitality they provided to the travelers and merchants. In the context of the prevalence of sexual immorality and prostitution in the Greco-Roman

---

63. Gordon D. Fee, *The First Epistle to the Corinthians*, NICNT (Grand Rapids, MI: Eerdmans, 1987), 2.
64. Fee, 3.
65. McGinn, *Economy of Prostitution*, 57.

world and of sexual pervasiveness in Corinth and its background, it is possible to consider that prostitution was one of the culturally accepted practices among the people in Corinth. However, Paul was against such a practice. While in 1 Corinthians 5:1–13 he used the cultural practice for condemning incest—particularly, the practice of a man sleeping with his father's wife—in 6:12–20, he exhorts against the common cultural practice of prostitution.

3. Culture and Sexual Immorality in Paul's 1 Corinthians 5 and 6

Culture is nothing but the shared values and practices found in a community. Edward Burnett Tylor defines culture as "that complex whole which includes knowledge, belief, art, morals, law, custom, and any other capabilities and habits acquired by man as a member of society."[66] For United Nations Educational, Scientific and Cultural Organization (UNESCO), "culture is the whole complex of distinctive spiritual, material, intellectual, and emotional features that characterize a society or social group."[67] These common cultural values found in a society are not rigid, unbreakable codes. Milena Ivanovic states, "Cultures are not fortresses with rigid demarcation line but fluid entities with porous boundaries allowing for the constant exchange of different cultural elements. Because culture is constantly changing and is influenced by exogenous and endogenous elements, it is regarded as a dynamic system."[68] This change does not happen instantaneously. It takes time, perhaps generations. Ivanovic further states, "'The totality of culture' has been acquired and transmitted over generations through symbols and shared meanings by a process of learning. . . . When carried by tradition, culture

---

66. Edward Burnett Tylor, *Primitive Culture: Researches into the Development of Mythology, Philosophy, Religion, Art, and Custom* (New York: Harper & Row, 1958), 1.

67. World Commission on Culture and Development, *UNESCO—Our Creative Diversity: Report of the World Commission on Culture and Development* (Paris: World Commission on Culture and Development, 1995).

68. Milena Ivanovic, *Cultural Tourism* (Cape Town: Juta, 2008), 26.

characterizes a human group called a community. A community is clearly defined when its members recognize a considerable number of shared meanings."[69] Therefore, cultural values are shared beliefs and practices found in a community.

When talking about sexual immorality, particularly incest and prostitution, the values found in the Roman world and in Corinth indicate that there was a consensus about these two practices in the culture of Corinth. The practice of a man having his father's wife was taboo, according to Corinthian culture, while prostitution was one that was accommodated. The many aforementioned sources from the Greco-Roman world on both these topics would validate this statement. It is taken for granted, then, in this chapter that the acceptance of prostitution and the prohibition of incestuous behavior were cultural norms of that society. For example, in Tamil culture, a girl can marry her maternal uncle or paternal aunt's son; however, marrying her father's brother or her father's brother's son is considered taboo. In contrast, in Filipino culture, marrying any nephew or uncle is considered taboo. What defines an act as sexually immoral and what makes it acceptable in a community are determined by shared values held for a long period of time. Therefore, the practices and taboos of a society are cultural in nature. Similarly, in Corinth, prostitution was common in the society because it was available as a cheaper alternative to adultery, which was considered a taboo in that culture. So it became an accepted cultural practice in the community. However, the incestuous practice of a man marrying his father's wife was considered a cultural taboo. While Paul agreed with them in the latter, he condemned the practice of prostitution. The rest of this chapter will deal with the reasons behind Paul's acceptance of one cultural practice and his condemnation of the other.

3.1. Paul's View of Incest

Paul's reason for his agreement with the cultural belief of the pagans in the aspect of incest is rooted in his view of incest. Paul was a Jew. He was a rabbi. His worldview and cultural shared values were

---

69. Ivanovic, 26.

formed from the Torah and the traditions of the Jews. The Torah spoke strongly against the practice of incest. Prohibitions against incest are found in Leviticus 18:6–18 and 20:11–21.

3.2. Incest and Jewish Culture

In Leviticus 18:6–8, several incestuous relationships are prohibited. While Leviticus 18:6 is an introduction to the rest of the incestuous behaviors that are mentioned in 18:7–18, 18:7, and 18:8 discuss the matter at hand. The first two prohibitions the author of Leviticus discusses concern sleeping with one's father's wife. Leviticus 18:7 pertains to the mother, and 18:8 applies to the stepmother: "You shall not uncover the nakedness of your father's wife; it is your father's nakedness" (Lev 18:8). Sleeping with one's father's wife means uncovering the nakedness of one's father. Then the rest of the incestuous behaviors are mentioned in the following verses: sister (9), granddaughter (10), stepsister (11), aunt (12–14), daughter-in-law (15), brother's wife (16), stepdaughter (17), and wife's sister (18).

In Leviticus 20:11–21, the prohibitions against incestuous relationships are included with other immoral sexual behaviors. Nevertheless, the prohibition against sleeping with one's father's wife comes first on the list.[70] Following this, other immoral behaviors are mentioned: sex with a daughter-in-law (12), sister/stepsister (17), aunt (19–20), and sister-in-law (21).[71] Perhaps this shows the seriousness of this sin. This passage also explains the punishments that are to be given for the sexual sins mentioned. Leviticus 20:11 says, "If a man lies with his father's wife, he has uncovered his father's nakedness; both of them shall surely be put to death; their blood is upon them." The punishment for this kind of incest is death. The death penalty is also called for incestuous relationships with a daughter-in-law (12), homosexuals (13), a mother-in-law (14), and animals (15–16).

---

70. This assumes Lev 20:10 as the introductory verse.
71. Intermittently, other sexually immoral behaviors and their punishments are mentioned as well: homosexuality (13), sex with a woman and her mother (14), sex with animals (15–16), and sex with menstruating women (18). This indicates that this passage is not just about incest but about the punishments to be rendered for immoral behaviors.

Paul, a serious adherent of the Torah, prodded his believers to follow the admonition in 1 Corinthians 5:1–13. In addition, when this teaching is paralleled with the pagan culture, he harnessed that cultural practice to strengthen his argument that this man, who has his father's wife, should be excommunicated from the church. This is a lesser judgment than the one prescribed in Leviticus 20:11.

In *Jubilees*, the author mentions that it is an unforgivable sin to sleep with one's father's wife. *Jubilees* 33:10 says, "For this reason it is written and ordained on the heavenly tablets that a man should not lie with his father's wife . . . for this is unclean: they shall surely die together, the man who lies with his father's wife and the woman also, for they have wrought uncleanness on the earth." This sin is considered unclean before God (*Jub.* 33:11). Further, *Jubilees* 33:12–14 articulates,

> And again, it is written a second time: "Cursed be he who lies with the wife of his father, for he has uncovered his father's shame"; and all the holy ones of the Lord said "So be it; so be it." And do you, Moses, command the children of Israel that they observe this word; for it (entails) a punishment of death; and it is unclean, and there is no atonement forever to atone for the man who has committed this, but he is to be put to death and slain, and stoned with stones, and rooted out from the midst of the people of our God. For to no man who does so in Israel is it permitted to remain alive a single day on the earth, for he is abominable and unclean.

The punishment for this sin is so severe that there is no atonement *forever* for this man. Jewish laws allow for atonement for all sins except for apostasy.[72] When a person brings the sacrifice on the Day of Atonement, all sins are forgiven, according to the Jewish laws (*Jub.* 33:13). However, the author of *Jubilees* states that there is no atonement for a man who sleeps with his father's wife. In addition, the

---

72. E. P. Sanders, *Paul and Palestinian Judaism: A Comparison of Patterns of Religion* (Philadelphia: Fortress, 1977), 180. Philo treats his nephew as an apostate because he did not even offer sacrifice on the day of the atonement. Philo, *De Providentia*, 2.

judgment on this man is capital punishment (*Jub.* 33:13). Further, the severity of this sin is intensified by the exhortation to punish him swiftly by the death penalty *on the same day* (*Jub.* 33:14). The writer of the *Jubilees* points out that the people should not ask for an excuse by citing Reuben and his sins (33:15–16) because the law was not given to them at that time. But as the law is instituted from Moses onward, the Jewish believers should follow the law, as it is required by Moses in Leviticus 18:6–18 and 20:11–21. The writer of *Jubilees* reiterates this thought in 33:17, saying, "And for this law there is no consummation of days, and *no atonement for it,* but they must both be rooted out in the midst of the nation: *on the day* whereon they committed it they shall slay them" (emphasis mine). In light of the severity shown in this passage, Paul's command to excommunicate the man in 1 Corinthians 5:1–13 seems reasonable.

In the *Testament of Reuben*, Reuben testifies about his sin with Bilhah, the maidservant of Rachel and the wife of Jacob. As he slept with his father's wife, the *Testament of Reuben* relates the plagues he received as punishment and judgment upon him (1:7–10). Only because of the prayer of Jacob did the Lord spare Reuben (1:7). The punishment for this sin is serious in Jewish culture. Similarly, Josephus in *Antiquities* says, "As for adultery, Moses forbade it entirely. . . . He also abhorred men's lying with their mothers, as one of the greatest crimes; and the like for lying with the father's wife" (3.12.1). For Josephus, this is one of the greatest crimes.

Philo, in *On the Special Laws*, says, "But our law guards so carefully against such actions as these that it does not permit even a stepson, when his father is dead, to marry his step-mother, on account of the respect which he owes to his father . . . for the man who is thought to abstain from her who has been the wife of another man, because she is called his step-mother, will much more abstain from his own natural mother" (3.3.20–21). For Philo, by not sleeping with his father's wife, a man preserves his "wholeness and integrity" (3.3.21). This also demonstrates the "respectful awe" for his stepmother (3.3.21), which is considered as the appropriate behavior of the stepson. With these detailed descriptions and exhortations, his culture taught Paul that a man sleeping with his father's wife is considered a shameful and ignominious act. In addition, it is also against the law. Therefore, Paul's cultural worldview, shaped by the Torah and the writings based on the Torah, made him condemn the practice of incest (particularly, a man having his father's wife) in 1 Corinthians 5:1–13. When his cultural worldview was in agreement with that of the pagans, he harnessed their worldview to validate his argument in 1 Corinthians 5.[73]

3.3. Paul's View of Prostitution

Prostitution was prohibited in the Old Testament. Leviticus 19:29 forbids parents from forcing their daughters into prostitution. According to the Torah, the prevalence of prostitution in the land means it will also be "full of depravity" (Lev 19:29). The priests were not allowed to marry a prostitute or an immoral woman (Lev 21:7, 14). Similarly, a priest's daughter who was involved in prostitution was commanded to be burned with fire (Lev 21:9). Though it is particularly commanded of the Levites' daughters, the custom seems to have been present from the time of the patriarchs. When Tamar slept with Judah (her father-in-law) without his knowledge and became pregnant, the village told him that she was immoral and that she was pregnant through immorality (Gen 38:24). When Judah heard this, he said, "Bring her out, and let her be burned" (Gen 38:24). Even at the time of Judah, the sentence for immorality was the death penalty. Therefore, the death penalty in Leviticus 21:9 could be applied to all prostitutes and not just the Levites' daughters. Similarly, Deuteronomy 22:13–21 demonstrates how a woman found immoral before marriage is to be considered a prostitute and stoned to death. According to Deuteronomy 22:20–21, the punishment for immorality and prostitution ("whoring") is the death penalty. Deuteronomy 23:17 interdicts anyone's involvement in cult prostitution. Several other texts, such as Proverbs 23:27 and 29:3, warn against prostitution. Therefore, prostitution is considered taboo in the Old Testament.

---

73. In addition, there could have even been a sarcastic element here. Paul's argument could have been this one: even when the sexually promiscuous pagan culture prohibits this kind of incest, how much more the Christian believers should have prohibited this incestuous act.

In addition, the punishment for prostitution, in several instances, is death.[74]

In 1 Corinthians 6:12–20, Paul does not invoke the aforementioned passages to exhort the Corinthians to forbid prostitution. Instead, Paul brings up a broader passage, which speaks against all sexual immorality, to speak against prostitution. In 1 Corinthians 6:15–16, Paul says that the believers should not enjoin themselves with a *prostitute*. However, in 1 Corinthians 6:18, Paul says that the believers should "flee from sexual immorality." Though he did not use the word *harlot* in 1 Corinthians 6:18, it is understood in the context (esp. from 6:15–16). However, Paul's augmentation of the idea from prostitution to sexual immorality, in 1 Corinthians 6:18, only strengthens his argument because there are many verses in the Old Testament that support Paul's exhortation against sexual immorality. In fact, 1 Corinthians 6:18 echoes the sixth commandment ("You shall not commit adultery") from the Ten Commandments mentioned in Exodus 20:14 and Deuteronomy 5:18. As with the prohibition of prostitution, adultery is also prohibited in the Torah. Leviticus 18:20 commands against adultery just as Exodus 20:14 and Deuteronomy 5:18 do. Similar to prostitution, Leviticus 20:10 and Deuteronomy 22:22 declare the death penalty as the punishment for adultery. Apart from these, verses such as Jeremiah 7:9–14; 23:14–15; Hosea 4:23; and Malachi 3:5 also pronounce judgment against adultery. Therefore, Paul's broadening the aspect to the general term, *sexual immorality*, in 1 Corinthians 6:18 could have been motivated by his desire to back his exhortation with strong biblical support from the Old Testament.

---

74. Nevertheless, it must be said that there were few instances where prostitutes were accommodated in the society, such as Rahab (Josh 2:1; 6:17, 22, 25), who helped the Israelites in Jericho. Jepthah was the son of a harlot (Judg 11:1). And the two prostitutes asked Solomon to adjudicate them over a child (1 Kgs 3:16). The wife of the priest Amaziah was forced into prostitution to survive after he was taken into exile (Amos 7:17).

4. Paul and Culture

In this light, Paul's reasons for appreciating the culture in prohibiting incest and exhorting against the cultural practice of prostitution could have originated from his strong belief in the Torah and the culture it created. This way, the reason for Paul's exhortation against a common cultural practice such as prostitution in 1 Corinthians 6:12–20 could be based on his desire to follow the Torah carefully. Therefore, when a cultural practice concurs with his interpretation of the Torah, Paul employs it for his exhortation, as it is displayed in 1 Corinthians 5:1–3. However, when a cultural practice goes against his view of the Torah, he condemns it, as he does in 1 Corinthians 6:12–20.

For Paul, the Torah is the supreme guide that should shape the worldview of a Christian. The life of a believer should be shaped by the Scripture. When the Scripture acknowledges a cultural practice, Paul does not hesitate to use it as an argument, as it is found in 1 Corinthians 5:1. However, when a cultural practice is found to be against Scripture, he does not hesitate to stand against it even though it is practiced all over the empire (1 Cor 6:12–20). Therefore, Paul here demonstrates his indisputable allegiance to the Torah.[75]

This chapter has explained Paul's apparent conflicting approach to culture in 1 Corinthians 5 and 6 in the areas of incest and prostitution. It also asserted that Paul's view on culture is varied because it is based on his allegiance to Scripture. The Christian believer could learn from Paul that our individual cultures should be transformed by the word of God. When a cultural practice is against the word of God, we may have to stand against it, even if it is prevalently practiced in our culture, as Paul did in his time.

---

75. Martin Luther, *A Commentary on St. Paul's Epistle to the Galatians*, trans. Theodore Graebner (Grand Rapids, MI: Zondervan, 1949), 129.

Bibliography

Copleston, Frederick. *History of Philosophy: Greece and Rome*. Vol. 1. New York: Image, 1993.

Engels, Donald. *Roman Corinth: An Alternative Model for the Classical City*. Chicago: University of Chicago Press, 1990.

Fee, Gordon D. *The First Epistle to the Corinthians*. NICNT. Grand Rapids, MI: Eerdmans, 1987.

Fitzmyer, Joseph A. *First Corinthians*. AYB. New Haven, CT: Anchor Yale Bible, 2008.

Grosheide, F. W. *The First Epistle to the Corinthians*. NICNT. Grand Rapids, MI: Eerdmans, 1979.

Ivanovic, Milena. *Cultural Tourism*. Cape Town: Juta, 2008.

Johnson, Alan F. *1 Corinthians*. IVPNTC. Leicester, UK: InterVarsity, 2004.

Keener, Craig S. "Adultery." In *Dictionary of New Testament Background: The IVP Bible Dictionary Series*, edited by Craig A. Evans and Stanley E. Porter, 6–16. Leicester, UK: InterVarsity, 2000.

———. *1–2 Corinthians*. NCBC. Cambridge: Cambridge University Press, 2005.

Knapp, Robert. *Invisible Romans: Prostitutes, Outlaws, Slaves, Gladiators and Others*. London: Profile, 2011.

Luther, Martin. *A Commentary on St. Paul's Epistle to the Galatians*. Translated by Theodore Graebner. Grand Rapids, MI: Zondervan, 1949.

McGinn, Thomas A. J. *The Economy of Prostitution in the Roman World: A Study of Social History and the Brothels*. Ann Arbor: University of Michigan Press, 2004.

Morris, Leon. *The First Epistle of Paul to the Corinthians*. TNTC. Leicester, UK: InterVarsity, 1983.

Murphy-O'Connor, Jerome. *St. Paul's Corinth: Texts and Archaeology*. Collegeville, MN: Liturgical, 2002.

Sanders, E. P. *Paul and Palestinian Judaism: A Comparison of Patterns of Religion*. Philadelphia: Fortress, 1977.

Thiselton, Anthony. *The First Epistle to the Corinthians*. NIGTC. Grand Rapids, MI: Eerdmans, 2000.

Tylor, Edward Burnett. *Primitive Culture: Researches into the Development of Mythology, Philosophy, Religion, Art, and Custom*. New York: Harper & Row, 1958.

World Commission on Culture and Development. *UNESCO—Our Creative Diversity: Report of the World Commission on Culture and Development*. Paris: World Commission on Culture and Development, 1995.

6

Culture Dynamics in the Johannine Community Context

JOHNSON THOMASKUTTY

The cultural dynamics of the Johannine community can be delineated with a focus on the way Christ and gospel are presented within the narrative framework of the Fourth Gospel.[1] A polyvalent analysis that takes into consideration the narrative developments, the plot structures, the progress of the discourse, the characterization, the community aspects, and the theological expansion can help the reader understand the gospel and the cultural interaction within the Gospel. A polyvalent analysis shall enable the reader to understand the power of the text and its persuasiveness from multiple angles. An interdisciplinary approach that takes into consideration the theological and cultural deliberations of Richard Niebuhr (1894–1962), the Johannine community paradigms, and the contemporary Indian realities can take the discussion to a different level of understanding of the text. The dynamic interlocking of Christ/gospel and culture within the narrative framework of John can be foregrounded by looking at the development of discourse in the text. Niebuhr's understanding of Christ's relationship with the culture can be adequately conceptualized from the Johannine

---

1. This is a largely revised and updated version of my previous presentation at the Nepal Theological Forum, August 2020. It is also a revised version of the article "'Gospel' and 'Culture' from a Johannine Community Perspective," *Theological and Ethical Issues in Nepal: Papers Presented at Nepal Theological Forum*, ed. Akumtila Jamir and Chubamongba Ao (Kathmandu: Samdan, 2021), 111–34.

narrative framework. In the analysis of John, the interconnection between the life situation of Jesus (*Sitz im Leben Jesu*) and the life setting of the Johannine community (*Sitz im Leben Kirche*) enable us to understand the broader spectrum of the gospel message. A reader of the Fourth Gospel can make a clear demarcation between the "insider" and the "outsider" narrative rhetoric as they explore the Johannine community dynamism. In the following sections, I will attempt to see John's narrative framework through that lens.

I. A Preliminary Discussion

A large number of scholars dealt with the subject matter of cultural and supracultural aspects in relation to the gospel. Among them, Bruce J. Nicholls, Chris Sugden, and D. S. Amalorpavadass are noteworthy.[2] All of them describe how culture is an integral part to be analyzed and understood properly. Culture is the characteristics of a particular group of people that includes language, religion, cuisine, social habits, music, and art.[3] In the process of studying the culture of a particular group, we need to assess their total lifestyle in relation to other communities around.[4] According to Bobbie Kalman, "Culture is the way we live. It is the clothes we wear, the foods we eat, the languages we speak, the stories we tell, and the ways we celebrate. It is the way we show our imaginations through art, music, and writing. Culture is also about our roots."[5] People's thought patterns, behaviors, mannerisms, and usage of language and other related aspects are shaped by the culture in which they are part and parcel. An Indian reader of the New Testament can understand the

---

2. Bruce J. Nicholls, *Contextualization: A Theology of Gospel and Culture* (Vancouver: Regent College, 1979); Chris Sugden, *Gospel, Culture, and Transformation*, Regnum Studies in Mission (Oxford: Regnum, 2000); D. S. Amalorpavadass, *Gospel and Culture: Evangelization, Inculturation, and "Hinduisation"* (Bengaluru: National Biblical Catechetical and Liturgical Center, 1978).

3. See Stephanie Pappas and Callum McKelvie "What Is Culture?," Live Science, accessed September 18, 2020, https://www.livescience.com/21478-what -is-culture-definition-of-culture.html.

4. See Nicholls, *Contextualization*, 7–19.

5. Bobbie Kalman, *What Is Culture?* (Catharines, ON: Crabtree, 2009), 4.

cultural phenomena of the gospel communities and their dynamic relationship with the culturally varied Indian contexts. The cultural dynamism of the Johannine community, the presentation of Christ and the gospel as per the community demands, and the integration of Christ/gospel in the emerging new situation in India today are to be analyzed and understood.

The relationship between religion and culture is another significant area to be discussed to develop an understanding of Christ/gospel in the Johannine community context. Culture is a significant aspect that takes into account people and their lifestyles in closer relationship with their contextual realities. It is a determining factor when we attempt to understand a person in their totality. The queries such as "Who?" "What?" "Where?" "How?" and "Why?" are important demarcations in the process of social identity. Culture also comprises a person's religious identity. While Ernst Troeltsch (1865–1923) maintained that culture is the soil of religion, Paul Tillich (1896–1965) believed that religion is the soul of culture.[6] Here we see both Troeltsch and Tillich attribute an integral relationship between religion and culture. In that sense, religion cannot flourish without having a cultural framework.

One of the most influential definitions of culture is given in the book *Primitive Culture* by Edward Tylor, who defined it as "that complex whole which includes knowledge, belief, art, law, morals, custom, and any other capabilities and habits acquired by [hu]man as a member of society."[7] From Tylor's viewpoint, we come to know that culture is a more inclusive term that can be understood on the basis of multiple categories of human involvement in society. We can even state that within the canvas of culture, faith and religion remain as

---

6. Domenic Marbaniang, "The Gospel and Culture: Areas of Conflict, Consent, and Conversion," *Journal of the Contemporary Christian* 6, no. 1 (August 2014): 9–10; cf. Ernst Troeltsch, *Writings on Theology and Religion*, ed. and trans. Robert Morgan and Michael Pye (Atlanta: John Knox, 1977). See also Paul Tillich, *Theology of Culture*, ed. Robert C. Kimball (Oxford: Oxford University Press, 1959); cf. Marbaniang, "Gospel and Culture," 3.

7. E. B. Tylor, *Primitive Culture: Researches into the Development of Mythology, Philosophy, Religion, Art, and Custom*, vol. 1 (London: John Murray, 1871), 1. Cf. Marbaniang, "Gospel and Culture," 3–4.

key factors. On the other hand, Niebuhr's fivefold classification of the relationship between Christ and culture does point to the fact that the religious can be distinguished from the cultural.[8] Niebuhr's classification sees fivefold ways in which Christ encounters culture.

2. Christ and Culture Dynamism in the Johannine Community

Niebuhr understands Christ and culture as both integrally connected and distinct from each other. A reader of the Fourth Gospel can make use of the fivefold models of Niebuhr to understand the dynamic relationship and the distinctive aspects of Christ and culture. This reading may further enable us to see how both are at work in the contemporary realities of the Indian context.

3. Christ against Culture

In this model, Niebuhr places Christ over against human culture. As per this approach, culture is viewed with a high degree of suspicion and considered as antagonistic to Christ and the gospel. In order to exemplify his stance, Niebuhr takes the positions of Tertullian, Leo Tolstoy, the Mennonites, and various voices from the monastic traditions as they paid loyalty to Christ and the church and rejected the culture and the society.[9] Though the sincerity of the adherents is remarkable, their position brings a clash between the gospel and the culture.[10] A reading of the Fourth Gospel with an emphasis on the community theory enables us to understand this phenomenon.

The Gospel of John places Christ as the agent of creation. The preincarnate Logos existed *in the beginning* (John 1:1; cf. Gen 1:1). The Word

8. H. Richard Niebuhr, *Christ and Culture* (San Francisco: Harper & Row, 1951). Cf. Marbaniang, "Gospel and Culture," 4.
9. Trevin Wax, "'Christ and Culture'—an Overview of a Christian Classic," Gospel Coalition, February 25, 2015, https://www.thegospelcoalition.org/blogs/trevin-wax/christ-and-culture-an-overview-of-a-christian-classic/.
10. Marbaniang, "Gospel and Culture," 5.

was with God and it *was* God (John 1:1).[11] The entire universe and all things in it came into being through the initiative of the Word. The ethical and ideological differences between "the world from above" and "the world from below" make distinctions between eternal and temporal, divine and human.[12] The preincarnate nature of the Word demonstrates that Christ came as an agent of God to attune the culture of the earthly world with the culture of the heavenly world. As God's begotten "from above," "with God," and "was God," Jesus exemplified the heavenly values and virtues in the world.[13] As a performer of signs, teacher of the heavenly message, and the resurrected God, Jesus showcased the heavenly culture that is above and beyond the human culture.[14] It was the heavenly God's culture that was revealed through Jesus's words and deeds.

In John, often Jesus places the heavenly ideological position over against the worldly cultural phenomena. This divergence is brought up through the means of Jesus's utterances. The dualistic master plan of John helps the narrator foreground the conceptual clash between Jesus the protagonist and the antagonistic religious authorities.[15] As Jesus's message was not rooted in the principles of the world "from below," an ideological conflict emerged between the messages of Jesus and of the religious elites.[16] The Jews are placed in juxtaposition to the heavenly realities and against those who confess their faith in Jesus (cf. John 9:22; 12:42; 16:2). The antagonistic trends of the Jews are widespread within the narrative framework (cf. John

---

11. Paul N. Anderson, *The Riddles of the Fourth Gospel: An Introduction to John* (Minneapolis: Fortress, 2011), 3, 5, 9, 22–23, 68–69, 103–4.

12. G. F. Shirbroun, "Light," in *Dictionary of Jesus and the Gospels*, ed. Joel B. Green, Scot McKnight, and I. Howard Marshall (Downers Grove, IL: InterVarsity, 1992), 472–73.

13. D. H. Johnson, "Logos," in Green, McKnight, and Marshall, *Dictionary of Jesus*, 481–84.

14. M. M. Thompson, "John, Gospel Of," in Green, McKnight, and Marshall, *Dictionary of Jesus*, 472–73.

15. Johnson Thomaskutty, *Dialogue in the Book of Signs: A Polyvalent Analysis of John 1:19–12:50*, BINS 136 (Leiden: Brill, 2015), 433–46.

16. Thomaskutty, 478–79.

11:45–53; 18:28–19:16; 19:17–22; 20:19).[17] F. J. Moloney says, "The conflict between Jesus and 'the Jews' are more the reflection of a Christological debate at the end of the first century than a record of encounters between Jesus and his [Jesus's] fellow Israelites in the thirties of that century."[18] This aspect of the gospel demonstrates the narrator's typical vantage point that realigns the story of Jesus within the story of the Johannine community.[19]

The time and space details and the eyewitness statements of the Fourth Gospel provide ample evidence concerning the attachment of the beloved disciple to the mission initiatives of Jesus.[20] The narrator portrays Jesus as the incarnated Word, the agent of God, the savior of the world, and the glorious child of God.[21] This portrait of Jesus introduces a conflicting situation between the traditional Judaism and the newly emerged Christian community.[22] John's two-level drama introduces a situation in which the Johannine community confronts opposition.[23] The community of John existed as a resistance movement that emphasized an ideological clash between the "from above" and the "from below" aspects.[24]

17. F. J. Moloney, *The Gospel of John*, Sacra Pagina Series, ed. D. J. Harrington (Collegeville, MN: Liturgical, 1998), 9–11; also see Cornelis Bennema, "A Comparative Approach to Understanding Character in the Gospel of John," in *Character and Characterization in the Gospel of John*, ed. C. W. Skinner (London: Bloomsbury, 2013), 44.

18. Moloney, *Gospel of John*, 10. See also G. R. Beasley-Murray, *John*, WBC 36 (Waco, TX: Word Books, 1987), xliv; and R. E. Brown, *The Gospel according to John (i–xii)*, Anchor Bible 1 (Garden City, NY: Doubleday, 1966), lxx–lxxv.

19. Johnson Thomaskutty, *The Gospel of John: A Universalistic Reading* (Delhi: Christian World Imprints, 2020), 157; also see D. Tovey, *Jesus, Story of God: John's Story of Jesus* (Adelaide, Australia: ATF, 2007).

20. See J. C. S. Redman, "Eyewitness Testimony and the Characters in the Fourth Gospel," in *Character and Characterization in the Gospel of John*, ed. C. W. Skinner (London: Bloomsbury, 2013), 59–78.

21. See M. W. G. Stibbe, *John*, Readings: A New Biblical Commentary (Sheffield, UK: Sheffield Academic, 1993), 16–17.

22. A. J. Kelly and F. J. Moloney, *Experiencing God in the Gospel of John* (New York: Paulist, 2003), 44–48.

23. J. Louis Martyn, *History and Theology in the Fourth Gospel* (Nashville: Abingdon, 1968), 24–36.

24. Cf. Johnson Thomaskutty, "Glo[b/c]alization and Mission[s]: Reading John's Gospel," *New Life Theological Journal* 5, no. 1 (January–June 2015): 57.

The narrator of the story uses the ipsissima vox (very voice) of Jesus rather than the ipsissima verba (very own words) of Jesus in order to narrate it in John's own idiom.[25] This narratorial trend enables John to delineate the synagogue-church conflict in a dynamic way with the help of dialogue at the intradiegetic (i.e., among the characters within the story) and metadiegetic (i.e., between the narrator and the reader) levels.[26] The narrator of the story convinces the reader with the underlying disputation and through the narratorial phenomenon called conflict and characterization. The agent-of-God schema where Jesus comes from the world "from above" over against the prevailing schema of the world "from below" introduces the conflicting situation.[27] This is more obvious when Jesus utters, "My kingdom is not from this world" (John 18:36 NRSV).

In the story of the man born blind (in John 9:1–41), the synagogue-church conflict comes out in convincing terms. One of the noticeable factors in the progress of the man is his apprehension about the person of Christ (John 9:11, 17, 30–33, 38).[28] As a member of the local synagogue, he progresses in his understanding of Jesus. But the religious authorities categorically reject him and his new convictions.[29] This situation introduces a conflicting situation within the synagogue.[30] The emerging opposition in Jerusalem (John 5) and Galilee (6), the domination of the Pharisees (7–10) and the Chief Priests (11), and Jesus's trial and death (18–19) are the local manifestations of the

---

25. *Ipsissima vox* is a Latin expression meaning "the very voice" and describes the view that the New Testament Gospel accounts capture the concepts that Jesus expressed, but not the exact words. *Ipsissima vox* is contrasted with *Ipsissima verba*, meaning "the very words."

26. See Thomaskutty, *Dialogue*, x. These terms were introduced by G. Genette, *Narrative Discourse: An Essay in Method* (Ithaca, NY: Cornell University Press, 1980), 228–34.

27. Martyn, *History and Theology*, 24–36; Jan G. van der Watt, *An Introduction to the Johannine Gospel and Letters*, T&T Clark Approaches to Biblical Studies (New York: T&T Clark, 2007), 112–14.

28. See Thomaskutty, *Dialogue*, 349–50. Also see R. A. Culpepper, *Anatomy of the Fourth Gospel: A Study in Literary Design* (Philadelphia: Fortress, 1983), 140.

29. See Martyn, *History and Theology*, 24–36.

30. See Moloney, *Gospel of John*, 10.

plot of this world against the Johannine community.[31] The dualistic contrast and the performative linguistic phenomenon of the text dramatically foreground the community conflict in the first century CE context. The contrast between the "believing" and "unbelieving," "sons [and daughters] of light" and "sons [and daughters] of darkness," and "world from above" and "world from below" rhetorically introduces the Jewish-Christian polarity with the help of figurative language and sociopolitical and religio-cultural phenomena.[32]

The "sending out of the synagogue" (aposunagogē) and the struggle of the newly emerged Johannine community are portrayed in the Gospel with the help of both explicit and implicit terms.[33] As a marginal group expelled from the synagogue (John 16:2), the Johannine community had to deal with the issues of their relationship with Judaism and questions of self-identity, minority status, and oppression.[34] In John 6, the narrator plays a significant role as the text adds a dramatic setting to the conflict. The murmuring scene (John 6:41), argument scene (6:52), and grumbling scene (6:60–61) are implicitly introduced as "community dialogues."[35] The Jews' "hate language" is made obvious through their activity of naming Jesus a "deceiver" (John 7:12), "demonic" (7:20; 8:48, 52; 10:20–21), "Samaritan" (8:48), and "Child of Joseph" (6:42).[36] Other aspects of hate language such as diminution and reduction are also demonstrable in the language of the Jews (John 6:42, 52).[37] The narrator's memory of the actual speeches and events concerning Jesus is reproduced in light of the ongoing struggles of the community.[38]

---

31. See van der Watt, Introduction to the Johannine Gospel, 30–77.
32. See Moloney, Gospel of John, 11.
33. Martyn, History and Theology, 37–62. Cf. R. E. Brown, Community of the Beloved Disciple (New York: Paulist, 1979).
34. For more details, refer to Johnson Thomaskutty, Proefschrift: The Nature and Function of Dialogue in the Book of Signs (Nijmegen: Radboud Universiteit Nijmegen, 2014).
35. Cf. Culpepper, Anatomy, 127.
36. J. M. Roy explains four language structures: naming, diminutives, reduction, and metaphors. See J. M. Roy, Love to Hate: America's Obsession with Hatred and Violence (New York: Columbia University Press, 2002), 25–42.
37. Roy, 32.
38. Thomaskutty, Dialogue, 466–67.

4. Christ of Culture

In this model, Christ is seen as not against culture but comfortable and interpretable by its context. Niebuhr points back to the ancient Gnostics, Peter Abelard, Albrecht Ritschl, and Protestant liberalism to exemplify this model. He does not see any tension between the church and the world outside. It is a kind of accommodative principle that allows the church to be in agreement with the world.[39] As Christ is presented in agreement with the world, the uniqueness of the gospel is often disregarded in this model.[40] This layer of thought can be derived out of the Johannine narrative framework with more clarity.

Though there is a sense of antagonism between the world "from above" and the world "from below," Christ came as a mediator between the two worlds. As an agent of reconciliation between God and humanity, Jesus came to the *world below* and accommodated the life situation (John 1:1–5, 14; Col 1:19–20; Heb 1:1–3).[41] Jesus, as the only begotten child of the heavenly parent (*monogenēs*; John 1:18; 3:16), had to shift the *Sitz im Leben* from the heavenly culture to the earthly culture. In the mission, Jesus exercised the following cultural realities: fusing the heavenly culture with the earthly culture, placing Jesus's role and status as a reconciler between the two cultural realities, and propagating the heavenly culture in the local Palestinian context.[42] Jesus's earthly mission can be considered as a transfer of role and status from the preincarnate and heavenly to the incarnate and earthly cultural realities.[43] In essence, Jesus came from the *Sitz im Leben Gott* but accommodated and became part of the *Sitz im Leben Welt*.[44]

---

39. Niebuhr, *Christ and Culture*, 92.
40. Niebuhr, 110.
41. For more details about dualism in John's Gospel, see Howard M. Teeple, "Qumran and the Origin of the Fourth Gospel," in *The Composition of John's Gospel: Selected Studies from Novum Testamentum*, ed. David E. Orton (Leiden: Brill, 1999), 7–10.
42. Thompson, "John, Gospel Of," 376–77.
43. Johnson, "Logos," 481–84.
44. Here, the German expressions like *Sitz im Leben Gott* and *Sitz im Leben Welt* are expressed with a broader understanding of the spatial realities.

Within the modified dualistic framework of John, the earthly is placed under the control and authority of the heavenly.[45] Jesus came to that which was Jesus's own, but Jesus's own did not receive the one from heaven (John 1:11). The expression "[Jesus] came to [Jesus's] own" demonstrates Jesus's preincarnate role in creation and authority and possessiveness over the world "from below." Jesus revealed the heavenly identity to the world that Jesus was the Logos in flesh and dwelling among humanity (John 1:14).[46] As a complete human, Jesus accommodated the earthly cultural patterns and, as a Jew, attuned to the Jewish ethos and pathos. As the story unfolds within the Palestinian topographical and geopolitical canvas, the narrator delineates Jesus's identity as one among humanity.[47]

The dwelling of Jesus with diverse people groups exemplifies how the Word tabernacled among humanity (John 1:39b; 2:12; 4:40; 7:1–9). Jesus's eating and drinking with people (John 4:7; 12:1–8; 13:1–20; 19:28; 21:9–14) demonstrate Jesus's physical needs and human feelings. By walking with the disciples/people, Jesus modeled as a teacher. Jesus called out disciples—Andrew, Peter, Philip, Nathanael (John 1)—to be with the master and to carry out the heavenly message in the world.[48] By attending a wedding in Cana in Galilee and visiting the temple at Jerusalem, Jesus revealed the earthly identity in the world and connections with the institutions (John 2:1–11; 2:13–22).[49] These aspects show how Jesus was part and parcel of the human culture. Without associating Jesus with the human culture, it is almost impossible to interpret the narrative annals of John's Gospel.

Jesus's conversation with Nicodemus develops in the form of a dialogue between a "teacher from heaven" and a "teacher of Israel" (John 3:2, 10; my translation). As Nicodemus accepts Jesus as a rabbi and teacher, the reader understands Jesus's status and position in

---

45. Thompson, "John, Gospel Of," 382–83.
46. Rudolf Schnackenburg, *The Gospel according to St. John*, vol. 1 (Kent, UK: Burns & Oates, 1968), 259–60, 265–73.
47. Schnackenburg, 1:265–73.
48. Jo-Ann A. Brant, *John*, Paideia Commentaries on the New Testament (Grand Rapids, MI: Baker Academic, 2011), 48–54.
49. Brant, 55–59.

the world.[50] The Samaritan woman understands Jesus through her conversation: "How is it that you, a Jew, ask a drink of me, a woman of Samaria?" (John 4:9 NRSV).[51] While feeding the five thousand, Jesus understands the particular situation in life and behaves as per the needs and demands of the people (John 6:1–15).[52] Jesus was aware of the Jewish customs and background (John 4:9; 6:1; 11:16, 24; 18:10, 40; 19:13, 17), attending the festivals (2:13, 23; 4:45; 5:1; 6:4; 7:2, 37; 10:22; 11:55–56; 12:1, 12, 20; 13:1, 29; 18:28, 39) and transforming the society as an agent of liberation.[53] The public conversations of Jesus with the interlocutors resemble in several ways Platonic dialogues.[54] As a persuasive speaker, the rhetoric of Jesus was systematic and transformative as it was in the case of Socrates, Gautama Buddha, and Sri Ramakrishna.[55] In that sense, Jesus identified with and adopted a large number of worldly patterns, customs, idioms, and rhetoric.

The usage of the family metaphor—God as the parent, Jesus as the Son, the Holy Spirit as the comforter, and the believers as the children—provides the reader a worldly canvas with which to understand the divine mission in the world.[56] Jesus appears as a family friend of Lazarus (John 11:3, 11), a companion of Mary and Martha and one who weeps at the tomb (11:35), and a teacher who washes the feet of the disciples (13:1–20).[57] As it was in the case of Socrates, Jesus delivers a farewell discourse (John 13–17), and Jesus was arrested,

50. Brant, 74–77.
51. Brant, 84.
52. Ben Witherington, *John's Wisdom: A Commentary on the Fourth Gospel* (Louisville, KY: Westminster John Knox, 1995), 151–53.
53. Paul N. Anderson, *From Crisis to Christ: A Contextual Introduction to the New Testament* (Nashville: Abingdon, 2014), 142, 148.
54. Thomaskutty, *Dialogue*, 444–45.
55. R. M. Wenley, *Socrates and Christ: A Study in the Philosophy of Religion* (Adelaide, Australia: Cambridge Scholars, 2002), 1–9, 170–90; Marcus Borg, ed., *Jesus and Buddha: The Parallel Sayings* (Brooklyn: Ulysses, 2020); Swami Saradananda, *Sri Ramakrishna, the Great Teacher* (Mylapore, India: Sri Ramakrishna Math, 2008).
56. Jan G. van der Watt, *Family of the King: Dynamics of Metaphor in the Gospel according to John*, BINS 17 (Leiden: Brill, 2000), 161–392.
57. Jey J. Kanagaraj, *The Gospel of John: A Commentary* (Secunderabad, India: OM Books, 2005), 356–57, 360, 370–71, 429–44.

tried, crucified, and put to death as the law suggests.[58] All these narrative aspects take our attention to Jesus's accommodative role in the world.

5. Christ above Culture

This augmenting model neither considers Christ against culture nor accepts Christ and culture on equal terms. Church fathers like Justin Martyr and Clement of Alexandria were early adherents of this model. Thomas Aquinas attempted to find a relationship between reason and revelation, creation and redemption, and nature and grace. Later on, this became a predominant position among the Roman Catholics. As per this view of Niebuhr, cultural aspects are basically good, and they can be perfected by Christian revelation and the work of the church.[59] This third layer is placed with widespread narrative annals in the Fourth Gospel.

Although part of the human culture, Jesus elevates the role and status above the worldly culture. A reader can notice it as a unique feature in the mission and ministry of Jesus. Jesus is *accommodative* as part of the human culture but at the same time *disruptive* as Jesus is above the culture.[60] Jesus's status as God's child and the creator of the universe enables the protagonist to function as part of and at the same time above and beyond the cultural phenomena in the world. Jesus is introduced as the Word "in the beginning," "with God," and "was God" (John 1:1), but later on, the narrator describes that the Word "became flesh and dwelt among us" (1:14).[61] This tendency of *being God* and *becoming flesh* makes Jesus unique in character and

58. See "Socrates Final Speech," World Future Fund, accessed October 10, 2020, http://www.worldfuturefund.org/Reports/Socrates/socrates.html. Also see Charles Talbert, *Reading John: A Literary and Theological Commentary on the Fourth Gospel and the Johannine Epistles* (Macon, GA: Smyth & Helwys, 2005), 207–9.

59. Wax, "Christ and Culture." Also see Niebuhr, *Christ and Culture*, 145.

60. Simon Samuel, *A Postcolonial Reading of Mark's Story of Jesus* (New York: T&T Clark, 2007), 158–59.

61. Kanagaraj, *Gospel of John*, 34–41, 53–59.

role, as part of the heavenly culture and part of the earthly culture simultaneously.

At the wedding place in Cana, Jesus makes it obvious that the hour of God is the opportune time for the protagonist to reveal the glory. Jesus puts aside the concern of Mary and awaits the hour of the heavenly parent (John 2:4).[62] Jesus's constant relationship with the heavenly parent is made clear to the reader. While *everyone* serves the good wine first, Jesus introduces the best wine at last (John 2:10).[63] It is an indication of the Messianic banquet that Jesus prepares for the believing community. The Jerusalem temple is introduced as the house of the heavenly God, but the Jews turned the abode of God into a marketplace. While the society alters the temple as a marketplace, Jesus transforms it into the divine sanctuary.[64] Though the Jews claim that the temple was built in forty-six years, Jesus transforms the occasion and relates its significance with the protagonist's death and resurrection (John 2:19).[65] While the Jews were concerned with the earthly customs and patterns, Jesus transforms such occasions to demonstrate the heaven-earth relationship. On all these occasions, Jesus elevates the understanding of culture in spiritual and heavenly senses.

While Nicodemus appears as a teacher who comes to Jesus "by night" (John 3:2a, 10), Jesus is introduced as a teacher who came from God (3:2b).[66] In a culture in which gurus were highly regarded, both of them appear as gurus, one as a teacher "from below" and the other a teacher "from above." Their perspectives also differ, as Nicodemus is preoccupied with worldly things (John 3:4), and Jesus emphasizes the concerns of God (3:3).[67] Jesus's "from above" aspects are clearer through the expression "No one has ascended into heaven except the one who descended from heaven" (John 3:13

---

62. Kanagaraj, 99–100.
63. Kanagaraj, 102–3.
64. Raymond E. Brown, *An Introduction to the New Testament* (Bangalore: Theological Publications in India, 2009), 340–41.
65. Thomaskutty, *Dialogue*, 93–106.
66. Thomaskutty, 107–23.
67. Kanagaraj, *Gospel of John*, 117–18.

NRSV).[68] While the narrator states that "Jews do not share things in common with Samaritans" (John 4:9b NRSV), Jesus asks for water from a Samaritan woman (4:7). While Jews and the Samaritans consider Jacob as their forefather, Jesus reveals the protagonist's status even above Jacob. While Jacob gave the Samaritans the well, Jesus gives them eternal life (John 4:6, 11–14).[69] The woman's understanding of Jesus as "a Jew" (John 4:9), "sir" (4:11, 15, 19), "prophet" (4:19), "Christ" (4:25–26), and "the Savior of the world" (4:42) enables the reader to understand Jesus above the human cultural patterns.[70]

In the story of the royal man (John 4:46–54), Jesus critiques his pattern of believing on the basis of signs and wonders (4:48).[71] Believing Jesus and God based on earthly conditions is altogether against the pattern of the heavenly culture.[72] While the Jews strictly observed the Sabbath regulations, Jesus breaks those regulations to make a person whole on a Sabbath day (John 5:1–9). Stating that "my [Parent] is still working, and I also am working" (John 5:17), Jesus proves self-authority above the existing cultural standards (5:19–47).[73] This is also obvious in the story of the man born blind (John 9:1–41). The customs and the interpretative tenets of the religious authorities stood in sharp contrast with Jesus's "from above" understanding (John 7–8).[74] While the poor, the Samaritans, and the blind were neglected in the society, Jesus elevates their lives and gives them a new identity.[75] Jesus stands firm against the human tendencies of interpretation and cultural phenomena. Jesus interprets the culture and the society from the eternal-life perspective.

---

68. Brown, *New Testament*, 341–42.
69. Thomaskutty, *Gospel of John*, 145–52.
70. Thomaskutty, 145–52.
71. Cornelis Bennema, *Encountering Jesus: Character Studies in the Gospel of John* (Bangalore: Primalogue, 2009), 94–99.
72. Bennema, 94–99.
73. Craig L. Blomberg, *The Historical Reliability of John's Gospel* (Downers Grove, IL: InterVarsity, 2001), 108–18.
74. Blomberg, 131–50.
75. Johnson Thomaskutty, "Johannine Women as Paradigms in the Indian Context," supplement, *Acta Theologica* 27 (2019): 79–100.

The raising of Lazarus (John 11:1–52) and, later on, Jesus's own resurrection (20:1–18) amply describe the position of the child of God above and beyond the cultural realities of the world.[76] Jesus's action of washing the feet of the disciples (John 13:1–20), the farewell discourse in a higher moral and ethical idiomatic tone (chaps. 13–17), the teachings on unity among the believers and oneness with God (15:1–5; 17:1–26), the passion and the glorious death on the cross (chaps. 18–19), the resurrection, and the breathing of the Holy Spirit on the disciples (chap. 20) foreground the method of spreading the heavenly culture in the world. As the "Word became flesh and dwelt among us" (John 1:14), Jesus emphasizes the eternal life principles of God.[77]

6. Christ and Culture in Paradox

This model was represented by Augustine (*Two Cities*), Martin Luther (*Two Governments*), and Søren Kierkegaard (*Faith and Absurd*), who saw in the relationship between Christ and culture a paradoxical tension between faith and reason.[78] This tension between Christ and culture does not advocate a total negation of culture but rather simultaneously embraces and rejects certain aspects of it.[79] For Niebuhr, though culture is understood as this-worldly and impermanent, Christ works in closer association with this world. The Fourth Gospel gives the reader ample evidence to prove this paradoxical existence.

The paradoxical relationship between Christ and culture is clearly stated right at the beginning of the Fourth Gospel. In John 1:10–11, the narrator states this aspect in the following way: first, Jesus was in the world, but the world did not know it; second, Jesus came to what was self own, but self own did not accept Jesus.[80]

---

76. Moloney, *Gospel of John*, 322–44.
77. Beasley-Murray, *John*, 222–307. Also see Thomaskutty, *Gospel of John*, 97–110, 191–208.
78. Niebuhr, *Christ and Culture*, 151; Marbaniang, "Gospel and Culture," 5.
79. Wax, "Christ and Culture." Cf. Niebuhr, *Christ and Culture*, 187.
80. Moloney, *Gospel of John*, 44.

The unknowing nature of the antagonists before the all-knowing protagonist introduces a paradox within John's narrative framework. The semantic domains of John function within a dualistic narrative master plan. The contrast between the "from above" and the "from below" develops within the macrostructure of the Gospel.[81] In the Gospel, the dualism of light and darkness, truth and untruth, and belief and unbelief appears paradoxical. Within the narrative framework, the protagonist is involved in the mission of attuning the "from below" to the "from above" culture.[82] This aspect is at the core of the Fourth Gospel.[83]

As Jesus was the true light, Jesus's presence was paradoxical to the falsehood that flourished in the world (John 1:9).[84] When John the Baptist introduces Jesus as "the Lamb of God who takes away the sin of the world" (John 1:29 NRSV), a reader can understand the contrasting nature of the sinful world before the true light.[85] Through the initiative of cleansing the temple, Jesus proved that the culture of this world is antagonistic to God and the heavenly kin(g)dom.[86] While the Jews convert the temple into a marketplace, Jesus considers it as God's house (John 2:16).[87] This aspect is an overarching phenomenon as the contrast between the believing and the unbelieving continues as a narrative strategy in John.

The paradoxical nature of Christ and culture comes into a sharp focus in John 7–8. The contrasting features, such as the work of Jesus versus the works of the world and believing over against unbelieving, remain significant within John's narrative.[88] Other aspects such as the hour of Jesus, revealing Jesus to the world, and the activities of testimony also bring forth the character contrasts. In John 7:1–9,

---

81. George Eldon Ladd, *A Theology of the New Testament* (Grand Rapids, MI: Eerdmans, 1993), 260–73.
82. Ladd, 260–73.
83. Ladd, 260–73.
84. Beasley-Murray, *John*, 12.
85. Beasley-Murray, 24–25.
86. Beasley-Murray, 38–42.
87. Blomberg, *Historical Reliability*, 87–91.
88. Blomberg, 131–50.

the narrator introduces the contrasting views of Jesus and the brothers.[89] In John 7–8, the central conflict of the dialogue is based on the parenthood of Jesus and the interlocutors. Two worldviews are in contrast with each other, the worldview of Jesus rooted in God versus the worldview of the Jews in relation to Abraham and Moses.[90] While the Jews claim that they are the children of Abraham (and also of God), Jesus declares that they are children of the devil (John 8:44).[91] The narrator develops the dialogue with the help of several ironies, misunderstandings, and dualistic language.

The Jesus movement in its own *Sitz im Leben* and the Johannine community in the *Sitz im Leben Kirche* followed new principles and methods. The teachings and praxes introduced by the new movements to the Jews and the gentiles were paradoxical to their existent cultural realities.[92] The involvements of both the Jesus movement and the Johannine community brought into effect some of the disputations, "outsider" and "insider" contrasts, and ultimately, dualistic tensions.[93] In John 11:45–53, the antagonism between the new movement and the Jewish community is stated in Caiaphas's words: "You do not understand that it is better for you to have one man die for the people than to have the whole nation destroyed" (John 11:50 NRSV).[94] The trial, crucifixion, and death of Jesus further reveal the paradoxical and antagonistic aspects of the Johannine narrative framework.[95]

7. Christ Transforming Culture

A more Calvinist and Reformed view sees the power of Christ to alter and ultimately transform the culture. In Niebuhr's view, culture is seen as tainted by human sinfulness and redeemable or

---

89. Thomaskutty, *Dialogue*, 253–58.
90. Thomaskutty, 305–9.
91. Rudolf Schnackenburg, *The Gospel according to St. John*, vol. 2 (Kent, UK: Burns & Oates, 1990), 210–24.
92. See Martyn, *History and Theology*.
93. Ladd, *A Theology of the New Testament*, 260–73.
94. Brant, *John*, 177–79.
95. Brant, 231–64.

transformable by the presence of Christ. According to Trevin Wax, "All of culture is under the judgment of God, and yet culture is also under God's sovereign rule."[96] That which is corrupted by human sinfulness and selfishness can be transformed by the initiative of Christ and the gospel. The Johannine narrator foregrounds this reality with more eloquence.

Jesus transforms human culture in a divine way. The purpose of Jesus's coming was to redeem the world and place it in harmony with the "from above" realities. A divine-human harmony in particular and a divine-world harmony in general were the ultimate concerns of Jesus's mission. John's realized eschatological framework describes the world from below in vertical interaction with the world from above. This vertical, realized, and constant relationship between the earthly and the heavenly is the expected goal of Jesus's mission in the world.[97] The holistic transformation intended through the mission and ministry of Jesus is foregrounded here with clarity. The cultural and social phenomena of the world deviated from the divine plan, and hence, Jesus was sent as the agent of God to fulfill the heavenly mission.

The Johannine community was composed of a transformed group of people with a new culture, morality, and principles. The newness motif of the Gospel demonstrates the transformative lifestyle that Jesus emphasized over against the existent social and cultural norms. The themes such as new wine (John 2:10), new temple (2:21), new birth (3:3), new water (4:10–15), new life (4:46–54), new Moses (6:31–48), new exodus (6:16–22), new manna (6:31), new tabernacle (1:14; 7–8), new sight (9:1–41), and others prefigure the expected norm given to the Johannine community as a transformed and liberated community of believers.[98] Over against a culture that was hate oriented and exclusive, Jesus's transformative model introduces a love-centered

96. Wax, "Christ and Culture." Also see Niebuhr, *Christ and Culture*, 191.
97. D. H. Johnson, "Life," in Green, McKnight, and Marshall, *Dictionary of Jesus*, 469–71.
98. W. L. Kynes, "New Birth," in Green, McKnight, and Marshall, *Dictionary of Jesus*, 574–76. Also see "John," United States Conference of Catholic Bishops, accessed October 12, 2020, https://bible.usccb.org/bible/john/0.

and inclusive pattern that accommodates people irrespective of their race, caste, color, gender, and national identity.[99]

Jesus transformed the lifestyle and the cultural phenomenon of many as they started following the one from heaven. The call narratives make it clear that through Jesus's initiative, people were brought to new levels of life. Their lifestyle was changed based on the new understanding they received about Jesus: Andrew states, "We have found the Messiah" (John 1:41); Peter says, "You are the Holy One of God" (6:69); Philip states, "We have found Jesus about whom Moses in the law and also the prophets wrote, Jesus the child of Joseph from Nazareth" (1:45); and Nathanael says, "Rabbi, you are the Child of God! You are the Kin[g] of Israel!" (1:49).[100] The event of temple cleansing demonstrates Jesus's initiative to replace the existing human culture with the divine principles (John 2:13–22).[101] Nicodemus, who came to Jesus by night, was changed as a disciple of the teacher from above (John 3:1–10; 7:50–52; 19:38–42).[102] The Samaritan woman was liberated from a biased human cultural background and shown the eternal life experience (John 4:1–26).[103] The woman became a change maker to bring the Samaritans to "the Savior of the world" (John 4:42).[104] A transformation based on people's faith in Jesus is obvious in the family of the royal man (John 4:46–54), the invalid person (5:1–18), those who heard the Word at the synagogue in Capernaum (6:25–59), those who gathered during the feast of the tabernacles (chaps. 7–8), the man born blind (9:1–41), the family of Lazarus (11:1–12:8), and the disciples who heard the voice of Jesus (chaps. 13–17).[105] The power of transformation is made obvious through the utterances of many: "I have seen the Lord[/ess]" (Mary Magdalene, John 20:18 NRSV), "We have seen the Lord[/ess]" (the disciples, 20:25 NRSV), "My Lord[/ess] and my God"

---

99. Thomaskutty, *Dialogue*, 466–70.

100. As discussed in Beasley-Murray, *John*, 27 and 97. These quotes are my own translations.

101. Brown, *New Testament*, 340–41.

102. Brown, 341–42.

103. Moloney, *Gospel of John*, 115–35.

104. Moloney, 149.

105. Moloney, 164–95.

(Thomas, 20:28 NRSV), and "It is the Lord[/ess]" (the beloved disciple, 21:7 NRSV).[106]

The Johannine community was transformed through their faith in Jesus, and they were rooted in the love of God. John's narrative framework gives the reader convincing clues about the transformation of various walks of people: the common fisher folk (the disciples),[107] the womenfolk (the mother of Jesus, the Samaritan woman, Mary and Martha, and Mary Magdalene),[108] the differently abled (the invalid and the man born blind), and the communities that followed Jesus (on various occasions).[109] These details enable us to understand the role and status of Jesus as a transformer of the earthly culture based on heavenly principles.

The previously stated models provide the following clues in the process of understanding Christ and the gospel in relation to culture: first, though there is an element of clash between Christ and culture, they are not mutually exclusive; second, though Christ and culture are viewed in relational terms, Christ has the autonomy to function independently; third, the supremacy of Christ above culture is an established factor, and hence Christ reveals self-esteem through the medium of culture; fourth, Christ and culture are in paradoxical positions, but the Word became flesh and dwelt in human history; and fifth, Christ transforms culture in order to save it from human sinfulness and selfishness. These aspects reveal the fact that the person and work of Christ can be understood in relationship to and distinction from the culture. This idea is important in understanding Jesus's work within the framework of John's Gospel.

8. Implications and Conclusion

The details of Niebuhr about Christ and culture are delineated with implications here in the Johannine community context. Niebuhr's fivefold method can be used as a theoretical framework to understand

---

106. Kanagaraj, *Gospel of John*, 648–63, 675.
107. Thomaskutty, *Dialogue*, 58–78.
108. Thomaskutty, "Johannine Women," 79–100.
109. Thomaskutty, *Dialogue*, 169–80, 310–40.

how Christ was understood and interpreted in the Fourth Gospel. A polyvalent and interdisciplinary approach that makes use of multiple literary tools and the paradigm of Niebuhr enables us to see the power of the Johannine text to foreground the layers of thought embedded within. As John's Gospel is a two-level drama, a reader can perceive the shift of emphasis from the life situation of Jesus (*Sitz im Leben Jesu*) to the life situation of the early Johannine church (*Sitz im Leben Kirche*).[110] The Johannine narrator demonstrates how the person of Jesus and the gospel were introduced to the emerging community in closer relationship with the sociocultural and politico-religious realities of the people. In the following sections, we will see how the Christ of the Fourth Gospel confronts the cultural phenomenon in a new idiom.

We attempted to understand Richard Niebuhr's perspectives on Christ and culture with evidence from Scripture. We explored several aspects of the Jesus movement and the Johannine community experiences to arrive at certain conclusions. The *Sitz im Leben Jesu* and the *Sitz im Leben Kirche* aspects were considered to delineate Christ/gospel and its dynamic relationship with the worldly culture. As Jesus introduces the heavenly principles in the earthly setting, Jesus emphasizes the aspects of the eternal life above all other concerns. As Jesus offers the gift of abundant life, people who are marginalized and dehumanized receive a new hope in the world. As the Word became flesh, Jesus accommodates the worldly culture to convey the heavenly message. On the other hand, Jesus distances himself from worldly patterns to communicate a unique message. Jesus fuses the "from above" message with the earthly to transform the world. In that sense, the Johannine community followed a rhetoric of difference as an alternative culture.

In the world, Christ/gospel functions in relation to the cultural phenomenon in multifarious ways: first, Christ/gospel exercises the heavenly power and authority over against the "from below" culture when it goes wrong; second, Jesus accommodates the worldly

---

110. For more details concerning the portrayal of John's Gospel as a two-level drama, see Martyn, *History and Theology*.

culture to communicate the message of eternal life in its own idiom and the patterns of the culture below; third, Jesus functions above the worldly culture as Jesus responds to the sinful nature of the world, attunes the earthly with the heavenly realities, and exists as the ideal for the world to follow; fourth, Jesus remains paradoxical to the human culture, as the sinless and sinful, light and darkness, and truth and untruth cannot coalesce; and fifth, Jesus transforms the human culture as God of heavens coming to the world as the creator of the universe. Being *against*, *of*, *above*, *paradoxical*, and *transformative*, Christ/gospel invites the attention of the world "from below" toward a life-affirming, liberative, and heavenly space of God.

In the process of interpreting the text, the realities of the suffering people in the Indian church and society should merge with the life setting of Jesus and the Johannine community to derive theological and contextual implications. The Gospel can be shared *above* and even *against* the culture, as Jesus is the true God (John 14:6). The Christ/gospel *of* the culture has to be explored, as the partial revelation of God is manifest in other religious and cultural practices in Indian society. The *paradoxical* nature of Christ/gospel is obvious when we emphasize the oneness aspect of God over against the systemic problems of the nation. The God of the Bible reveals the creator of the universe. Jesus appears as cocreator with God, the child of God who dies for humanity, and the resurrected Lord/ess and the savior of the world. These aspects of the Jesus movement are often considered paradoxical to the Indian culture. The *transforming* power of Christ/gospel can liberate the Indian culture and society from the clutches of the rich-poor dichotomy, tribal and Adivasi struggles, the dehumanization of women, and various other human-made and culture-bound taboos in the country and in the world.

The Christian identity in India should be demonstrated in dialogical and intertextual relationships with the surrounding socioreligious and politico-cultural realities so that the Christians can stand *against* the odds and the injustices of the cultural phenomena, accommodate the cultural values and be part *of* the prevailing realities of our neighbors, foreground the Christian ethical and moral aspects *above* and *beyond* in the context of existential struggles of the people, expose the *paradoxical* aspects of different people groups, enable a constructive dialogue among communities to lead all toward the common good, and *transform* the socioreligious and politico-cultural taboos and structures to liberate people from being marginalized and ostracized. An "insider" and "outsider" dynamism can be identified through the means of the aforementioned ways and means. By enabling a boundary mark between the "insider" and the "outsider," Christian communities can transform the culture by extending invitations to outsiders so that they may embrace the paradigmatic inside group. As the Covid-19 pandemic grips the people across the globe, the church as a community of the reformed can stand *against*, *of*, and *above* to liberate people irrespective of their caste, color, creed, gender, region, and ethnic identity. The church and the Christian community should foster the virtue of solidarity in the midst of turbulent situations. As it was done in the *Sitz im Leben Jesu* and in the *Sitz im Leben Kirche*, it should also be actualized in the *Sitz im Leben Indien* (life situation of the wider Indian community), with a special focus on the marginalized during the Covid-19 pandemic (*Sitz im Leben Covid-19*).

Bibliography

Amalorpavadass, D. S. *Gospel and Culture: Evangelization, Inculturation, and "Hinduisation."* Bengaluru: National Biblical Catechetical and Liturgical Center, 1978.

Anderson, Paul N. *From Crisis to Christ: A Contextual Introduction to the New Testament.* Nashville: Abingdon, 2014.

———. *The Riddles of the Fourth Gospel: An Introduction to John.* Minneapolis: Fortress, 2011.

Beasley-Murray, G. R. *John.* WBC 36. Waco, TX: Word Books, 1987.

Bennema, Cornelis. "A Comparative Approach to Understanding Character in the Gospel of John." In *Character and Characterization in the Gospel of John*, edited by C. W. Skinner, 36–58. London: Bloomsbury, 2013.

———. *Encountering Jesus: Character Studies in the Gospel of John.* Bangalore: Primalogue, 2009.

Blomberg, L. Craig. *The Historical Reliability of John's Gospel*. Downers Grove, IL: InterVarsity, 2001.

Borg, Marcus, ed. *Jesus and Buddha: The Parallel Sayings*. Brooklyn: Ulysses, 2020.

Brant, Jo-Ann A. *John*. Paideia Commentaries on the New Testament. Grand Rapids, MI: Baker Academic, 2011.

Brown, Raymond E. *Community of the Beloved Disciple*. New York: Paulist, 1979.

———. *The Gospel according to John (i–xii)*. Anchor Bible 1. Garden City, NY: Doubleday, 1966.

———. *An Introduction to the New Testament*. Bangalore: Theological Publications in India, 2009.

Culpepper, R. A. *Anatomy of the Fourth Gospel: A Study in Literary Design*. Philadelphia: Fortress, 1983.

Genette, G. *Narrative Discourse: An Essay in Method*. Ithaca, NY: Cornell University Press, 1980.

Johnson, D. H. "Life." In *Dictionary of Jesus and the Gospels*, edited by Joel B. Green, Scot McKnight, and I. Howard Marshall, 469–471. Downers Grove, IL: InterVarsity, 1992.

———. "Logos." In *Dictionary of Jesus and the Gospels*, edited by Joel B. Green, Scot McKnight, and I. Howard Marshall, 481–484. Downers Grove, IL: InterVarsity, 1992.

Kalman, Bobbie. *What Is Culture?* Catharines, ON: Crabtree, 2009.

Kanagaraj, Jey J. *The Gospel of John: A Commentary*. Secunderabad, India: OM Books, 2005.

Kelly, A. J., and F. J. Moloney. *Experiencing God in the Gospel of John*. New York: Paulist, 2003.

Kynes, W. L. "New Birth." In *Dictionary of Jesus and the Gospels*, edited by Joel B. Green, Scot McKnight, and I. Howard Marshall, 574–576. Downers Grove, IL: InterVarsity, 1992.

Ladd, George Eldon. *A Theology of the New Testament*. Grand Rapids, MI: Eerdmans, 1993.

Marbaniang, Domenic. "The Gospel and Culture: Areas of Conflict, Consent, and Conversion." *Journal of the Contemporary Christian* 6, no. 1 (August 2014): 9–10.

Martyn, Louis. *History and Theology in the Fourth Gospel*. Nashville: Abingdon, 1968.

Moloney, F. J. *The Gospel of John*. Sacra Pagina Series. Edited by D. J. Harrington. Collegeville, MN: Liturgical, 1998.

Nicholls, Bruce J. *Contextualization: A Theology of Gospel and Culture*. Vancouver: Regent College, 1979.

Niebuhr, H. Richard. *Christ and Culture*. San Francisco: Harper & Row, 1951.

Pappas, Stephanie, and Callum McKelvie. "What Is Culture?" Live Science. Accessed September 18, 2020. https://www.livescience.com/21478-what-is-culture-definition-of-culture.html.

Redman, J. C. S. "Eyewitness Testimony and the Characters in the Fourth Gospel." In *Character and Characterization in the Gospel of John*, edited by C. W. Skinner, 59–78. London: Bloomsbury, 2013.

Roy, J. M. *Love to Hate: America's Obsession with Hatred and Violence*. New York: Columbia University Press, 2002.

Samuel, Simon. *A Postcolonial Reading of Mark's Story of Jesus*. New York: T&T Clark, 2007.

Saradananda, Swami. *Sri Ramakrishna, the Great Teacher*. Mylapore, India: Sri Ramakrishna Math, 2008.

Schnackenburg, Rudolf. *The Gospel according to St. John*. 2 vols. Kent, UK: Burns & Oates, 1990.

Shirbroun, G. F. "Light." In *Dictionary of Jesus and the Gospels*, edited by Joel B. Green, Scot McKnight, and I. Howard Marshall, 472–473. Downers Grove, IL: InterVarsity, 1992.

Socrates. "Socrates Final Speech." World Future Fund. Accessed October 10, 2020. http://www.worldfuturefund.org/Reports/Socrates/socrates.html.

Stibbe, M. W. G. *John*. Readings: A New Biblical Commentary. Sheffield, UK: Sheffield Academic, 1993.

Sugden, Chris. *Gospel, Culture, and Transformation*. Regnum Studies in Mission. Oxford: Regnum, 2000.

Talbert, Charles. *Reading John: A Literary and Theological Commentary on the Fourth Gospel and the Johannine Epistles*. Macon, GA: Smyth & Helwys, 2005.

Teeple, Howard M. "Qumran and the Origin of the Fourth Gospel." In *The Composition of John's Gospel: Selected Studies from Novum Testamentum*, edited by David E. Orton, 1–10. Leiden: Brill, 1999.

Thomaskutty, Johnson. *Dialogue in the Book of Signs: A Polyvalent Analysis of John 1:19–12:50*. BINS 136. Leiden: Brill, 2015.

———. "Glo[b/c]alization and Mission[s]: Reading John's Gospel." *New Life Theological Journal* 5, no. 1 (January–June 2015): 56–77.

———. "'Gospel' and 'Culture' from a Johannine Community Perspective." In *Theological and Ethical Issues in Nepal: Papers Presented at Nepal Theological Forum*, edited by Akumtila Jamir and Chubamongba Ao, 111–134. Kathmandu: Samdan, 2021.

———. *The Gospel of John: A Universalistic Reading*. Delhi: Christian World Imprints, 2020.

———. "Johannine Women as Paradigms in the Indian Context." Supplement, *Acta Theologica* 27 (2019): 79–100.

———. *Proefschrift: The Nature and Function of Dialogue in the Book of Signs*. Nijmegen, Netherlands: Radboud Universiteit Nijmegen, 2014.

Thompson, M. M. "John, Gospel Of." In *Dictionary of Jesus and the Gospels*, edited by Joel B. Green, Scot McKnight, and I. Howard Marshall, 368–383. Downers Grove, IL: InterVarsity, 1992.

Tillich, Paul. *Theology of Culture*. Edited by Robert C. Kimball. Oxford: Oxford University Press, 1959.

Tovey, D. *Jesus, Story of God: John's Story of Jesus*. Adelaide, Australia: ATF, 2007.

Troeltsch, Ernst. *Writings on Theology and Religion*. Edited and translated by Robert Morgan and Michael Pye. Atlanta: John Knox, 1977.

Tylor, E. B. *Primitive Culture: Researches into the Development of Mythology, Philosophy, Religion, Art, and Custom*. Vol. 1. London: John Murray, 1871.

van der Watt, Jan G. *Family of the King: Dynamics of Metaphor in the Gospel according to John*. BINS 17. Leiden: Brill, 2000.

———. *An Introduction to the Johannine Gospel and Letters*, T&T Clark Approaches to Biblical Studies. New York: T&T Clark, 2007.

Wax, Trevin. "'Christ and Culture'—an Overview of a Christian Classic." Gospel Coalition, February 25, 2015. https://www.thegospelcoalition.org/blogs/trevin-wax/christ-and-culture-an-overview-of-a-christian-classic/.

Wenley, R. M. *Socrates and Christ: A Study in the Philosophy of Religion*. Adelaide, Australia: Cambridge Scholars, 2002.

Witherington, Ben. *John's Wisdom: A Commentary on the Fourth Gospel*. Louisville, KY: Westminster John Knox, 1995.

7

The Gospel and Truth
Predicates in a Hindu Context

ARUTHUCKAL VARUGHESE JOHN

There is a popular sentiment that conceives of the Semitic religions and Indic religions as polar opposites on the matter of truth perception. Unlike Indic religions, the Semitic religions, and Christianity in particular, are identified as possessing theological doctrines that have true/false predicates. There is little contention about Christian doctrinal beliefs also being truth claims. As Bruce D. Marshall argues, "As I am using the term, a *belief* is an attitude or disposition expressible by holding a sentence true. Thus one cannot have the concept of belief without having the concept of truth.... Believing is thus a *propositional attitude*, that is, an attitude (in this case, holding true) toward a sentence the meaning or interpretation of which the believer understands or has specified; there are many other propositional attitudes, such as hoping, doubting, and wishing."[1] In contrast, it is claimed that in the Hindu context, "truth and falsity do not apply to human traditions." This is not a claim that Hinduism has no conception of truth; in fact, it has a robust idea of truth. The term *Satyameva Jayate* popularized by Pandit Madan Mohan Malviya was derived from the *Mundaka Upanishad* (3.1.6): "Truth alone triumphs; not falsehood. Through truth the divine path is spread out by which

---

1. Bruce D. Marshall, *Trinity and Truth* (Cambridge: Cambridge University Press, 1999), 10.

the sages whose desires have been completely fulfilled, reach to where is that supreme treasure of Truth."[2]

Further, truth is intertwined with dharma in the Hindu tradition.[3] While "truth-telling, and by implication promise-keeping, were particularly appropriate acts for good Brāhmaṇas,"[4] Krishna's discourse in the *Mahabharata* contends that where truth telling is purely pursued as following the letter of the law, it can become an immoral act. Kauśika, by his immature vow, "Satyaṃ mayā sadā vācyam iti tasyābhavad vratam" (I shall always tell the truth), gave up the men hiding from bandits in the forest, resulting in their death.[5] In such complex scenarios, Krishna "endorse[s] *context* as key to determining the relative merits of what seem to be temporarily incompatible dharmic goods."[6]

If Hinduism has a robust idea of truth associated with the ultimate reality, how shall we understand the proposal that the Hindu doctrines do not possess true/false predicates? In this chapter, I shall claim that truth predicates are not unique to Christianity or the Semitic religions. The Hindu religious texts have similar truth

---

2. *Satyameva Jayate* was adopted in 1950 as the official motto for the Indian State. For the quote, see *Satyameva jayate nānṛtaṁ, satyena panthā vitato devayānaḥ | yenākramantyṛṣayo hyāptakāmā, yatra tat satyasya paramaṁ nidhānam* II, trans. Swami Krishnananda (Sivananda Ashram, India: Divine Life Society, n.d.), 54, http://www.swami-krishnananda.org/mundak/Mundaka_Upanishad.pdf.

3. It is hard to find a semantic equivalent in English for *dharma*. It can carry a wide range of meanings, such as "duty," "religion," "justice," "law," "ethics," "religious merit," "principle," and "right." Jaimini, a commentator of the Mimamsa school describes dharma as "an obligation, declared by the *Veda*, to perform ritual action (*karma*), which brings of itself no reward other than that its non-performance would be 'that which is not *dharma*' (*adharma*) and result in retribution or 'sin' (*papa*)." See Gavin Flood, "*Dharma*," in *India's Religions, Perspectives from Sociology and History*, ed. T. N. Madan (Delhi: Oxford University Press, 2004), 231–32.

4. Julius Lipner, "The Truth of Dharma and the Dharma of Truth: Reflections on Hinduism as a Dharmic Faith," *International Journal of Hindu Studies* 23, no. 3 (2019): 213–37.

5. Lord Krishna instructs, "As for Kauśika, by that immoral act (*adharmeṇa*), by that highly ill spoken word, he went to a ghastly hell. A fool, he was not knowledgeable enough of the authoritative texts and unable to distinguish the realities of *dharma* (8.49.46)." Lipner, 223.

6. Lipner, 221.

claims that are equally exclusive in nature. I shall also claim that it is in the very nature of beliefs, religious or otherwise, to have truth predicates. Yet I shall argue that the historical and nonhistorical natures of religious beliefs in the two traditions entail an essential difference. Finally, I shall explore certain bridge concepts within the Hindu cultural aspirations of truth for the gospel and briefly suggest a way of navigating the difficult terrain of religious conversion. Let me first state the problem.

I. The Problem of Truth Predicates and Religious Conversion

For brevity, I shall briefly explore two publications, articulated by Balagangadhara and others from Ghent University in Belgium. In their 2007 article "The Secular State and Religious Conflict: Liberal Neutrality and the Indian Case of Pluralism," S. N. Balagangadhara and Jakob De Roover argue that we "consider the following two propositions about religious truth: (a) religion revolves around the truth of its doctrine; (b) the predicates 'truth' and 'falsity' do not apply to human traditions. These views have been held by two different kinds of groups: the Semitic religions such as Christianity and Islam; and the 'pagan' traditions of the Antiquity and the Hindu Indians."[7] These two propositions, according to the authors, illustrate two divergent sets of attitudes toward religions and human traditions.

Similarly, in their 2008 paper, Sarah Claerhout and Jakob De Roover argue that the "strictness of ritual might generate temporary conflicts within traditions, but it does not transform different religions into rivals. Truth claims do so."[8] Consequently, the problem with Christianity and Islam, the authors argue, is that they view religions as "competitors because they revolve around

---

7. S. N. Balagangadhara and Jakob De Roover, "The Secular State and Religious Conflict: Liberal Neutrality and the Indian Case of Pluralism," *Journal of Political Philosophy* 15, no. 1 (2007): 73.
8. Sarah Claerhout and Jakob De Roover, "Conversion of the World: Proselytization in India and the Universalization of Christianity," in *Proselytization Revisited: Rights Talk, Free Markets and Culture Wars*, ed. Rosalind I. J. Hackett (London: Equinox, 2008), 62.

doctrines, which can be either true or false. Since such truth predicates apply to them, they are engaged in a perpetual competition over religious truth. Christianity and Islam claim that—because they are the unique revelations of the biblical God to humankind—they are true. They believe there is one true God, who is the Creator and Sovereign of the world."[9] Contrary to Christianity and Islam, the Indic religions espouse that "different cultural traditions could never be religious rivals, because truth predicates do not apply to them. The various traditions are part of a human search for truth and the different practices are paths in this ongoing quest."[10]

In this portrayal, the authors are not suggesting that there are conflicting views about truth that are equally plausible; rather, they highlight the attitudes that the two different religious traditions have toward truth. Their contention is not about the nature of truth—whether it corresponds to reality or whether it can be propositionally represented. Their claim is that Christianity is fundamentally defined by doctrines with truth predicates, whereas Hinduism is not. Yet it is not clear whether the contrast that the authors draw between Semitic and Indic traditions pertains to claims within the religious texts or whether they pertain to the attitudes of people regardless of the religious texts.

To illustrate the exclusive conception of the truth of Christianity through appeal to divine authority, they cite *The Epistle to Diognetus*, composed around 124 CE, as a case in point:

> The doctrines they [the Christians] profess is not the invention of busy human minds and brains, nor are they, like some, adherents of this or that school of human thought. As I said before, it is not an earthly discovery that has been entrusted to them. The thing they guard so jealously is no product of mortal thinking, and what has been committed to them is the stewardship of no human mysteries. The Almighty Himself, the Creator of the universe, the God whom no eye can discern, has sent down His very own Truth from heaven,

---

9. Claerhout and De Roover, 65.
10. Claerhout and De Roover, 65.

His own holy and incomprehensible Word, to plant it among men and ground it in their hearts.[11]

Conversely, for Indic religions, the authors argue, "The idea that a certain religion is true, while others are false, is improper. In the view of these traditions, there is no one true God who has revealed His will, which should be accepted by humankind."[12] They further argue,

> Historically, the Hindu traditions have generally tried to make sense of the Christian claims about religion and truth from their traditional perspective, which cannot assign truth predicates to traditional practices. The result is the often-repeated claim that all religions are true. This does not reflect a pluralistic notion of religious truth, but an attempt to translate the attitude of one culture into the language of another. The Hindu view does not see the different traditions of humanity as either true or false. Consequently, the belief that the diversity of traditions reflects a rivalry over religious truth is confined to religions like Christianity and Islam.[13]

Consequently, the authors argue that the assumptions that guide Semitic religions and Hinduism are antithetical to each other: "One side is the logical negation of the other: (1) The Hindu traditions and Islam and Christianity are phenomena of the same kind, or they are not. (2) As such, they are religious rivals, or they are not. (3) As rivals, they compete with each other regarding truth or falsity, or they do not. They can do so because *some* religion is false, but they never could if *no* religion is false."[14] Following this prognosis, the authors conclude that these three assumptions, which shape "today's view of religious conversions," remain a "universal problem." For them, "the conclusion is inevitable: conversion becomes a vital problem of religious diversity, if and only if one looks at the world the way

11. Quoted in Balagangadhara and De Roover, "Secular State," 73.
12. Claerhout and De Roover, "Conversion of the World," 65.
13. Claerhout and De Roover, 66.
14. Claerhout and De Roover, 66.

Christianity and Islam do. In other words, the problem of religious conversion exists only within the experiential world of these religions."[15] The argument is that the application of a secular constitution precludes the possibility of equal footing for Hinduism with Christianity before the law as regards conversion. I have engaged with that argument elsewhere.[16]

In what follows, I shall look at *Śivapurāṇa*, one of the most authoritative texts, to illustrate that the religious doctrines articulated therein do possess true/false predicates, implying that the Ghent school position would have to be nuanced in the light of the Hindu scriptures.

2. Textual Level: Do Hindu Religious Texts Claim Truth Predicates for Beliefs?

To argue that the Hindu texts have truth predicates, I shall first draw from McComas Taylor's detailed analysis of *Śivapurāṇa*[17] to show that contrary to the Ghent school understanding, this Hindu text warrants the association of truth predicates with Hindu religious belief. Quite similar to the exclusive nature in which truth is conceived in Christianity, *Śivapurāṇa* also makes exclusive truth claims.

The exclusive truth claim justified by appeal to divine authority illustrated in *The Epistle to Diognetus* earlier is not unique to Christianity. Romaharsana, one of the composers of *Śivapurāṇa*, argues that it "was created by Siva himself in a thousand million verses at the time of the creation of the Universe."[18] According to him, "the text, and indeed the entire body of *purāṇic* lore, 'the nectar by the name of *purāṇa*', was produced by Śiva at the time of the first creation of

---

15. Claerhout and De Roover, 66.
16. See Aruthuckal Varughese John, "Religious Freedom: Freedom of Conversion or Freedom from Conversion?," *International Bulletin of Mission Research* 45, no. 4 (October 2019): 388–96, https://doi.org/10.1177/2396939319882160.
17. McComas Taylor, "'This Is the Truth—the Truth without Doubt': Textual Authority and the Enabling of 'True' Discourse in the Hindu Narrative Tradition of the Śivapurāṇa," *Religions of South Asia* 2, no. 1 (2008): 69.
18. Taylor, 69.

the cosmos (0.1.27, 1.2.48, 1.2.57)."[19] These verses lay a claim to authority by invoking the divine origins of *Śivapurāṇa*, where Śiva, the god himself, is its author. On the passing on of divine revelation, it follows a clear succession, where "Śiva conferred this corpus on Sanatkumāra, the son of Brahma, the four-faced creator-deity (see 7.41), who in turn imparted it to Vyāsa. Later, after Vyāsa had divided the corpus into the 18 great purāṇas (1.2.58), he narrated the *Śivapurāṇa* to Romaharsana, who subsequently related it to the sages assembled at Prayāga. This is to say, the purāṇic narrative passed from Śiva to Sanatkumāra to Vyāsa to Romaharsana to the sages."[20]

What sort of validation do the composers of religious texts employ to make them authoritative? If the religious texts narrate events pertaining to a real historical person, then such an account can be verified from historical and geographical records. Where such corroboration is not possible, the authors must rely on some other means to make the texts authoritative. Although a mythical sage, Vyāsa lends "canonicity" to the text. For Taylor, "this is one of the strategies that enable a text to function as 'true.' As Narayana Rao astutely observes, '[a]uthorship by such a superhuman person elevates the Purāṇa to an infallible status and endows them with a coherent meaning' (Narayana Rao 1993:93; 2004:97)."[21]

Taylor rightly observes, "In the absence of external sources of authorization and validation, purāṇic authors resorted to internal, textual strategies to legitimize and empower their texts, and to perpetuate their traditions."[22] In addition to elevating the authority of *Śivapurāṇa* through divine authorship, the text also advances a tenor of exclusivity and rivalry. On the question of purification from sins, it argues, "There is nothing other than the *Śivapurāṇa* for purifying the minds of those born in the age of Kali (0.1.10)."[23] Slighting other texts rhetorically, it asks, "What is the use of many Vedic texts, scriptures and perplexing purāṇas? The *Śivapurāṇa* alone resounds with the

---

19. Taylor, 70.
20. Taylor, 70.
21. Taylor, 71.
22. Taylor, 66.
23. Taylor, 74.

gift of liberation' (0.1.37). It is the nectar produced by Siva as a result of 'churning the ocean of the Upanisads' (1.2.41), and is 'derived from all doctrines' (0.1.7–8). 'Hundreds of Vedic texts, remembered texts, purāṇas, histories and sacred doctrines are not worth even as little as a sixteenth part of this Śivapurāṇa' (1.2.64)."[24] Further, Śivapurāṇa claims to be the ultimate answer to all human problems: "Until the Śivapurāṇa becomes the pre-eminent scripture, the world will labor under adharmic chaos. All the normative scriptures will contradict one another and all the other purāṇas will clamour for prominence. There will be disputes over which are the most efficacious sacred sites, mantras places of pilgrimage, gifts, gods and doctrines (1.2.11–17). All these disputes will be settled with the rise of the Śivapurāṇa and the establishment of true religion that will inevitably accompany that auspicious advent."[25]

On the efficacy to "'cleanse all sins' (0.1.40, 1.2.23) and 'destroy the sins of the Kali age' (1.2.3),"[26] the Śivapurāṇa claims exclusivity by rendering all other traditions ineffectual.[27] The propositional structure and the metaphysical presuppositions of the Śivapurāṇa, which relegate other texts to a lower status, present a starkly different picture of Hinduism from the Ghent school portrayal of an inclusive Hindu theological formulation without truth predicates.

After all, the doctrinal claims of the Hindu scriptures are intended to be taken as true. To suggest otherwise would be discourteous to a good majority of Hindus who believe the scriptural teachings as true, which is the reason why people strenuously order their lives around those religious beliefs. In short, the Ghent school argument that for "the 'pagan' traditions of the Antiquity and the Hindu Indians," "the predicates 'truth' and 'falsity' do not apply to human traditions" may be textually contested.

---

24. Taylor, 73.
25. Taylor, 74.
26. Taylor, 73.
27. Yet it may be noted that the exclusive truth claims of Śivapurāṇa or Christianity are not technically opposed to other traditions equally holding similar exclusive notions of truth.

3. Meta Level: Do Human Beliefs Possess Truth Predicates?

In addition to showing that the Hindu scriptures make truth claims similar to those of Semitic religions, in this section, I shall explore how truth predicates are integral to beliefs—religious or otherwise.

3.1. On Belief as Assent

It may be argued that irrespective of culture, all our beliefs follow a structure, where "it is simply impossible to believe . . . two things which you *know* are inconsistent with each other. It seems we are obliged to believe only what we *think* is consistent."[28] Someone—say, S—holding belief P need not entail a conscious assent that is propositionally articulated that "*P* is true"; it only entails that S acts as if P is true. Unlike knowledge, which is objectively examined for truth, belief can only be subjectively assessed. Yet every belief, even where no explicit truth claim is made, has an internal structure that assumes it as true. Accordingly, one finds it impossible to hold a belief that is known to be false. For instance, where S knows that earth is spherical, it is impossible for S to believe that the earth is flat even if S were offered a tempting bribe.

According to the disquotational principle, asserting a statement inevitably carries with it the imprint that the statement is true. Every belief that is articulated, whether in religious texts or rituals, is a manifestation of a belief, which involves the assent that the belief is true even though the nature of that assent may vary on the level of certitude. On one end, one may believe, hoping that her belief is true, and on the other end, one may believe with absolute certitude. Yet in both cases, a belief is truth predicated.

Those who find the traditional disquotational principle overbearingly propositional may consider a modified version of the same.[29] Even though believing could be distinguished from assent-

---

28. Wilfrid Hodges, *Logic* (New York: Penguin, 1977), 15.
29. As Ruth Barcan Marcus argues, "If a normal speaker of a language L assents to '*p*' and '*p*' is a sentence of L and '*p*' describes a possible state or states of affairs, i.e., *p* is possible, then that speaker believes that *p*." Ruth Barcan Marcus, "Rationality and Believing the Impossible," *Journal of Philosophy* 80, no. 6

ing, one may surmise that since a belief is translatable into language, it amounts to a form of assent for all language users.[30] According to Donald Davidson, "Someone cannot have a belief unless he understands the possibility of being mistaken, and this requires grasping the contrast between truth and error—true belief and false belief." He further remarks, "The notion of a true belief depends on the notion of a true utterance, and this in turn there cannot be without a shared language."[31]

As Ruth Barcan Marcus argues, "It is likely that, for language users, there is an essential connection between the notions of truth and falsity as applied to utterances and being in the believing relation to actual and nonfactual states of affairs—language users do have such notions as true and false taken as properties of linguistic entities."[32] Where speech acts belong to "sincere, reflective, non-conceptually-confused language users . . . there is an essential connection between the assents of such agents and believing."[33] Indic religionists, similar to their Semitic counterparts, have articulated responses such as certitude, doubt, trust, fallibility, and the like with respect to their religious beliefs. Rational and logico-semantic articulations are eminently manifest within the robust Hindu philosophical schools. We may thus surmise that a belief, religious or otherwise, articulated in a language possesses truth predicates.

(June 1983): 330. While this excludes the overt claim that one's assent to p is also a claim to p being the actual state of affairs or being true, it nevertheless makes the claim that p is possible and that they believe that p.

30. Those who make a distinction between belief and assent appeal to the fact that certain animals seem to have beliefs that produce certain behaviors, removing language as a necessary condition for beliefs. Yet where language users hold beliefs, there seems to be an undeniable connection between assent and belief.

31. Donald Davidson, "Thought and Talk," in Mind and Language, ed. Samuel Guttenplan (New York: Oxford, 1975), 22–23.

32. Marcus, "Rationality and Believing," 333.

33. Marcus, 333.

3.2. *Pramāṇas* to Discriminate Truth from Falsehood

That a religion makes a truth claim is different from the question of it being true. However, it is possible to establish the legitimate "conditions in which we might properly take some proposal as a candidate for being true."[34] The field of religious epistemology has existed alongside the formulation of beliefs and religious texts.[35] In the Hindu context, the task of *pramāṇas* has been to formulate the conditions under which beliefs may be considered warranted. All the major Indian philosophical schools, both orthodox and heterodox, have a strong emphasis on *pramāṇas* that defines valid and reliable sources/means of knowledge. If the task of *pramāṇas* is to distinguish between beliefs that are warranted and unwarranted, then we may legitimately presuppose that there are beliefs that are warranted and those that are not.

The *pramāṇas* provide the means of reliable knowledge by presupposing a standard by which beliefs may be validated on the basis of accuracy, reliability, or utility; likewise, they may be invalidated because they are inaccurate, unreliable, or impractical. By extension, disagreements about truth claims pertaining to doctrinal beliefs are possible, and truth predicates are essential components of such disagreements.[36] Let us suppose that someone, S, holds the belief that the Vedas are authoritative, and S also holds that she is warranted by the *pramāṇas* to hold such a belief. If another person, B, believes that the Vedas are not authoritative irrespective of the *pramāṇas* or because of a different interpretation of the *pramāṇas*, then we have

---

34. Patrick John Mahaffey, "Religious Pluralism and the Question of Truth: An Inquiry in the Philosophy of Religious Worldviews" (PhD diss., University of California, 1988), 254. Mahaffey uses W. A. Christian's proposal that "suggests four conditions. The proposal must (1) be capable of self-consistent formulation, (2) be liable to significant disagreement, (3) permit a reference to its logical subject, and (4) permit some support for the assignment of its predicate to its subject." W. A. Christian, "Truth-Claims in Religion," Journal of Religion 42, no. 1 (1962): 52–62.

35. See Keith E. Yandell, *The Epistemology of Religious Experience* (Cambridge: Cambridge University Press, 1993).

36. Mahaffey argues, "The important point about religious disagreements is this: if genuine disagreements are not possible, then significant truth claims are not possible." Mahaffey, "Religious Pluralism," 253.

a case of genuine disagreement about the doctrinal belief concerning the authority of the Vedas. While one may not be able to settle the question about the authority of the Vedas in this manner, it can be argued that both *S* and *B* have applied truth predicates to their respective beliefs.

A proper disagreement is possible only if both parties recognize the category in question. So if two religions are conceptually different, then it is hard to "bring out significant disagreements between religions which have little or no obvious point of contact between their doctrines. . . . An example would be Theravada Buddhism and Islam. If Nirvana and Allah are taken to be central concepts, it is unpromising to look for a common reference in these concepts and thus to formulate a doctrinal disagreement."[37] Conversely, insofar as basic doctrinal disagreements are possible between different Hindu philosophical schools and between different Indic religions, truth predicates can legitimately be assumed to be part of Hindu religious beliefs.

Śaunaka Ṛṣi Dāsa makes a perceptive observation about how Swami Vivekananda categorizes beliefs that are contrary to the neo-Vedantic position as lower in the epistemic and spiritual hierarchy.[38] Vivekananda argues, "The same God whom the ignorant man saw outside nature [those who follow *Dvaita*], the same whom the little-knowing man [those who follow *Viśiṣṭādvaita*] saw as interpenetrating the universe, and the same whom the sage realizes as his own Self [those who follow *advaita*], as the whole universe itself—all are One and the same Being, the same entity seen from different standpoints, seen through different glasses of Maya, perceived by different minds, and all the difference was caused by that."[39] While each of the three schools of thought represents unique epistemic positions that

---

37. Mahaffey, 253.
38. Śaunaka Ṛṣi Dāsa [formerly, Timothy Kiernan], "Conversion in Hindu Culture: A Talk by Shaunaka Rishi Das of the Oxford Centre for Hindu Studies," Oxford Center for Hindu Studies, April 6, 2016, https://www.youtube.com/watch?v=qUq3CF4Pdb4.
39. Swami Vivekananda, *The Complete Works of Swami Vivekananda*, vol. 3, *San Francisco 1900* (Champawat, India: Advaita Ashrama, 2016), https://www.ramakrishnavivekananda.info/vivekananda/volume_3/lectures_from_colombo_to_almora/the_vedanta.htm.

people can choose from, identifying opposing positions as either "ignorant" or "little-knowing" presupposes a standard by which they may be distinguished thus as well as truth predication on the basis of which the opposing views are relegated to a lower status as they miss the truth about reality. Truth predicates are as essential to the Hindu traditions as they are for Semitic traditions, various Hindu philosophical schools within the orthodox tradition or the birth of Buddhism predicated on the explicit denial of authority to the Vedas (indicating a rival doctrinal formulation against Puranic/Vedic Hinduism) notwithstanding.

4. Practical Level: Truth, Historicity, and Religious Beliefs

Through both textual and philosophical analysis, we have explored how truth predicates are essential parts of religious beliefs. However, the point of departure between the two sets of religions seems to exist at a practical level, where truth predicates seem differently relevant. I shall explore two factors as possible reasons for this.

4.1. Eclectic Pragmatism of the Polytheistic Frame
In a quasi-tautologous sense, we may state that the nature of truth predication of Hindu religious beliefs corresponds to its polytheistic frame. This means not that the Indic religionists do not desire truth predicates in religious beliefs but rather that the multiple parallel traditions with alternate doctrines make it impossible to create a single creed that may be referred to as *the Hindu* religious doctrine. It is sometimes assumed that Indic religions are noncreedal. However, belief in god(s) involves belief about their nature and character, which in a polytheistic context entails a multiplicity of creeds arranged contiguously with some overlap.[40]

Given the parallel arrangement of gods and goddesses and their corresponding creeds, eclecticism becomes part and parcel of the

---

40. While Carvaka and the other heterodox schools do not believe in the existence of a god, beliefs about the world and reality are nevertheless posited doctrinally.

Hindu culture. Any treatment that spotlights a single doctrine that ignores the multiplicity and the contiguous arrangement of beliefs becomes problematic. Likewise, any critique of a single creedal belief is like bursting a single bubble in a cluster—the cluster merely rearranges by mutual shifting. Such doctrinal rearrangement has been observed several times. Influenced by Christian missionaries, Hindu reformers like Raja Ram Mohan Roy appropriated the critique of idol worship, sati, and child marriage and incorporated these changes within his neo-Hindu reformed movement of Brahmo Samaj. Such doctrinal flexibility has been described as "the religion's greatest strength. Hinduism has survived for millennia precisely because it proved eclectic, agglomerative, all-embracing."[41]

Yet even in the polytheistic context, a well-known Rig Vedic text asks a pertinent question: "Kasmai devāya havisa vidhema?" (Which god shall we worship with offerings?; 10.121).[42] Its semblance to Joshua's question to Israel, also beset by polytheism, is obvious: "Choose for yourselves this day whom you will serve, whether the gods your ancestors served beyond the Euphrates, or the gods of the Amorites, in whose land you are living. But as for me and my household, we will serve the Lord" (Josh 24:15 NIV). To a wayward Hebrew, Joshua's question was not as much a suggestion to look around and choose whatever he liked; it was a reminder to turn back to Yahweh. Thus, they answered, "Far be it from us to forsake the Lord to serve other gods" (Josh 24:16 NIV).

Why, then, did not the Rig Vedic question similarly lead to monotheism? Karve argues that the Rig Vedic prayer "was merely of a rhetorical nature. It was answered on behalf of certain gods by their priests. Each priesthood claimed its god to be not only the highest, but the only true god."[43] Since each god/goddess could be called upon to address a specific context, the Rig Vedic question "Which is

---

41. Shashi Tharoor, "Nature of the Faith," Shashitharoor.in, July 8, 2007, https://shashitharoor.in/writings_my_essays_details/219.

42. Quoted in Irawati Karve, *Hindu Society: An Interpretation* (Poona, India: Deccan College, 1961), 79.

43. Karve, 80.

the most beneficial god for us to worship?" still had practical utility. After all, as gods cater to different vocations, a fisherman would be inclined to answer the question very differently from a businessperson or an educator. This pragmatic reality legitimized the presence of a rain god, a sun god, a god of knowledge, a god of financial profit, and many more.

Although each priest would desire that the god and the temple in question attained universal acceptance, no momentum toward universal acceptance is possible when their truth claims were comparable to other available alternatives. The persistence of a polytheistic framework was a consequence of the comparable nature of doctrines, where no single god presented so unique a prospect that stood out to draw universal acceptance.

4.2. Historicity of Religious Beliefs and Truth Predication

Religious faith and truth claims complement and mutually shape each other. If doctrines that are fundamental to a religious belief are held as true, the trueness of the doctrine imposes itself upon a believer and the culture. Such faiths cannot help but be evangelistic. Christian mission is not only a response in obedience to "being sent" into the world; it is also framed by the belief that the gospel is "good news" for everybody.

That is the reason why deceit, coercion, and allurement as methods of religious expansionism, if and where they happen, are a betrayal of Christianity. Persuasion, rather than coercion, has been the characteristic of a better part of Christianity, given that the Evangelists who witnessed the resurrection and other miracles were compelled to believe in Jesus as the Messiah. Luke "followed all things closely for some time past" and set out to "write an orderly account . . . that you may have certainty concerning the things you have been taught" (Luke 1:3–4), and Paul argued that they avoided underhanded means of communicating the gospel (2 Cor 2:17). Yet a willful obliteration of the distinction between persuasion and coercion seems to be a problem that is widespread in contemporary times. As Jean Bethke Elshtain argues, "Somewhere along the line—certainly in the last thirty years or so—a view of power took hold that disdains distinctions between coercion, manipulation, and persuasion."[44]

A reason why apologetic defense became an essential part of Christian religious belief is that it is vigorously contested. Whether it was the sociopolitical accusations against the early Christians or the onslaught of the modern Enlightenment milieu, the challenge to the Christian faith constantly required believers to "be prepared to make a defense to any one who calls [them] to account for the hope that is in [them]" (1 Pet 3:15 RSV). As Marshall writes, "In the modern world the church's claim that its chief doctrines are true has been challenged more vigorously than at any time since the first centuries of Christianity. This challenge has focused to a considerable degree on the right of the Christian community to hold beliefs which seem not to meet the epistemic standards of modernity—broadly speaking, of those views about what we have the right to believe which stem from the Enlightenment. . . . Great intellectual ingenuity has gone into this effort, as we will see. But it has persistently tended to yield unsatisfying results."[45] A more fundamental distinction in truth claims between Hinduism and Christianity lies in the historical nature of Christian religious beliefs over against the ahistorical/mythical nature of Hindu beliefs.[46] The historical revelation of Jesus entails that Christian religious beliefs are also historical beliefs, which come with their own set of characteristics. The historical nature of Christian religious beliefs makes historical rigor an essential epistemic feature of Christian faith, where the warrant for historical truth claims requires the whetting of religious beliefs via historical corroboration.

Conversely, the mythological nature of Hindu religious beliefs entails an absence of historical verification, where theological warrant

---

44. Jean Bethke Elshtain, "Toleration, Proselytizing, and the Politics of Recognition," in *Charles Taylor*, ed. Ruth Abbey (Cambridge: Cambridge University Press, 2004), 134.

45. Marshall, *Trinity and Truth*, 4.

46. For further discussion, see Varughese John, "A Sense of History and Apologetics in a Hindu Context," *Missiology: An International Review* 34, no. 2 (April 2008): 219–26.

is tracked for coherence along logical and philosophical lines. Consequently, Hindu beliefs are doctrinally flexible, whereas rigid boundaries are drawn for ritual practices. As Swami Animananda says, one might "observe the rules of Hindu society and you may believe in anything or nothing at all."[47] Beliefs are deemed sacred for their moral value rather than for their historical reliability. On the significance of mythology in the Hindu context, Jawaharlal Nehru argues,

> Indian mythology and old tradition crept into my mind and got mixed up with all manner of other creatures of imagination. I don't think I ever attached very much importance to these stories as factually true, and I even criticized the magical and supernatural element in them. But they were just as imaginatively true for me to draw so much. It influenced my mind so much and I realized how much more old mythology and tradition work on the minds of others and, especially, the unread masses of our people. That influence is a good influence both culturally and ethically, and I would hate to destroy or throw away all the beauty and imaginative symbolism that these stories and allegories contain.[48]

Understandably, where historical validation becomes part of religious belief, it introduces the risk of falsifiability.[49] In this sense, Christianity is most vulnerable to falsification: "If Christ has not been raised, then our preaching is in vain and your faith is in vain" (1 Cor 15:14 RSV). Yet risk may have its own lure for human religious experience in that it motivates one to probe whether the object of faith is real.[50]

---

47. Quoted in Hans Staffner, *The Significance of Jesus Christ in Asia* (Anand, India: Gujarat Sahitya Prakash, 1985), 99.
48. Jawaharlal Nehru, *The Discovery of India* (New Delhi: Oxford University Press, 1946), 101.
49. For further discussion on historical vulnerability and Christian faith, see Aruthuckal Varughese John, *Truth and Subjectivity, Faith and History: Kierkegaard's Insights for Christian Faith* (Eugene, OR: Pickwick, 2012).
50. As Søren Kierkegaard writes, "For without risk, no faith; the more risk, the more faith." See his [pseud. Johannes Climacus], *Concluding Unscientific*

Further, the life of Jesus Christ was characterized by indescribable pathos. The Roman mock trial and the subsequent crucifixion—the most gruesome manner of death invented by the Romans "to serve as a deterrent" to any form of uprising or revolt—are of unparalleled significance for the religious experience of a Christian believer.[51] The unexpected exponential rise of Christians in the early years, when persecution was extensive, has led scholars to underline the significance of eyewitness experience and accounts of the early disciples of the resurrected Jesus.[52] The Christian understanding of truth, in short, cannot be severed from historical events surrounding Jesus.

As Marshall writes, "By undertaking to speak in the name and on behalf of a God who is 'the truth,' this community accepts the task of saying in a reflectively explicit way what truth is, and by what right it claims to speak the truth. In this sense truth is a theological problem."[53] However, the Christian idea of truth is not limited to truth predicates of its theological doctrines. The tragic and inspiring death and resurrection of Christ entails that Christian *witness* (Greek: *martyria*) to the truth moves beyond the realm of *speech act* and into the realm of *play acting* martyrdom, as its Greek etymology suggests. Unlike Krishna's inspiring teaching that enlightens Arjuna, Christ's claim to *being the truth* is intricately tied to his *death and resurrection*. As A. G. Hogg argues, the "reason why the historical element is not still fundamental in Hindu religion is simply the absence from Indian history of a sufficiently tragic and universally inspiring figure."[54]

Since Hindu religious beliefs are not historical beliefs, they cannot be falsified and thus are protected from being disproved. Yet for the same reason, the veracity of religious beliefs will elude a

Postscript to "Philosophical Fragments," vol. 1, ed. and trans. Howard Hong and Edna Hong (Princeton, NJ: Princeton University Press, 1992), 209.

51. Tom Holland, *Dominion: The Making of the Western Mind* (London: Little, Brown, 2019), xiv.

52. See Rodney Stark, *The Rise of Christianity* (Princeton, NJ: Princeton University Press, 1996).

53. Marshall, *Trinity and Truth*, 3.

54. A. G. Hogg, *Karma and Redemption* (Madras, India: Christian Literature Society, 1909), 8.

probing believer, as they cannot be validated either, which leaves gaps in the question of reliability. We may conclude that the divergent attitudes pertaining to religious beliefs between Semitic and Indic religions seem to be rooted not in any a priori predisposition within cultures about religious beliefs but also in the historical nature of religious beliefs or the absence thereof. The Ghent school description of Asiatic religions as not being preoccupied with truth predicates may thus be understood in context.

5. Truth as a Cultural Bridge for the Gospel

Several explorations of cultural bridges have been undertaken in the attempts to contextualize the gospel. The early twentieth century witnessed the articulation of Christianity as *The Crown of Hinduism*[55] by J. N. Farquhar, and Sadhu Sundar Singh stated, "Christianity is the fulfilment of Hinduism. Hinduism has been digging channels. Christ is the water to flow through these channels."[56] Today, there is "a widespread appropriation of the fulfilment concept as a unifying phenomenon among converts"[57] from Hinduism. While the fulfillment scheme fits well with those that are proud of their traditions, especially the upper-caste converts, Dalits have often sought to break from the tradition, which they feel is responsible for their dreadful condition.[58] Dalit "discontinuity" with the Hindu tradition is often evidenced in visible outward changes, often of name and dress.[59] Yet while emphasizing discontinuity from the upper-caste

---

55. John Nicol Farquhar, *The Crown of Hinduism* (Oxford: Oxford University Press, 1913).
56. Quoted in Ivan Satyavrata, *God Has Not Left Himself without Witness* (Oxford: Regnum, 2011), 167.
57. Satyavrata, 26.
58. For further discussion on this idea, see Aruthuckal Varughese John, "Religious Conversion in India: Four Portraits of a Complex and Controversial Phenomenon," *Journal of Asian Evangelical Theology* 25, no. 1 (March 2021): 97–118.
59. I have elsewhere argued that the Dalit reaction may also be understood as a "subversive political statement in the context of caste oppression." See Aruthuckal Varughese John, "Christian Missions and Missionary Guilt," in *Theological Formation for Christian Missions*, ed. Aruthuckal Varughese John and Roji T. George (Bangalore: SAIACS, 2019), 167–88.

traditions, a Dalit may still find aspects from their tradition that are continuous with the Christian faith.[60]

While Raimon Panikkar's *The Unknown Christ of Hinduism* has some radical views, he rightly argued that one does not have to be "spiritually Semitic and intellectually Greek" to appropriate the gospel.[61] While the apostle Paul's articulations constantly establish bridges between the cultural aspirations of his hearers and the truth of Christ, a unique convergence of "desirability characterizations" are drawn from within the Hebrew, the Greek, and the Roman cultures, all of which converged in the city of Corinth.[62]

What conceptual bridges may we build between the truth discourse of Hinduism and Christ as the truth? The concept of *satyam* (truth) articulated in the Upanishad is refreshingly rich in that the scope of its meaning is not limited to a propositional rendition of truth. The term finds its etymological roots in *Sat*, connoting both an ontological and an ethical dimension. Ontologically, *Sat* means "to be" or "true essence/self," and ethically, it refers to purity as one that is not corrupt. As a central theme in both the Vedas and the Upanishads, *Sat* is a common prefix that qualifies various categories. The *Bṛhadāraṇyaka Upanishad* (1.4.xiv) states, "Even a weak man hopes (to defeat) a *stronger* man through righteousness, as (one contending)

---

60. For instance, Dalit theology has emphasized the experience of brokenness as being identified in the suffering servant songs that point to Christ as the one who takes upon himself their suffering.

61. Raimon Panikkar, *The Unknown Christ of Hinduism: Towards an Ecumenical Christophany*, rev. ed. (Bangalore: Asian Trading Corporation, 1982). For "spiritually Semitic and intellectually Greek," see "The Unknown Christ of Hinduism," Raimon Panikkar, accessed April 26, 2022, https://www.raimon-panikkar.org/english/X-2-Il-Cristo.html.

62. Following Elizabeth Anscombe, Taylor describes "desirability characterizations" as follows: "I come to understand someone when I understand his emotions, his aspirations, what he finds admirable and contemptible in himself and others, what he yearns for, what he loathes, and so on. Being able to formulate this understanding is being able to apply correctly the desirability characterizations which he applies in the way he applies them." Charles Taylor, *Philosophy and the Human Sciences: Philosophical Papers 2* (Cambridge: Cambridge University Press, 1985), 119. See also 2 Cor 4:6: "For it is the God who said, 'Let light shine out of darkness,' who has shone in our hearts to give the light of the knowledge of the glory of God in the face of Christ."

with the king. That righteousness is verily truth. Therefore they say about a person speaking of truth, 'He speaks of righteousness,' or about a person speaking of righteousness, 'He speaks of truth,' for both these are but righteousness."[63] The context for this text is the action of the *Kṣhatriya*. Yet the unity of *righteousness* and *truth*, envisaged both ontologically and ethically, provides substantial legitimacy to view Christ as personifying this Upanishadic representation of truth.

A better known Upanishadic prayer states, "Asato mā sad gamaya; tamaso mā jyotir gamaya; mṛtyor mā amṛtam gamaya" (Lead me from delusion to truth; lead me from darkness to light; lead me from mortality to eternal life; *Bṛhadāraṇyaka Upanishad* [1.3.28]). One cannot help but wonder if this *sloka* was spoken precisely of the person of Jesus Christ.[64] Three passages from the Gospel of John locate truth (14:6), light (8:12), and eternal life (11:25) self-referentially in the person of Jesus Christ.

Whether one takes the approach that identifies Jesus Christ as the fulfillment of the spiritual aspiration within the Upanishadic text or merely uses the text as a bridge, identifying continuity between spiritual aspirations within a culture and the truth of Christ brings in an element of authenticity, enabling a gospel appropriation that has deep cultural roots. By focusing on the historical figure of Christ as the one in whom specific spiritual aspirations are fulfilled, we bring together the rich Hindu traditions to meet the person of Christ. Yet these continuities are undertaken not as a pan-Indian phenomenon, although that may be possible, but as identifying bridges to Christ from within specific Hindu traditions.

Building bridges between truth descriptions in the Upanishad and the person of Jesus not only satisfies certain spiritual aspirations but also sanctifies what is "desirable" within the culture. In this

---

63. *Bṛhadāraṇyaka Upanishad* 1.4.4. See Swāmī Mādhavānanda, trans., *Brihadaranyaka Upanishad: The Bṛhadāraṇyaka Upaniṣad (with the Commentary of Śaṅkarācārya)* (Khat Khutam, India: Advaita Ashrama, 2018), https://www.wisdomlib.org/hinduism/book/the-brihadaranyaka-upanishad/d/doc117939.html.

64. A *sloka* is a Sanskrit verse, usually in a couplet form.

sense, the cultural appropriation of the gospel is a two-way process that not only establishes continuities between Christ and culture for identification but also brings the culture under Christ's influence for sanctification.

6. The Problem of Conversion and the *Krista Bhakta* Identity

Conversion has increasingly become a contentious issue in India. One of the main reasons has been the perceived break with the family and culture that conversion entails. Thus, Gandhi observed, "If I had the power and could legislate, I should certainly stop all proselytizing. . . . In Hindu households the advent of a missionary has meant the disruption of the family coming in the wake of change of dress, manners, language, food and drink."[65] Although Gandhi's comment can be legitimately critiqued, often the changes in "dress, manners, language, [and] food" are nonessentials to the question of conversion, which is fundamentally a change of heart toward greater spiritual devotion.

To address this concern, one may take a cue from Balagangadhara's view of Hinduism as a culture rather than a religion. Balagangadhara argues that the idea of "religion" is a uniquely European Christian construct invented as "an explanatorily intelligible account of the Cosmos and itself."[66] This entails that "Hinduism as a religion" is also a European depiction. If "religion has brought forth one configuration of learning; other things have brought forth other configurations of learning as well."[67] He further asserts that in the Asian context, the "ritual, just like religion, brings about a culturally specific way of going-about in the world. In a configuration of learning generated by it, performative learning dominates."[68]

---

65. M. K. Gandhi, "Interview to a Missionary Nurse," in *Collected Works*, vol. 67 (New Delhi: Publications Division e-Book, 1935).
66. S. N. Balagangadhara, *"The Heathen in His Blindness . . ." Asia, the West & the Dynamic of Religion*, Studies in the History of Religions 64 (Leiden: Brill, 1994), 354.
67. Balagangadhara, 446.
68. Balagangadhara, 415.

Contestable as they are, these concepts establish a legitimate way of exploring the possibility of a Hindu-Christian identity. Kali Charan Banerjee articulates this view in the very first issue of the *Bengal Christian Herald*: "In having become Christians, we have not ceased to be Hindus. We are Hindu-Christians, as thoroughly Hindu as Christian. We have embraced Christianity, but we have not discarded our nationality. We are intensely national as any of our brethren of the native press can be."[69] Today, the term *Hindu-Christian* (signifying accent on the *religio*) is more aptly described as the *Hindu Krista Bhakta* (signifying accent on the *traditio*), where one retains the Hindu culture and tradition as a follower of Christ. On the one hand, this entails challenges of problematic traditions such as the caste system that has confronted the life of the church; on the other, it initiates a way for the gospel to refine the culture.

Unlike the Ghent school's portrayal of Christianity as one that views Hinduism as a "rival," the growing *Krista Bhakta* movement in India practices the act of following Christ as a Hindu. Consequently, the movement envisages a socioreligious identity where being a *Hindu* and being a *Christ follower* are coterminous and converging movements rather than rivals. Raghav Krishna provides helpful pointers where cultural continuity may be observed in diet, worship, baptism, communion, and other rituals.[70] Although such redefinitions of local cultural traditions to fit the teachings of Christ involve the risk of syncretism, not engaging the local culture in this way entails a greater danger of abandoning one's culture and adopting alien cultural baggage as necessary features of following Christ.

A local, culturally appropriate term for *Messiah* that is conceptually close in meaning would have to be adopted. By paying attention to the *sense and reference* of a term and its meaning within a cultural context, one may navigate the complex phenomenon of cultural appropriation by adopting cultural concepts where they converge and by redefining the sense to converge with the intended reference where

69. Cited in Kaj Baagø, "The First Independence Movement among Indian Christians," *Indian Church History Review* 1, no. 1 (1967): 67.

70. Raghav Krishna, "From 'Krishna Bhakti' to 'Christianity' to 'Krista Bhakti,'" *International Journal of Frontier Missiology* 24, no. 4 (2007): 173–77.

they vary.[71] For instance, a preexisting local term, say, *Muktinath* (God who saves/liberates), or its equivalent becomes readily accessible. However, *Muktinath* as the referent may be presumed to be loaded with meaning—for example, in the Vaishnava tradition. Yet it is also true that *Muktinath* does not have a singular meaning and can generically and etymologically mean "God who saves." Further, what *God who saves* can mean may still need to be redefined to articulate the nature of Christ's work that brings about salvation in those who believe in him. Any contextual appropriation requires the use of existing terminologies with clearly defined meanings clarified through the constant articulation of the character of Jesus Christ. A *Krista Bhakta*, Krishna argues, "identifies himself/herself as part of the Hindu community, all festivals are celebrated with the community.... This is not to say that this celebration is without boundaries, however. A *Krista Bhakta* will not go against his or her convictions concerning God in matters involving things like bowing to deities, etc., and sometimes may pass on being included in certain festival activities. This is acceptable in Hindu tradition, however, as followers of certain Hindu gods refuse to bow before idols of other gods."[72] The suspicion and the problematizing of *Krista Bhakta* identity within traditional Indian Christianity often betrays the nonrecognition of complexities in human identity formation, which inevitably combines sociocultural features with the act of following Christ.

7. Epilogue

An examination of the Hindu religious texts and the nature of human beliefs illustrates that truth predicates are integral parts of religious beliefs. The Ghent school's argument, "the Hindu view does not see the different traditions of humanity as either true or false. Consequently, the belief that the diversity of traditions reflects a rivalry over religious truth is confined to religions like Christianity

---

71. This distinction was originally articulated by the German philosopher Gottlob Frege in 1892 in his paper "On Sense and Reference [Über sinn und bedeutung]," *Zeitschrift für philosophie und philosophische kritik* 100 (1892): 25–50.
72. Krishna, "From 'Krishna Bhakti,'" 176.

and Islam,"[73] seems to be grossly mistaken. In presuming to identify "the Hindu view," it tends to present Hinduism as a singular religious phenomenon. Rather, a more appropriate way to conceive of Hinduism is to view it as a composite, integrated by geographic proximity and cultural overlap of multiple traditions that were often at odds with one another, both doctrinally and in ritual practice. Conversion to and from various Hindu schools of thought, insofar as it involved changes in belief and rivalry, is evident, just as there is some continuity among them.

The cultural continuity with the Hindu traditions that the *Krista Bhakta* movement endorses does not view Hinduism as a rival. Rather, it envisages a continuity by recognizing the fulfillment of certain Hindu aspirations in the person of Jesus Christ. Further, if there are no specific creedal beliefs that essentially make one a Hindu, then one's devotion to Christ should not exclude a Christ devotee for that reason from being *Hindu Krista Bhakta*. This message is pivotal in the context of alienating rhetoric within the society that seeks to vilify religious conversions as a form of betrayal.

Bibliography

Baagø, Kaj. "The First Independence Movement among Indian Christians." *Indian Church History Review* 1, no. 1 (1967): 67.

Balagangadhara, S. N. *"The Heathen in His Blindness..." Asia, the West & the Dynamic of Religion*. Studies in the History of Religions 64. Leiden: Brill, 1994.

Balagangadhara, S. N., and Jakob De Roover. "The Secular State and Religious Conflict: Liberal Neutrality and the Indian Case of Pluralism." *Journal of Political Philosophy* 15, no. 1 (2007): 67–92.

Christian, W. A. "Truth-Claims in Religion." *Journal of Religion* 42, no. 1 (1962): 52–62.

Claerhout, Sarah, and Jakob De Roover. "Conversion of the World: Proselytization in India and the Universalization of Christianity." In

---

73. Claerhout and De Roover, "Conversion of the World," 66.

Proselytization Revisited: Rights Talk, Free Markets and Culture Wars, edited by Rosalind I. J. Hackett, 53–76. London: Equinox, 2008.

Davidson, Donald. "Thought and Talk." In *Mind and Language*, edited by Samuel Guttenplan, 7–23. New York: Oxford, 1975.

Elshtain, Jean Bethke. "Toleration, Proselytizing, and the Politics of Recognition." In *Charles Taylor*, edited by Ruth Abbey, 127–139. Cambridge: Cambridge University Press, 2004.

Farquhar, John Nicol. *The Crown of Hinduism*. Oxford: Oxford University Press, 1913.

Flood, Gavin. "*Dharma*." In *India's Religions, Perspectives from Sociology and History*, edited by T. N. Madan, 231–232. Delhi: Oxford University Press, 2004.

Frege, Gottlob. "On Sense and Reference [Über sinn und bedeutung]." *Zeitschrift für philosophie und philosophische kritik* 100 (1892): 25–50.

Gandhi, M. K. "Interview to a Missionary Nurse." In *Collected Works*, vol. 67. New Delhi: Publications Division e-Book, 1935.

Hodges, Wilfrid. *Logic*. New York: Penguin, 1977.

Hogg, A. G. *Karma and Redemption*. Madras, India: Christian Literature Society, 1909.

Holland, Tom. *Dominion: The Making of the Western Mind*. London: Little, Brown, 2019.

Karve, Irawati. *Hindu Society: An Interpretation*. Poona, India: Deccan College, 1961.

Kierkegaard, Søren [pseud. Johannes Climacus]. *Concluding Unscientific Postscript to "Philosophical Fragments."* Vol. 1. Edited and translated by Howard Hong and Edna Hong. Princeton, NJ: Princeton University Press, 1992.

Krishna, Raghav. "From 'Krishna Bhakti' to 'Christianity' to 'Krista Bhakti.'" *International Journal of Frontier Missiology* 24, no. 4 (2007): 173–177.

Lipner, Julius. "The Truth of Dharma and the Dharma of Truth: Reflections on Hinduism as a Dharmic Faith." *International Journal of Hindu Studies* 23, no. 3 (2019): 213–237.

Mādhavānanda, Swāmī, trans. *Brihadaranyaka Upanishad: The Bṛhadāraṇyaka Upaniṣad (with the Commentary of Śaṅkarācārya)*. Khat Khutam, India: Advaita Ashrama, 2018. https://www.wisdomlib.org/hinduism/book/the-brihadaranyaka-upanishad/d/doc117939.html.

Mahaffey, Patrick John. "Religious Pluralism and the Question of Truth: An Inquiry in the Philosophy of Religious Worldviews." PhD diss., University of California, 1988.

Marcus, Ruth Barcan. "Rationality and Believing the Impossible." *Journal of Philosophy* 80, no. 6 (June 1983): 321–338.

Marshall, Bruce D. *Trinity and Truth*. Cambridge: Cambridge University Press, 1999.

Nehru, Jawaharlal. *The Discovery of India*. New Delhi: Oxford University Press, 1946.

Panikkar, Raimon. *The Unknown Christ of Hinduism: Towards an Ecumenical Christophany*. Rev. ed. Bangalore: Asian Trading Corporation, 1982.

Satyavrata, Ivan. *God Has Not Left Himself without Witness*. Oxford: Regnum, 2011.

Śaunaka Ṛṣi Dāsa. "Conversion in Hindu Culture: A Talk by Shaunaka Rishi Das of the Oxford Centre for Hindu Studies." Oxford Center for Hindu Studies, April 6, 2016. https://www.youtube.com/watch?v=qUq3CF4Pdb4.

Staffner, Hans. *The Significance of Jesus Christ in Asia*. Anand, India: Gujarat Sahitya Prakash, 1985.

Stark, Rodney. *The Rise of Christianity*. Princeton, NJ: Princeton University Press, 1996.

Taylor, Charles. *Philosophy and the Human Sciences: Philosophical Papers 2*. Cambridge: Cambridge University Press, 1985.

Taylor, McComas. "'This Is the Truth—the Truth without Doubt': Textual Authority and the Enabling of 'True' Discourse in the Hindu Narrative Tradition of the Śivapurāṇa." *Religions of South Asia* 2, no. 1 (2008): 65–82.

Tharoor, Shashi. "Nature of the Faith." Shashitharoor.in, July 8, 2007. https://shashitharoor.in/writings_my_essays_details/219.

Varughese John, Aruthuckal. "Christian Missions and Missionary Guilt." In *Theological Formation for Christian Missions*, edited by Aruthuckal Varughese John and Roji T. George, 167–188. Bangalore: SAIACS, 2019.

———. "Religious Conversion in India: Four Portraits of a Complex and Controversial Phenomenon." *Journal of Asian Evangelical Theology* 25, no. 1 (March 2021): 97–118.

―――. "Religious Freedom: Freedom of Conversion or Freedom from Conversion?" *International Bulletin of Mission Research* 45, no. 4 (October 2019): 388–396. https://doi.org/10.1177/2396939319882160.

―――. "A Sense of History and Apologetics in a Hindu Context." *Missiology: An International Review* 34, no. 2 (April 2008): 219–226.

―――. *Truth and Subjectivity, Faith and History: Kierkegaard's Insights for Christian Faith*. Eugene, OR: Pickwick, 2012.

Vivekananda, Swami. *The Complete Works of Swami Vivekananda*. Vol. 3, *San Francisco 1900*. Champawat, India: Advaita Ashrama, 2016. https://www.ramakrishnavivekananda.info/vivekananda/volume_3/volume_3_contents.htm.

Yandell, Keith E. *The Epistemology of Religious Experience*. Cambridge: Cambridge University Press, 1993.

8

One Gospel, Many Cultures

Continuity, Change, and Christianity in India

PRABHU SINGH VEDHAMANICKAM

> Before the bread of life (the Christian faith) came to our part
> of Africa, it stayed in Europe for over a thousand years. There
> the Europeans added a plastic bag (their own customs) to the
> bread. And when they came to southern Africa, they fed us
> the bag along with the bread. Now, the plastic bag is making
> us sick! The plastic is theirs. We know that God planned for us
> to receive the bread just as he planned for them to receive it.
> We can remove the plastic and enjoy the bread.
>
> —Makhathini

I. An "Experiment with Truth"

In his personal memoir, *An Autobiography: The Story of My Experiments with Truth* (1956), Mahatma Gandhi claims that he showed tolerance for all other faiths from a very early age but "developed a sort of dislike" for Christianity.[1] He shares the reasons for his dislike by recounting his childhood experience:

> In those days Christian missionaries used to stand in a corner near
> the high school and hold forth, pouring abuse on Hindus and their

---

1. Mahatma Gandhi, *An Autobiography: The Story of My Experiments with Truth* (Ahmedabad, India: Navajivan, 1956), 33.

gods. I could not endure this. I must have stood there to hear them once only, but that was enough to dissuade me from repeating the experiment. About the same time, I heard of a well-known Hindu having been converted to Christianity. It was the talk of the town that, when he was baptized, he had to eat beef and drink liquor, that he also had to change his clothes, and hence forth he began to go about in European costume including a hat. *These things got on my nerves. Surely, thought I, a religion that compelled one to eat beef, drink liquor and change one's own clothes did not deserve the name. I also heard that the new convert had already begun abusing the religion of his ancestors, their customs and their country. All these things created in me a dislike for Christianity.*[2]

Gandhi was very critical of Christianity and Christian missions even though he openly declared his admiration for Christ and his teachings, particularly the Sermon on the Mount.[3] His critiques of Christianity need to be located in the sociohistorical context of the colonial era, and several of them are valid and must be acknowledged, accepted, and addressed.[4]

Yet his allegation of the new convert "abusing the religion of his ancestors, their customs and their country" is perilous, particularly in the present milieu. Hence, it is imperative to explore further to authenticate the veracity of this incident, as many continue to use this Gandhian claim to portray Christians as "antinational" and Christianity as an alien faith inclined to destroy local cultures.

---

2. Gandhi, 33–34 (emphasis added).

3. Although Gandhi openly declared his admiration for Jesus Christ as a great teacher and the Sermon on the Mount as his inspiration for nonviolent action, one could argue that he never fully grasped the Christian faith. As E. Stanley Jones, Gandhi's friend, commented, "The Mahatma was influenced and molded by Christian principles, particularly the Sermon on the Mount. But he never seemed to get to Christ as a person." E. Stanley Jones, *Mahatma Gandhi: An Interpretation* (New York: Abingdon-Cokesbury, 1948), 60.

4. Striving for freedom during the colonial era, when the colonizers' official religion was Christianity, as well as the active presence of hundreds of missionaries from different parts of the world and the emergence of mass movements among the marginalized communities with their social, religious, and political implications all undergird the Gandhian critique of Christianity.

Robin Boyd, in his work *A Church History of Gujarat*, sheds some light on this Gandhian claim. He pointedly asks, "The question arises, was Gandhiji referring to actual events or was he being led astray by false propaganda, of the kind which has always been used against the Christian faith, and is still used today?"[5]

H. R. Scott, an erudite scholar of Gujarati and also the only missionary in Rajkot during the period Gandhi referred to, questioned Gandhi regarding the accuracy of his account. Scott wrote, "I was the only missionary in Rajkot during those years (from 1883 to 1897), and what you say about Christian missionaries in Rajkot standing at a corner near the High School and pouring abuse on Hindus and their gods fills me with a painful wonder. I certainly never preached 'at a corner near the High School,' my regular preaching station was under a banyan tree in the Para Bazar; and I certainly never 'poured abuse on Hindus and their gods.' That would be a strange way to win a hearing from Hindus."[6]

Referring to the enforced consumption of beef and drinking of alcohol, Scott wrote, "Well, I have been over 42 years in India, and I have never heard of such a thing happening, and indeed I know it to be quite contrary to what all missionaries with whom I am acquainted teach and believe and practice."[7] Gandhi replied to Scott and "accepted Scott's repudiation," and he also added, "About beef-eating and wine-drinking at baptism, I have merely stated what I heard."[8]

Gandhi was candid enough to admit that it was only hearsay. But by failing to edit the passage in the subsequent publishing of his autobiography or even including a footnote highlighting Scott's repudiation of his version, Gandhi contributed to the perpetuation of the negative stereotyping of Christianity as he "lent authority to what in fact was only a commonly-circulated but unsubstantiated rumor."[9] Was it really an oversight on Gandhi's part, or was it an "experiment with truth," as the title of his autobiography suggests?

5. Robin H. S. Boyd, *A Church History of Gujarat* (Madras, India: Christian Literature Society, 1981), 133.
6. Boyd, 134.
7. Boyd, 134.
8. Boyd, 134.
9. Boyd, 134.

The Gandhian conflation of these three themes—religion, customs, and country—have also been consistently employed by contemporary Hindu nationalists, who tend to malign Christians as a community involved in destroying local religion, desecrating Indic culture(s), and destabilizing the nation.[10]

As this negative narrative has been deeply embedded and successfully deployed against the Christian community, it is imperative to engage in the arduous twin tasks of contesting spurious claims as well as challenging the Christian community to be culturally sensitive and discard any dubious methods.

This incident also raises some vital, valid questions regarding gospel and culture. Are cultures dynamic or static? Does the Christian gospel engender culture change and thereby endanger local cultures? How do the gospel and culture interact and what are the missional implications?

While a detailed answer to these questions is beyond the limited scope of this chapter, I shall briefly highlight some of the important ideas regarding gospel, culture change, and culturally relevant missional engagement in the Indian context.[11]

2. The Cultural Embeddedness of Humans

The term *culture* is probably one of the most used, misused, and abused words in the English lexicon. Some of the confusion and controversy that surround this term emanate from the diverse ways in

---

10. Hindu nationalism is an exclusivist ideology that seeks to essentialize and homogenize India as a Hindu *rashtra* (nation) by reconfiguring Indianness on the basis of religion. For more details, see Christophe Jaffrelot, *The Hindu Nationalist Movement in India* (New York: Columbia University Press, 1996). This strange convergence between Gandhi and the Hindu nationalists has been highlighted by scholars like Gauri Viswanathan, "Literacy in the Eye of India's Conversion Storm," in *Conversion: Old Worlds and New*, ed. Kenneth Mills and Anthony Grafton (Rochester, NY: University of Rochester Press, 2003), 273.

11. This chapter is a product of my academic education, teaching profession, and field training of cross-cultural witnesses as well as an amplification of my published article, "Living Water in Indian Cups: A Call for Cultural Relevance in Contemporary Missions," *Asbury Journal* 66, no. 2 (2011): 57–66.

which it has been defined and employed in both the popular and academic realms.[12] The complexity is multiplied manifold due to the current iteration of globalization, migration, information technology, and easy access to media as well as the increased proximity and intermingling of various cultural groups.[13]

In this chapter, I seek to present culture from a nonreductionist, holistic, systemic perspective, primarily from the field of cultural anthropology.[14] Culture is the way of life of a group of people. It is more than mere arts and artifacts. Culture is a system of systems that consists of values, beliefs, behavior patterns, material products, and the underlying worldview that ties them all and provides coherence and meaning to a group of people. It is distinct (identifiable with a group of people), distributed (key features are shared more or less by all people in a group), and dynamic (carries the possibility for culture change).[15]

Humans produce culture, which in turn shapes and sustains them. As Clifford Geertz, a symbolic anthropologist, describes, "Man

12. Way back in 1952, Alfred Kroeber and Clyde Kluckhohn came up with a collection of 164 different definitions of culture. T. K. Oommen, "Culture Change among the Tribes of North East India," in *Christianity and Change in North East India*, ed. T. B. Subba, Shaji Joseph Puykunnel, and Joseph Puthenpurakal (New Delhi: Concept, 2009), 3.

13. A recent empirical study among young people in Bangalore revealed that the urban youth exhibited an "amalgamation" of local (subculture), national (culture), and foreign (other) cultures, and "the co-existence of three streams" of cultures "were influencing decision-making across multiple contexts." Ray Titus, *Yuva India: Consumption and Lifestyle Choices of a Young India* (Gurgaon: Random House India, 2015), xxiii, xxiv.

14. A wholistic view seeks to avoid the twin dangers of reductionist as well as stratigraphic view of human beings. Paul G. Hiebert, *Anthropological Insights for Missionaries* (Grand Rapids, MI: Baker, 2001), 22–27.

15. Some of the classic works of Christian anthropologists in this field are Eugene A. Nida, *Customs and Cultures: Anthropology for Christian Mission* (New York: Harper & Row, 1954); Louis J. Luzbetak, *The Church and Cultures: New Perspectives in Missiological Anthropology* (Maryknoll, NY: Orbis, 1988); and Paul G. Hiebert, *Cultural Anthropology* (Grand Rapids, MI: Baker, 1983). Some of the recent works include Brian M. Howell and Jenell Williams Paris, *Introducing Cultural Anthropology: A Christian Perspective* (Grand Rapids, MI: Baker Academic, 2011); and Michael Rynkiewich, *Soul, Self, and Society: A Postmodern Anthropology for Mission in a Postcolonial World* (Eugene, OR: Cascade, 2011).

is an animal suspended in webs of significance he himself has spun, and I take culture to be those webs, and the analysis of it to be therefore not an experimental science in search of law but an interpretive one in search of meaning."[16]

While Geertz locates culture externally in the social realm as a context that needs to be interpreted for meaning, the spider web is an apt metaphor for our consideration.[17] Spiders weave their externally visible webs with silky threads secreted from their own internal glands. They not only spin their own webs; they are also suspended in them. Similarly, human cultures include both visible (arts, artifacts, rituals) and invisible (ideas, beliefs, values, worldview assumptions) dimensions. Humans not only produce their culture but also are shaped and sustained by the very culture they create.

All cultures are dynamic, as they undergo change, primarily through two processes—externally through diffusion and internally through innovation. However, the pace of change and the components of the culture in which the change occurs vary from time to time and from one culture to another. For instance, the conative dimension of a culture may be more open to change than the cognitive and normative dimensions.[18]

3. Gospel Interacts with Culture

Christian missions do not occur in a vacuum, as the receptors of the gospel are deeply embedded in their respective cultures. As the Christian gospel seeks to transform the whole person and also communities, we need to have a better understanding of culture in its totality.

The Scripture teaches that God has created humans as creative beings with the capacity to produce culture. Humans, who are created

---

16. Clifford Geertz, *The Interpretations of Culture* (New York: Basic Books, 1973), 5.
17. Scholars differ in their views as to whether to locate culture primarily in the cognitive, social, or material realm. For various schools of thought within the field of cultural anthropology, see L. L. Langness, *The Study of Culture*, 3rd rev. ed. (Novato, CA: Chandler & Sharp, 2005). For various metaphors of culture and its critique, see Howell and Paris, *Introducing Cultural Anthropology*, 38–42.
18. Oommen, "Culture Change," 5.

in the image of God, are also tainted by sin due to their fallen state. Hence, all cultures, as human products, have both good and bad elements. No single culture is fundamentally good or fundamentally bad. Therefore, in its dynamic interaction with a particular culture, the gospel affirms what is good (contextual) and judges what is bad (countercultural), resulting in cultural continuity and discontinuity and thereby transforming the whole culture (see the chart in this chapter's appendix).

While the Christian gospel is *supracultural* (it is not a cultural construct, as it is the revelation of God) and also *transcultural* (applicable and translatable to all cultures), it is also *incultural*, as it can be understood, accepted, and expressed primarily through one's own cultural categories. The Christian gospel's engagement with human cultures will inevitably result in culture change. As mentioned earlier, because all cultures have both good and bad elements, the transformation of cultures by the gospel will result in both cultural continuity and discontinuity. Too often, Christians tend to swing to both extremes—viewing all of culture as bad and thereby developing an antagonistic approach, resulting in the demonization of the local culture, or uncritically embracing all of culture as good, which results in syncretism and split-level Christianity.[19]

We need to avoid viewing culture as a monolithic entity that demands a singular Christian response. In his classic book *Christ and Culture*, Richard Niebuhr presents a fivefold typology of the interaction between Christ and culture.[20] Even after several decades, it has proved to be an enduring, seminal work. However, one of the key critiques of his idea is that the typology tends to portray culture as a monolithic entity, thereby necessitating a singular response, like Christ against culture or Christ of culture.[21] The gospel calls for a multidimensional, holistic approach. We must avoid an either/or position (either contextual or countercultural), as each element of the

---

19. Paul G. Hiebert, R. Daniel Shaw, and Tite Tienou, *Understanding Folk Religion* (Grand Rapids, MI: Baker, 1999), 15.

20. H. Richard Niebuhr, *Christ and Culture* (New York: Harper & Row, 1951).

21. Dean Flemming, *Contextualization in the New Testament: Patterns for Theology and Mission* (Downers Grove, IL: InterVarsity, 2005), 126n21.

culture may need a particular response, which results in the total transformation of the whole culture.

4. Culturally Relevant Christian Missions in Contemporary India

The need for cultural relevance and sensitivity has gained greater ascendancy in contemporary India. I shall briefly highlight a few contextual factors necessitating a culturally relevant missional engagement in India.

4.1. The Heterogeneous Cultural Reality of India

India is an ancient civilization known for its rich heritage of cultural diversity and religious plurality. As Indian scholar Shashi Tharoor states it well, "The singular thing about India is that you can only speak of it in the plural."[22] The anthropological survey of India's People of India project has enumerated 4,693 communities in India.[23] It claims that Indian diversity is marked by linguistic heterogeneity, ecological diversity, biological variation, and cultural pluralism.[24]

While some argue that the hegemony of globalization is inevitably shaping the world into a homogenized Western mold, we need to take into consideration the fact that globalization and economic liberalization have also led to the fragmentation and tribalization of the Indian population, with each community attempting to assert its identity. This is evidenced by the formation of numerous caste organizations, regional political parties, and religious outfits in the last two decades.

Indian Christians must celebrate the diversity of Indian cultures, as this is a bulwark against the homogenizing forces that threaten to create a monocultural, monoreligious Hindu *rashtra*. Also, we need to be cautious with our contextualization approaches. Too often, missional

---

22. Shashi Tharoor, *India: From Midnight to the Millennium* (New Delhi: Penguin, 2000), 8.
23. K. S. Singh, *People of India: Introduction*, rev. ed. (New Delhi: Anthropological Survey of India / Oxford University Press, 2003), 289.
24. Singh, 61.

contextualizers have privileged the high-caste Brahminic stream of Hinduism as representative of Indian culture.[25] This not only negates the cultural reality of India but also undermines the legitimate cultural expressions of Dalits, Adivasis, and other marginalized communities, thereby contributing to the ideological hegemony of the Hindu nationalists. Christian witnesses are called to incarnate the gospel so that the 4,693 communities may understand, appropriate, and celebrate Christ within their particular cultural contexts.

4.2. The Prevalence of Negative Portrayals of Christians

The issue of the rootedness of Christianity in the native soil that reflects the local culture has become all the more pertinent in light of the orchestrated attacks and noisy negative propaganda against Christians. Indian Christian scholar Felix Wilfred calls for soul-searching among the Christian community. He writes, "The recent incidents of attack on the churches, Christians, religious personnel—condemnable and painful as they are—are also an occasion for the Christian community for a critical self-examination about its rootedness in the soil."[26]

One of the reasons for the persecution of the church in the Indian context is the cultural insensitivity of Christians, which has adversely undermined their valuable contribution to the society. Even though it does not absolve the perpetrators of the heinous crimes against the Christian community, we cannot accept uncritically the Hindutva-inspired conception of Indian culture, and it is important for Indian

---

25. Brahmabandhab Upadhyaya's interpretation of the Trinity as *Saccidananda Brahman*, Appasamy's portrayal of Christianity as *Bakti Marga*, Chenchiah's appropriation of Aurobindo's philosophy for Christian theology, and the various attempts by different scholars to present Christ as *Ishvara*, *Avatara*, *Saguna Brahman*, *Sabda Brahman*, *Vedic Prajapati*, and so on are a few examples of the contextual efforts in the theological realm. See Robin H. S. Boyd, *An Introduction to Indian Christian Theology* (Delhi: ISPCK, 1969). Also, the Ashram movement, Sadhu ideal, Yesu Bhaktas, and other movements are efforts to incarnate the gospel in Indian settings. However, most of them are geared toward the Brahminic stream of Hinduism.

26. Felix Wilfred, *Asian Dreams and Christian Hope: At the Dawn of the Millennium* (Delhi: ISPCK, 2003), 189.

Christians to take cultural issues seriously and not give room for others to legitimately malign us.

4.3. The Third-Wave Shift in Indian Christian Missions

The call for cultural relevance is also heightened due to the paradigmatic shift happening in the Indian mission scenario. While Christianity in India is as old as Christianity itself, the Protestant Christian missions in India—spanning three centuries—can be broadly classified into three waves:[27] the first wave of foreign cross-cultural missions during the colonial period (1706–1946), the second wave of Indian cross-cultural missions in postindependent India (1947–90), and the third wave of Indigenous missions[28] in postliberalization India (1991–onward).[29]

The first wave started with the arrival of Bartholomäus Ziegenbalg, the first Protestant missionary to Tamil Nadu in South India.[30] The next 250 years saw a steady influx of cross-cultural witnesses from different parts of Europe and America to India, which was then under colonial rule. This wave began to ebb by the beginning of the twentieth century and lost its thrust by the mid-twentieth century. Mission was primarily understood as monodirectional during this period, as the major missional emphasis came from foreign

27. "Wave" as an analogy has been employed by scholars and historians—like Kenneth Latourette, Alvin Toffler, and Robert Schreiter—to categorize and periodize history. Waves are a suitable analogy, as they represent the ebb and flow of time as well as the crest and trough of key actors and events in a particular period. However, it reminds us that the periodizations are not watertight compartments, as they tend to overlap with each other.
28. The term *Indigenous* is used here to mean "local" and not "primal."
29. As mentioned earlier, this classification of the three waves is not a watertight compartmentalization but a conceptual tool to analyze and understand Protestant missions in India that stretch over three centuries. The three key markers are: (1) 1706, with the arrival of the first Protestant missionary to India, Bartholomäus Ziegenbalg; (2) 1947, when India attains Independence; and (3) 1991, when India liberalizes its economy, which paves the way for rapid globalization and westernization.
30. For an excellent work on the life of Ziegenbalg, see Brijraj Singh, *The First Protestant Missionary to India* (New Delhi: Oxford, 1999).

missionaries.[31] However, new studies show that Indian Christians too played a crucial, catalytic role in the rapid spread of the gospel.[32]

After the independence of India in 1947, resistance to the presence of foreign missionaries due to various factors resulted in their phased withdrawal in the 1950s and 1960s. While many wondered what would happen to Christianity in India,[33] a new wave of Indian cross-cultural mission movements were started, particularly from the 1960s onward in South India[34] and other places, with the ambition to take the gospel to the unreached people groups, particularly the Adivasis in North and Central India.[35] This second wave ebbed by the

31. During this period, there have been many Indian mission stalwarts, like Bishop Azariah, the first Indian Anglican bishop who played a crucial role in the formation of the Indigenous Indian Missionary Society in 1903 and National Missionary Society in 1905. However, a mono-directional understanding of missions (from the West to the rest of the world) was predominant during this period. This is also one of the key reasons for Christianity being viewed as a Western colonial religion in India. For an excellent biography of Azariah, see Susan Billington Harper, *In the Shadow of the Mahatma: Bishop V.S. Azariah and the Travails of Christianity in British India* (Grand Rapids, MI: Eerdmans, 2000).

32. Many mission stories and histories were written by Western missionaries for the consumption of their donor base in their homeland. Hence, some of the critical roles played by Indian Christians have not been highlighted. However, fresh studies are throwing more light on this phenomenon. See Robert Eric Frykenberg, *Christianity in India: From Beginnings to Present* (New York: Oxford University Press, 2008); and Rowena Robinson and Sathiyanathan Clarke, eds., *Religious Conversion in India: Modes, Motivations and Meanings* (New Delhi: Oxford University Press, 2003), 336–38.

33. A similar apprehension happened in China when Mao Zedong came to power and threw out most of the Western missionaries, but Christianity continued to grow exponentially. Authentic Christian mission is God's mission—*missio Dei*—and it will continue to thrive, as God is the author as well as the resource for the movement, even as he uses frail humans to accomplish his purposes for the flourishing of all of God's creation during particular epochs in human history.

34. Some of the major Indian cross-cultural movements that emerged from South India, such as Friends Missionary Prayer Band, Blessing Youth Mission, Vishwa Vani, and so on, are from Tamil Nadu. There were also similar movements from Kerala as well as many church-based mission agencies from northeast India.

35. *Adivasi* is a term often used to denote the various Indigenous tribal communities in different parts of India. It means "original, primal inhabitants" (*adi*, "first"; *vasi*, "inhabitant").

1990s as India underwent cataclysmic changes during that decade.[36] While this wave has seen significant success, there have been serious limitations as well.[37]

The third wave began in the 1990s as India liberalized its economy, unleashing a new era of globalization. In spite of the increase in persecution during this wave, Christianity continues to grow in fresh ways across various groups of people. From the 1990s onward, there has been an ongoing shift in emphasis from Indian cross-cultural movements to local Indigenous movements and personnel. Nearly fifty years of Indian cross-cultural efforts have borne fruit, evidenced by a vast array of diverse churches thriving in different parts of the country, thereby necessitating the rise of local leadership. This has also significantly contributed to the welfare and holistic development of the Adivasi communities.

Unfortunately, in some places, due to a combination of ignorance and arrogance, Indian cross-cultural witnesses have replicated the mission models of the colonial era, evidenced by several instances where South Indians have uncritically transported and transplanted their cultural form of Christianity, seemingly oblivious to what the context demands. One of the important reasons for the prevalence of the high attrition rate among new *believers* in this third wave—in my personal experience, sometimes 30 to 50 percent—can be attributed to the alienation felt by these new followers who have experienced a form of Christianity that lacks a cultural fit.

In this third wave, the matrix of mission in contemporary India has dramatically changed. This has brought fresh opportunities as well as specific challenges to Indian Christianity, thereby demanding new missiological paradigms and innovative approaches.

---

36. While South Indian cross-cultural witnesses continue to exist, their influence is diminished, as many local Christian leaders and movements have emerged across the country.

37. Some of the major limitations during this wave are as follows: the focus was primarily on tribal and rural settings, resulting in neglect of the urban context; there was inordinate attention paid to "numbers," which resulted in lack of discipleship and attrition of new believers; there was an uncritical importation of South Indian (Tamil/Kerala) cultures and worship patterns; and there was a failure to intentionally develop the next generation of leaders from local contexts, which has also resulted in discord in some places in the contemporary third wave.

5. Four Flawed Conceptions of Culture

In the contemporary scenario, there are many misconceptions regarding culture that can be traced to colonial times, and I shall briefly highlight four popular flawed views of culture.

5.1. The Elitist View: "The Other Has No Culture"

The elitist view claims that there are people without any culture. This is due to a fallacious understanding, where culture is equated with the elite's understanding of literacy, fine arts, and highly developed technology. This perspective was common among many early Euro-American missionaries and scholars during the colonial period, who equated culture with Western classical music, art, and other etiquettes that were considered refined and sophisticated.

Such a view tends to treat the other as a "blank slate" or "empty vessel."[38] As members of their own specific societies and communities, there is no person without culture. People are neither blank slates on which we etch our cultural narrative nor empty vessels to be filled with our cultural way of life. In Christian witness, adhering to this view leads to the obliteration of the local culture and an uncritical importation of the evangelizer's culture.

5.2. The Ethnocentric View: "The Other Has Culture, but It Is at a Lower Level Than Mine"

While the first view reveals an elitist mindset, this second misconception highlights an ethnocentric attitude, where one's own culture is exalted and made the norm against which other cultures are evaluated. Ethnocentrism is universal, as we all tend to think that our way of life and forms of expressing our faith are better than others. This is a slight improvement from "no culture" thinking, but it is still seriously flawed.

This view was common among many early Western anthropologists like Lewis Henry Morgan, Edward Tylor, and others, who

---

38. Everett M. Rogers, the diffusion studies scholar, calls it "the fallacy of the empty vessels." See Everett M. Rogers, *Diffusions of Innovation*, 4th ed. (New York: Free Press, 2010), 240–41.

espoused the theory of cultural evolutionism. Culture, often equated with Western civilization, was portrayed as a monolithic entity that is in various stages of a unilineal evolution, with the European countries perched at the apex in a highly developed state.

Many missionaries hailing from Euro-America, who fanned out to different parts of the world during the colonial era, were influenced by this cultural evolutionism that tried to "uplift" and "liberate" the people from their culture—which is at the lower level of evolution—so that they could resemble that of the developed Western culture. This led to the classic mission slogan of the colonial era: the twin task of Christianizing and civilizing the world.

This view has resulted, at times, in situations where the new believer is encouraged to adopt uncritically the cultural practices of the evangelizer, which are perceived to be at a higher level. Hence, the believer is more conformed to the image of the missionary rather than transformed into the image of God.

5.3. The Exorcist View: "Culture Is Evil and Demonic; It Must Be Replaced with the Christian Culture"

In this view, the culture of the other is perceived to be under the total dominion of evil, and hence, it has to be totally rejected and replaced with the "Christian" culture. Unfortunately, in most instances, "Christian" culture tends to be the culture of the evangelizer.

As a result of this, there are instances in Indian church history where new believers are encouraged to shun their cultural songs, stories, festivals, and musical instruments like drums, as they are portrayed as evil. Definitely, there are evil influences in a culture that have to be addressed, and some need to be eliminated. However, portraying all of culture as evil is lopsided and demeans the people in that culture.

5.4. The Exotic View: "All of Culture Is Good; Therefore, Preach the Gospel, but Do Not Change the Culture"

Reacting to the criticism that Christians tend to negatively portray the cultures of others, as seen in the previous three views, some swing to the other extreme of the spectrum and consider that everything in a culture is good, and therefore, any culture change is undesirable.

This romanticized notion results in the uncritical absorption of all of culture and falls prey to syncretism. As mentioned earlier, all cultures have good as well as bad elements, and the gospel affirms the good, confronts the evil, and thereby transforms the whole culture.

Another popular perspective that is associated with this view is advocated by those who distinguish between religion and culture and claim that change must happen only in the religious and not in the cultural realm. However, from a systemic view of culture, this perspective is reductionist, as it fails to consider religion as one of the subsystems of culture, which is also inextricably intertwined with the social, economic, and other subsystems of that culture. Hence, change in one subsystem will invariably affect the others. Also, the possibility of evil in the social, economic, and other subsystems of a culture cannot be denied or disregarded.

This exotic and exalted concept of culture fails to consider that all cultures are dynamic and not static. It continues to undergo changes through the twin processes of diffusion and innovation, even though the rate of change may vary from one culture to another.

A Christian is a change agent in the culture where they serve.[39] However, the culture change that the dynamic gospel ushers in is not the complete overthrow or total obliteration of the culture but positive, beneficial changes that facilitate shalom and the flourishing of all of God's creation.

6. Serving in Such a Time as This

The Bible clearly exhorts God's people to understand and appropriate the times they live in. The matrix of Christian mission in India is no longer the same as during the previous waves or eras, and we must be sensitive to the shifting moods and the seismic changes that are happening in Indian society. I shall suggest some general principles that help us serve Christ effectively in "such a time as this" (Esth 4:14).

---

39. For an excellent study of culture change ushered in by Christianity within a particular community and its long-term implications, see K. N. Sahay, *Christianity and Culture Change in India* (New Delhi: Inter-India, 1986).

6.1. Learn to View People through the Eyes of Jesus

An authentic Christian community, following in the footsteps of Jesus, keeps genuine love central to its task of evangelization.[40] Jesus Christ, the incarnation of the awesomely holy God, unconditionally loved humanity, even in its sinful state. Therefore, the Great Commandment to love God and people must always precede the Great Commission to evangelize and make disciples.

We need to see people through the eyes of Jesus. At times, Christians tend to view others as a *territory* to be conquered, or a *target* to be achieved, or a *trophy* to be won. We objectify people and reduce evangelism to the slick gimmicks of a salesperson. Our language and the metaphors we employ betray such an attitude.

How do we view the other? Alicja Iwańska, an anthropologist, researched the attitudes and relationships of the people living in the northwestern United States. She discovered that people in that area tend to categorize their world into three broad domains of experience. The first is "scenery." This includes nature, weather, politics, sports, and other events over which they have little control. The issues and events that fall under the "scenery" offer them topics for casual conversation.

The second domain is "machinery." This includes "tools"—they are anything people use to accomplish a task. Tools are to be cared for as long as they are needed and repairable. If not, they can be discarded. They include tractors, livestock, chairs and beds, pencils and books, clothes and homes, and so on. The third domain is "people." These are human beings who often think and feel like themselves and to whom they can relate.

However, the most important finding of Iwańska was that the people whom she researched did not view all humans as "people." They viewed people who were different from them, like Native American Indians, as scenery. They visited the reservation to see the native Indians in the same way they would go to a zoo. They also viewed workers, like the migrant Mexican laborers in their area, as machinery. They are like tools that can be used and discarded when they are no longer useful for them. The only humans they saw as real people were their

---

40. Paul rightly reminds us of this fact in his masterpiece, 1 Cor 13.

family and friends who resembled them and to whom they could easily relate. This study highlights the perilous possibility of seeing others not as humans based on our biased cultural lenses.[41]

Similarly, Raj Mohan Gandhi, the grandson of Mahatma Gandhi, in his work *Revenge and Reconciliation*, traces the aspect of revenge as a driving force in South Asian history from Kurukshetra to Kargil. Even though reconcilers like Buddha and Ashoka came periodically, they were not able to stem the violence. One of his critical diagnoses that account for the perpetual cycle of revenge and retribution in South Asian history was a failure to see the other as a person. He writes, "This blindness, the inability to see individuals as individuals, each with a unique set mix of gifts and defects, emerged from our survey as one of South Asia's defining—and disabling—features."[42]

How do we see the other and their culture? Do we exhibit an elitist, ethnocentric view of others? Jesus challenged his disciples to shed their scales of Jewish pride and prejudice and exhorted them to see the Samaritans and their culture, who were moving toward him, through his eyes (John 4:30, 35).

6.2. Develop the Art of Double Listening

The art of listening is indispensable to learning. Unfortunately, often we tend to speak more than listen. Amartya Sen, Indian thinker and Nobel laureate, begins his best seller *The Argumentative Indian* with these words: "Prolixity is not alien to us in India. We are able to talk at some length. . . . We do like to speak."[43] Sen points to V. K. Krishna Menon's record-setting nine-hour speech in the UN assembly nearly half a century ago as well as the Sanskrit epic the *Mahabharata*, which is about seven times as long as the *Iliad* and *Odyssey* put together, as evidence of the loquacity of Indians.[44] Raj Mohan Gandhi, in the

41. Alicja Iwańska, "Some American Values" (paper presented at the American Anthropological Association annual meeting, Chicago, IL, 1957).

42. Raj Mohan Gandhi, *Revenge and Reconciliation: Understanding South Asian History* (New Delhi: Penguin, 1999), 393.

43. Amartya Sen, *The Argumentative Indian: Writings on Indian Culture, History and Identity* (New Delhi: Penguin, 2005), 3.

44. Sen, 3.

work cited earlier, advocates "listening, with the heart as well as the ear, to what is said and also to what is unsaid."[45]

John Stott writes that Christians have a propensity to talk more and listen less: "Everybody finds listening difficult. But are Christians for some reason (perhaps because we believe ourselves called to speak what God has spoken) worse listeners than others?"[46] He calls Christians to develop the ability of "double listening," which is the "faculty of listening to two voices at the same time, the voice of God through Scripture and the voices of men and women around us."[47] Listening to the voices of others around us implies that we take their views and ways of life seriously. It reveals our desire to learn not only about the other but also from the other. Without listening to the sighs, groans, doubts, and questions of a hurting, broken world around us, we would perennially be answering questions that people are not asking and not answering the real questions they are asking.

6.3. Cultivate Cultural Competency

In the Indian context, there seems to be an affinity for mission strategies that emanate from overseas. The uncritical acceptance and uncontextualized application of some of these mission strategies and megaprojects may have serious ramifications for the future of Christian missions in India. Some mission programs are conceived and executed in a militaristic manner by "mapping" the local area, fixing "targets," and conducting "campaigns." The militarization of Christian rhetoric is particularly offensive for people living in countries that have experienced colonial subjugation.

Organizing large public meetings with a foreigner flown in to preach the gospel alienates the Christian community and perpetuates the stereotyping of Indian Christianity as a West-dependent faith. Some of the evangelizers' sloganeering like "India for Christ in ten years," bombastic claims, and statistical hypes are also causes of

45. Gandhi, *Revenge and Reconciliation*, 401, 402.
46. John Stott, *The Contemporary Christian* (Chennai, India: Evangelical Literature Service & UESI, 2001), 28.
47. Stott, 29.

concern. The obsession with statistics leads to the objectification of people as members of a community are reduced to mere numbers.

Some of the evangelical megamission movements have come under severe scrutiny. For instance, the Joshua Project is portrayed as a threat to Indian national security due to the collection of strategic statistics regarding the demography of India, which is then stored in the database of Western agencies. Indian Christians were often portrayed as traitors, colluding with their Western counterparts in this process of national destabilization. While there is room for Western Christians' contribution to Indian Christianity in many areas, some of these highly publicized, West-initiated mission methods and megamovements tend to create suspicion and antagonism in the minds of many Indians.

Indian Christians need to reexamine their rootedness in the local soil without severing themselves from the global body of Christ, as the church is both *swadeshi* (indigenous) and *sarvadeshi* (universal).[48]

6.4. Live Authentically to Augment the Appeal of the Gospel

The Christian community that incarnates the gospel must exhibit the mind of Christ and embody the love of Christ. A Christ-centered, other-oriented, authentic Christian living is imperative to make an impact in our nation and the world.

In the latter part of the nineteenth century, Narayan Vaman Tilak, a Chitpavan Brahmin from Maharashtra, was drawn to Jesus Christ miraculously after reading the New Testament—particularly the Sermon on the Mount—which was handed to him by a stranger on a train.[49] A man of great brilliance and poetic genius, he endured severe persecution for his new faith, including an attempt on his life. As an ardent lover of his nation, his lifelong passion was to make Christ intelligible to his own people. Having failed in an earlier attempt to

---

48. C. V. Mathew, "To Be or Not to Be," in *Free to Choose: Issues in Conversion, Freedom of Religion and Social Engagement*, ed. Richard Howell (New Delhi: Evangelical Fellowship of India, 2002), 56–58.

49. This narration of the life story of Narayan Vaman Tilak is from Hans Staffner, *Jesus Christ and the Hindu Community: Is a Synthesis of Hinduism and Christianity Possible?* (Anand, India: Gujarat Sahitya Prakash, 1988), 58–71.

formulate a common religion for the transformation of his nation, he believed that Christ must be the foundation for national renewal. Through a series of contextualized efforts like *bhajans*, Bhakti literature, and donning the saffron robes of a sannyasi, he attempted to present Christ in a manner that his own people could understand and appreciate. Yet he knew that ultimately, people will be drawn to Christ primarily through the credible lives of Christians, including himself.

In a memorable poem, he expressed his deepest desire to redeem not only his own people but also their cultural features. However, he culminates this longing for national transformation with a prayer of personal surrender, offering himself as "a living garland"[50] at the "lotus feet" of Jesus Christ:

> When shall these longings be sufficed
> > That stir my spirit night and day?
> > When shall I see my country lay
> Her homage at the feet of Christ?

> Yea, how behold that blissful day
> > When all her prophets' mystic lore
> > And all her ancient wisdom's store
> Shall own His consummating sway?

> Of all I have, O Saviour sweet—
> > All gifts, all skill, all thoughts of mine,—
> > A living garland I entwine,
> And offer at Thy lotus feet.

---

50. This is a brilliant Indian analogy that is reminiscent of Paul's "living sacrifice" in Rom 12:1.

Appendix

Image 1.1 Transformation of culture

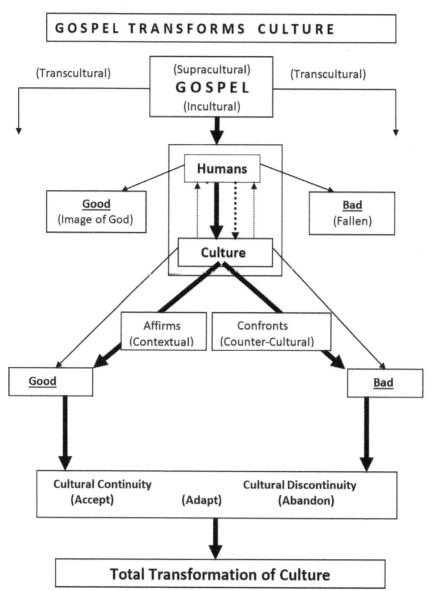

Bibliography

Boyd, Robin H. S. *A Church History of Gujarat*. Madras, India: Christian
Literature Society, 1981.
———. *An Introduction to Indian Christian Theology*. Delhi: ISPCK, 1969.
Bradshaw, Bruce. *Bridging the Gap: Evangelism, Development and Shalom*.
Monrovia, CA: MARC, 1993.
Flemming, Dean. *Contextualization in the New Testament: Patterns for Theology and Mission*. Downers Grove, IL: InterVarsity, 2005.
Frykenberg, Robert Eric. *Christianity in India: From Beginnings to Present*.
New York: Oxford University Press, 2008.
Gandhi, Mahatma. *An Autobiography: The Story of My Experiments with Truth*. Ahmedabad, India: Navajivan, 1956.
Gandhi, Raj Mohan. *Revenge and Reconciliation: Understanding South Asian History*. New Delhi: Penguin, 1999.
Geertz, Clifford. *The Interpretations of Culture*. New York: Basic Books, 1973.
Harper, Susan Billington. *In the Shadow of the Mahatma: Bishop V.S. Azariah and the Travails of Christianity in British India*. Grand Rapids, MI: Eerdmans, 2000.
Hiebert, Paul G. *Anthropological Insights for Missionaries*. Grand Rapids, MI: Baker, 2001.
———. *Cultural Anthropology*. Grand Rapids, MI: Baker, 1983.
Hiebert, Paul G., R. Daniel Shaw, and Tite Tienou. *Understanding Folk Religion*. Grand Rapids, MI: Baker, 1999.
Howell, Brian M., and Jenell Williams Paris. *Introducing Cultural Anthropology: A Christian Perspective*. Grand Rapids, MI: Baker Academic, 2011.
Iwańska, Alicja. "Some American Values." Paper presented at the American Anthropological Association annual meeting, Chicago, IL, 1957.
Jaffrelot, Christophe. *The Hindu Nationalist Movement in India*. New York: Columbia University Press, 1996.
Jones, E. Stanley. *Mahatma Gandhi: An Interpretation*. New York: Abingdon-Cokesbury, 1948.
Langness, L. L. *The Study of Culture*. 3rd rev. ed. Novato, CA: Chandler & Sharp, 2005.
Luzbetak, Louis J. *The Church and Cultures: New Perspectives in Missiological Anthropology*. Maryknoll, NY: Orbis, 1988.

Mathew, C. V. "To Be or Not to Be." In *Free to Choose: Issues in Conversion, Freedom of Religion and Social Engagement*, edited by Richard Howell, 56–58. New Delhi: Evangelical Fellowship of India, 2002.

Nida, Eugene A. *Customs and Cultures: Anthropology for Christian Mission*. New York: Harper & Row, 1954.

Niebuhr, H. Richard. *Christ and Culture*. New York: Harper & Row, 1951.

Oommen, T. K. "Culture Change among the Tribes of North East India." In *Christianity and Change in North East India*, edited by T. B. Subba, Shaji Joseph Puykunnel, and Joseph Puthenpurakal, 3–14. New Delhi: Concept, 2009.

Robinson, Rowena, and Sathiyanathan Clarke, eds. *Religious Conversion in India: Modes, Motivations and Meanings*. New Delhi: Oxford University Press, 2003.

Rogers, Everett M. *Diffusions of Innovation*. 4th ed. New York: Free Press, 2010.

Rynkiewich, Michael. *Soul, Self, and Society: A Postmodern Anthropology for Mission in a Postcolonial World*. Eugene, OR: Cascade, 2011.

Sahay, K. N. *Christianity and Culture Change in India*. New Delhi: Inter-India, 1986.

Sen, Amartya. *The Argumentative Indian: Writings on Indian Culture, History and Identity*. New Delhi: Penguin, 2005.

Singh, Brijraj. *The First Protestant Missionary to India*. New Delhi: Oxford, 1999.

Singh, K. S. *People of India: Introduction*. Rev. ed. New Delhi: Anthropological Survey of India / Oxford University Press, 2003.

Staffner, Hans. *Jesus Christ and the Hindu Community: Is a Synthesis of Hinduism and Christianity Possible?* Anand, Gujarat: Gujarat Sahitya Prakash, 1988.

Stott, John. *The Contemporary Christian*. Chennai, India: Evangelical Literature Service & UESI, 2001.

Tharoor, Shashi. *India: From Midnight to the Millennium*. New Delhi: Penguin, 2000.

Titus, Ray. *Yuva India: Consumption and Lifestyle Choices of a Young India*. Gurgaon: Random House India, 2015.

Vedhamanickam, Prabhu Singh. "Living Water in Indian Cups: A Call for Cultural Relevance in Contemporary Missions." *Asbury Journal* 66, no. 2 (2011): 57–66.

Viswanathan, Gauri. "Literacy in the Eye of India's Conversion Storm." In *Conversion: Old Worlds and New*, edited by Kenneth Mills and Anthony Grafton, 271–291. Rochester, NY: University of Rochester Press, 2003.

Wilfred, Felix. *Asian Dreams and Christian Hope: At the Dawn of the Millennium*. Delhi: ISPCK, 2003.

9

Principles of Cultural Engagement

DARRELL BOCK

The intent of this chapter is to lay out some biblical roots for cultural engagement. As one from the West, I cannot apply these ideas to India—that is something local Indian theologians must do—but I can trace the biblical emphases that address how to approach cultural engagement. I will do this in various steps. I will examine the Christian's place in culture through a quick look at four texts. I will lay out some core tensions that are always a part of engagement. Then I will consider some key texts about engagement. Through these key texts, I will set forth a couple of metaphors that describe our role in engagement with a particular interest in the issue of tone in engagement. Finally, I will consider the issue of tone and mission.

Before I start, a few observations are necessary.

First, the church's situation in India is distinct from the situation in the United States. In the United States, the Christian presence has and continues to possess cultural power, even though the competition for that power has heightened in the last several decades. Indian Christianity operates as a cultural minority in the face of a strong Hindu presence. This is one of the reasons why the application of what I will discuss must come from within Indian theological circles and reflection.

Second, I want you to learn from the West's mistakes. We have been engaged in a culture war over the last several decades that has not been of help to the church, even though some leaders thought it to be necessary. In part, the failure was because the wrong enemy was identified, and so the effort was misdirected. I hope to show that misdirection in what I will argue here.

Third, culture is actually a complex entity. In essence, it is how we live as a society and the rules we go by. It involves institutions, customs, expectations, art, values, and a full array of factors. It is made up of many subcultures as well that bounce off one another, making culture both general and specific in its nature. So Hindu Indian culture will not be Christian Indian culture. Among believers, the Christian subculture will be different if one is Baptist, for example, or Charismatic. This makes it hard to speak about culture in many ways because which variation is in view is sometimes important. Most theologians are not careful students of culture because they live in a Christian "bubbled" subculture that distances itself from the general culture.

When I am speaking about cultural engagement, I have in mind interaction with this larger, mostly non-Christian culture that Scripture would refer to as "the world." However, the world is a big place, and the array of cultural manifestations in the world means that cultures can and do differ widely from place to place in the world. This is why a discussion of engagement has to take on both a global and a local flavor at the same time because culture is fluid, and the local flavor is the one anyone needs to be most sensitive about in considering engagement. The global issues here have been classically surveyed in Richard Niebuhr's *Christ and Culture*, noting five ways one can engage with culture. Most people working with his classifications have noted that any one approach he describes does not adequately convey the complexity of the relationship between culture and the church. Rather, his five ways show up in different ways in different places depending on what one is doing with culture. So one can put Christ against culture (as churches often do), speak of the Christ of culture in some heavily Christian contexts, present Christ as above culture in some settings, place Christ and culture in paradox (as often can happen in politics where nationalism and faith are mixed), or present Christ as a transformer of culture. We can even add a category that sometimes Christ and culture may walk together side by side in some harmony in the promotion of the common good or human flourishing. This additional category goes mostly missing in Niebuhr's work, which is being raised more often these days.

Fourth, we must also note that in speaking of transforming culture, there is a special danger biblically. Some who use this term do so thinking Christian values showing up in culture or in its laws means it is being transformed. But the mission of the church tells us clearly that without a heart change, any external rule is at best protective and largely artificial. This is why real transformation takes place only in the sacred space the Spirit creates in people and in the church that has embraced the gospel. So the church invites people into it through the offer of the gospel and recognizes that without that spiritual dimension, any "transformation" is incomplete, as the new life and its new capability so central to real transformation are not yet in place. This observation also means that when culture and Christ walk side by side without this spiritual component, the results will be limited and lack the ground to stand without the additional spiritual element.

All of this is preliminary yet crucial to our textual work, to which we now turn.

1. The Christian's Call in Engagement

The apostrophe in this section is important. As the church engages culture, it does so as individuals and together. Its effectiveness is directly related to how widespread this "together element" is in the engagement. So if we do not see the corporate importance of engagement, we will weaken its effect.

The place to begin is Philippians 3:20–21. Here believers are called citizens of heaven. This means the most basic passport and identity we have is as believers in God through Christ. It transcends any form of nationalism because the church itself is transnational in its origin and outreach, as it is global in its concerns for all of humanity. One of the tensions this identity introduces is the challenge of believers serving their home yet remaining ultimately loyal to the gospel. History has shown that when nationalism has precedence over faith, the result for the church has been disastrous. German nationalism was wedded to the church in the twentieth century and yet produced a distortion of the faith that showed itself in ethnic prejudice. It produced lethal results that were the reverse of what the church was to reflect. Without a strong sense of identity as a heavenly citizen that can check this nationalistic tendency to a risky and competitive national self-focus, engagement will, at worst, fail to be Christian at all. Its alternative is a nominal Christian engagement that has a Christian veneer but still falls short on God's concern for all that the Bible calls us to possess. It is in the historic church-state relationships of many Western countries that the failures of Christian faith have been most evident through the centuries.

A second key text is 2 Corinthians 5:20. Here the positive idea of the gospel being about reconciliation comes into view, as do the issues of tone and the picture of believers as ambassadors for the heavenly "country" they most represent. This means that even though I might have a US passport and you might have an Indian one, we all are called to represent our relationship to God faithfully as an "outsider" who resides in a particular place to serve people and represent God at the same time. The ambassador exists to reflect the values of their home, which is elsewhere. That picture is a good one for the church's engagement and protects against the excessive nationalism just noted. Note one other thing about this text. In 2 Corinthians 5:18, the tone of engagement involves a plea for people to be reconciled to God. That message comes as an invitation, not a demand. One can refuse it, but one does so with consequences. The plea to be reconciled to God through Christ summarizes our mission, our message as not just about avoiding hell but about gaining a reconnected relationship with the creator who made us in his image, a relationship all were designed to possess but do not get by default. We come to God knowing our need for him and responding to him with a humility that asks for and constantly seeks his help. So being an ambassador with a message of invitation is a core picture of what engagement is to involve. A core image of the gospel is here as well because Paul summarizes everything the gospel is with the term *reconciliation*, a term that looks to our reconnection to God and, as a result, to one another in a potentially more healthy and flourishing way that makes the church sacred (Eph 2:11–22).

First Peter 1:1 reinforces this picture by describing believers as temporarily residing where God has them. Our home is not in this world, so although we are called to it and are also directed to serve it, our allegiance is elsewhere. When one combines this observation with the call in a text like Jeremiah 29:7 to serve the city, we seek how God calls people to represent him in the world. The Jeremiah text is an instruction to Jews who had been taken to the very hostile culture of Babylon. Rather than be locked in despair or fear, the text and its context call on Jews to serve the city and pray for it, arguing that through their good behavior and engagement, the city will be helped. The Christian's primary role in culture is to engage it as positively as possible in service that also points to the character of God (Luke 6:35–36).

So the call of all of us is as ambassadors bringing a message of reconciliation, given as a somber invitation to outsiders to step into new, sacred space without which real transformation is not possible. In viewing things this way, one can immediately see the limitations of a political engagement that places society's solutions in a sphere that politics cannot meet because the requisite internal qualities to get there are missing. In the meantime, we serve the city as best we can, living in a distinct way that shows there is another way to live.

2. The Core Tension of Engagement and Reflecting the Design and Character of God

The core tension of engagement is that we are called to issue this invitation to reconciliation while also issuing a challenge to people for the way they live that is the basis for why the cross of Christ was necessary. We are called to represent God's standards of righteousness in a fallen world as we invite people to consider the faith and contemplate being reconciled. When all we do is confront people without the balance of the tone of invitation and service, we risk communicating that we do not care about them as people. People will be slow to take a critique of their lives seriously if they do not believe we genuinely care about them as people made in God's image. Our witness needs to have consistency here so that when we say God loves people, the actions of his ambassadors show it.

In living in this tonally sensitive way, we connect the Great Commission to take the gospel to the world with the Great Creation mandate given to all humans in Genesis 1:26–28 that we fill the earth and subdue it. This looks to the core call all humans have before God to steward his creation well. When God created Adam and Eve and asked them to engage the earth, he was showing how important it is to serve one another and steward what God has given to us. He created them not to compete with each other for supremacy but to complement each other so that together, they could manage the creation well.

I went several years in my theological career without any theology of stewardship. It was a Korean student of mine who introduced me to the idea. The more I looked, the more important the idea became, as managing the creation well and managing our relationships well is what the Great Commandment is all about, not to mention the fact that most of the fruit of the Spirit is defined by relational qualities. When we see how the Great Commission connects to the cultural call to every human to contribute to the management of the creation, we get more clarity on our call to serve in the world that is the garden God gave to us.

Our world is a fallen one. We live and minister in an imperfect, sometimes upside-down place. Although public space was designed to be sacred, it often is not. The church as an invitee and witness to God's grace reminds us that we do not live as independent adults. Our souls need the anchor that rightly being related to God provides, and we also need to live in a less self-focused way, something the spirit of God supplies within the believer who relies on what God is doing through the presence of that enablement. We will never transform public space into sacred space until the hearts of people are transformed from the inside out.

So our call (and challenge) in engagement is to reflect the caring character of Christ, the spirit of his incarnation in coming to die for those who had turned their backs on God. It is to show how the grace of God and graciousness are the best ways to confront injustice by mirroring an alternative. It is to live in the spirit of the early church, which, when confronted for the first time with persecution, did not pray to have the danger be taken away or ask that its enemies be destroyed but asked for boldness to share the message of what could bring real change and to give service to those who rejected them to show they meant what they were preaching, supporting it by action that showed their care. Acts 4:23–27 shows this spirit that is at the core of how to engage.

3. The Key Texts

I noted earlier how the culture war in the United States was misdirected. I want to show that point to you now. The lesson here comes from Ephesians 6:12. The context is the most famous battle section of the New Testament, the discussion on the armor of God in Ephesians 6:10–18. It identifies the nature of the battle and the enemy. It is not who we often think it is.

The text says our battle is *not* against blood and flesh but against principalities, against powers, against the world rulers of this present darkness, against spiritual hosts of wickedness in heavenly places. In other words, people are not the enemy. To fight the battle, we have to have the right target. People are not the enemy; they are the goal. It is they who we invite into sacred space because what God provides by his grace is what they need. When we make people the enemy, we make it harder to carry out our mission. To demonize people is to leave them in the devil's hands. To reach out to them as Christ did, even with a caring challenge wrapped in an invitation, is to love and care for them.

A spiritual battle also takes spiritual resources, not the resources of our current circumstances. So the solution is not the right political ideology or appeals that risk underscoring self-interest. Those resources, according to Ephesians 6, are truth, righteousness, the gospel of peace, faith, salvation, the Word, and prayer. Scripture is but one part of our protection. It is ideas and character, not just ideas. This is part of the reason why tone in engagement matters.

It reflects character. Who we are as people and how we live matter so that we have credibility. When we support things that are simply the way the world lives, we undercut our message that Christ not only saves but also makes a difference in life and how people live. Our use of Scripture in the public square is only as effective as our ability to reflect its way of life and engagement. When we protect power or seek it in the way the world fights, we make it a battle royal of competing strengths and self-interests, with spiritual values and their uniqueness tossed aside. That form of engagement becomes even more divisive than what we did previously. When the battle is fought in the right way, with the right target, and the right spiritual tools, the uniqueness of the church can shine forth.

There is a second metaphor here for us alongside the ambassador. As we think about the battle being a spiritual one, an unseen war in many ways, it means the military metaphor to use is that of the special forces. The picture is of infiltrating enemy space almost unseen because of the spiritual manner of the way the battle unfolds. The goal is one of rescuing people out of the clutches of an enemy who seeks to do them harm even if they do not recognize it.

This brings us to the passage that says more about how to engage than any other in the New Testament, 1 Peter 3:13–18. Our lives and style of engagement need to match the hope the gospel provides (1 Pet 3:15–16). As that passage teaches, we are to set Christ apart in our hearts as Lord and be ready to give a defense for the *hope* that is in us, but we must do so with gentleness and respect. Notice that there is content to our engagement and a tone we are to set. This text needs a little more detailed study. What a great passage. We are to be ready to explain what we believe, our hope. Our faith is not ultimately about ideas, though it certainly has those, but about hope, about understanding and appreciating why we are on earth and how we can connect to the creator who made us. It is an exciting call and a wonderful idea. But we often miss what is around it, and that helps us answer our question about what kinds of expectations we should have as we engage.

The unit starts in 1 Peter 3:13 NET picturing a world as it ought to be: "For who is going to harm you if you are devoted to what is good?" So if we do good, things should go well. Simple enough. Only we live in an upside-down world, so the next verse reads, "But in fact, if you happen to suffer for doing what is right you are blessed." Now just look at that verse. It anticipates that we will suffer for doing right. It sounds like Peter actually understood what Jesus taught the disciples in the second half of his ministry. That is the world we engage in and with, a world where one can do right and suffer. Read it and do not be surprised if pushback from the world is the result. Yet we are blessed because we are being who God asks us to be, and our understanding and acceptance do not come from the world. It is in our heavenly citizenship that we rest and where we reside for acceptance, an acceptance already received.

The next part of the verse is even more amazing: "But do not be terrified of them or be shaken" (1 Pet 3:14 NET). There is to be no fear as we engage even though we can anticipate rejection and injustice. Now, I have to be honest. A lot of what I see as the church responding to our culture in various places in the world, especially in the West, looks like fear or our being shaken. Those responses never help us engage well. We can become self-protective and focus on our own interests when this happens. Our hope and identity rest in God, so fear should not be present. It is at this point that the famous part of the passage I cited earlier appears. We connect to Christ as our hope and march into the world ready to engage.

Like reconciliation, here Peter chooses one word to summarize all we experience. *Hope* is the word he lands on to recapitulate it all. It is an important word. When we engage the world, we hope the world should hear what we are talking about. Often when we engage in order to get people convicted of sin, we focus on their need and failure. If we do not balance that with the provision God made in Christ and the love it showed when we did not deserve such provision, then we will not get to the message of hope that leads to a changed life. Our message of engagement is fundamentally positive, even when it challenges. However, if challenge is all we do, then hope can get drowned out, and love becomes harder to communicate. This is yet another reason why tone is important.

Often we stop reading in the passage right there. Be prepared to give a defense for the hope that is in us is our assignment. But how we do it also matters, so reading on is worth it. Look at 1 Peter 3:16 NET: "Yet do it with courtesy and respect, keeping a good conscience, so that those who slander your good conduct in Christ may be put to shame when they accuse you." There is a lot to digest here. Let me make three quick points: (1) Our engagement is to come with gentleness and respect—not fear, not anger, not resentment but hope for the hope we have experienced. As a result, we need not be threatened but can be gentle and respectful. This is another thing I see less of what I might hope to see from the church as it engages the world. We can do better here. "Gentleness and respect as we engage" is crucial as we interact with culture. Tone matters because it communicates our love for those we challenge with the gospel. (2) Our good behavior will be slandered. This is the second time Peter says our good will meet with bad. Do not be surprised. It comes with the territory. (3) We are to have a good conscience while knowing God knows the wrong we have experienced. The shame our accusers will have is before God. This is one of the reasons we need not fear as we engage. Peter explains why we can think this way in 1 Peter 3:17 NET: "For it is better to suffer for doing good [yet a third mention of injustice!], if God wills it, than for doing evil." We are not to respond to the world in kind, even in the face of the injustice of some responses. Disciples engage and show a different way of relating, even to those who reject them.

The reason for this way of engaging is shown in what Peter says next. It is the example of Jesus himself in 1 Peter 3:18. He was a just one who served to draw the unjust to God. He is our model. We suffer because we mirror that he suffered. We are never to forget where we came from. When we were unjust and he was just, he made provision for us. So we model the same kind of outreach.

We need to be not fighters but witnesses. We speak to hostility with hope. There is much more that could be said, but this is enough for now. Engage but expect pushback. Do not be surprised if it comes. Do not fear. Rest in the hope we have in God. Engage with gentleness and respect. Mirror the way God drew you to him when you were a sinner. Remember how Christ served you when you were not interested in him. Remember where we came from and how

God's grace and love turned us in a new direction. Model that. When we mirror the way of God in our engagement and leave the results to him, we are faithful to our calling and witness to the way of God being different than the world. The expectations of engagement are to live the call by mirroring him as a witness and leave the results to God. Mirror the call, and our engagement will be great in God's eyes.

Colossians 4:4–6 and Galatians 6:10 reinforce this emphasis. Colossians teaches that our speech is always to be gracious and seasoned with salt. I remind people when I talk about this that *always* is a technical term meaning "all the time": twenty-four hours a day, seven days a week, fifty-two weeks a year, 365 days a year (366 in leap years—no day off for the leap year!). Galatians 6:10 teaches that we are to do good to all, especially the people of the faith. This means we are to treat all people the same way, doing good to them all. How we are to treat believers is also how we are to treat those outside the belief. There is no difference. Jesus said the same in teaching on the parable of the good Samaritan when he said to be a neighbor; do not worry who your neighbor is. And by the way, neighbors can come in surprising packages, as the Samaritan shows.

This leaves us with a text that rarely gets discussed for this topic, 2 Timothy 2:22–26. Look at what it says: "And the Lord's servant must not be quarrelsome but kindly *to every one*, an apt teacher, forbearing, correcting his opponents *with gentleness*. God may perhaps grant that they will repent and come to know the truth, and they may escape from the snare of the devil, after being captured by him to do his will" (2 Tim 2:24–26 RSV; emphasis added). Both truth and tone matter a great deal, as does knowing the goal in the battle. This is how we engage with everyone, no exceptions. Gentleness is the clothing we are to wear. When it comes to the use of Scripture in the public square, we are to be inviting, tonally sensitive, bridge building to Jesus, challenging, truth proclaiming, and praying—all at the same time.

And look at the ending. The result may be an escape from the snare of the devil, that spiritual battle rescue that Ephesians 6:12 alludes to. Repentance brings that rescue, but this style of engagement makes it possible.

4. Two Lessons from the Text

This leaves us with two final texts to consider. Both show the new community in action.

In Luke 4:14–44, we see Jesus preaching in the synagogue in Nazareth, proclaiming the hope to those God called him to pursue—namely, the poor, the blind (to the spiritual realities), and the oppressed. But in Luke 4:30–44, we see Jesus serving through a ministry that shows caring. Yes, this involved miracles, but do not lose sight of what is also taking place. Jesus is backing up his words in the synagogue with deeds that show he means it. He is serving those he came to save, showing God's care for them concretely. In fact, that service shows that his words are not empty but come with a weight of credibility that the service gives to what has been preached. This is the kind of engagement we need from the church. Too often, the church is so engaged with its own discipleship that Jesus's kind of service to those outside of its walls is missing. As a result, the world only knows our words and claims and rarely sees what those claims look like.

In Acts 17, we see Paul reaching out to a fallen culture. Acts 17:16 tells us the idols had provoked him, so he was not happy with what the culture brought. We know his negative attitude about such idols from Romans 1:18–32. In that text, we get Paul describing the culture in scathing terms, but you would never know it from his opening in addressing that culture in Acts 17:22 NET: "I see that you are very religious in all respects." He opens gently and with respect. He builds a bridge that says, "I do see you are interested in spiritual things; now let's talk about that topic." He follows with observations designed to give his listeners pause about the way they pursue spirituality. He seeks to raise fresh points about how to walk with God, but the tone is modulated compared to Romans 1. He does not speak with outsiders harshly. He invites and challenges. In fact, he is so benevolent in his opening that liberal scholars say he cannot be the Paul of Romans 1! That move cancels out the lesson Paul and Luke together teach. It is that in engagement, respect can open doors.

5. Conclusion

So here are our principles of engagement: (1) We are ambassadors for Christ first, even over nationality or ethnic identity. (2) We are like the special forces; the rescue of people is the goal, even if those people are not aware they are in danger. These are our two key metaphors for engagement. (3) Our battle is not against people; it is a spiritual one requiring spiritual resources. (4) That we suffer for doing good is to be no surprise in a fallen world. (5) Transformation requires the gospel. Without it, all change is superficial. This shows the limits of any political answer to culture. (6) Our message is one of hope and reconciliation because relationships matter, all of them. (7) Our engagement is always to be with gentleness and respect. (8) We are to seek to serve most of all, for that service supplies the credibility for our message. (9) When we engage this way, we show the grace of God and reflect his character, for he rescued us, the just for the unjust. (10) Engagement, then, requires a humility that never forgets that we did not earn our salvation; it was God's mercy that brought us in. (11) So engagement is about not just ideas but relationships, and the pursuit of reconciliation is a key point for the gospel.

All that is left now is the contextual application of all of this. That is your job to figure out in an Indian context. But knowing the mission and the how and why of engagement can certainly help us get to where we ought to be and keep us on the right track by guarding us against fighting a war with the wrong aim with damaging results. After all, engagement is to seek to win people to the gospel by reflecting the love, care, and grace of God that God showed in Christ. In other words, the character of our engagement is as important as our engagement with the right facts and ideas. Tone matters as well as content. And invitation in the midst of challenge is the call God gave to us. Plead with the world in this way. Remember that all he asks of us is to be faithful. The results of our engagement are his to give.

Contributors

Darrell Bock (PhD, University of Aberdeen) is the executive director for cultural engagement, Howard G. Hendricks Center for Christian Leadership and Cultural Engagement. He is also a senior research professor of New Testament studies, Dallas Theological Seminary. He has earned recognition as a Humboldt scholar (Tübingen University in Germany); is the author of over forty books, including the recently released *Cultural Intelligence* (2020); and serves in cultural engagement as the host of the seminary's *Table Podcasts*. He was the president of the Evangelical Theological Society (ETS) from 2000 to 2001 and has served as a consulting editor for *Christianity Today*.

Paul Premsekaran Cornelius (PhD, Fuller Theological Seminary) currently serves as the regional secretary of the Asia Theological Association–India. After completing a BA from St. Stephen's College, Delhi University, and a bachelor of divinity at Union Biblical Seminary, Pune, he and his wife served with Youth for Christ in New Delhi for several years. He then went on to complete an MTh from the South Asia Institute of Advanced Christian Studies (SAIACS) and a doctorate in intercultural studies from Fuller Theological Seminary, California. Paul enjoys teaching courses related to globalization and mission, gospel and culture, and biblical theology of mission as well as conducting workshops in areas related to learning and education. Paul is grateful for his wife and their three adult children for supporting him and challenging him in his thinking.

Ken Gnanakan (PhD, London University) was the chancellor of the ACTS Group of Institutions, which includes primary and secondary schools and a theological college. He was an Indian educator, environmentalist, artist, musician, and theologian. He taught in universities in India and in other parts of the world on varied subjects such as management, environment, education, theology, and philosophy. He was also the vice-chairman of Global Challenges Forum based in Geneva, which collaborates with the United Nations Institute of Training and Research (UNITAR). He championed the philosophy of integrated learning and was heading up various initiatives on the theme worldwide. He wrote several books on philosophy and theology, including an internationally used textbook in theology, *Kingdom Concerns* (1989, 1993). He wrote *Integrated Learning* (2011) and *Wellness and Wellbeing* (2016).

Roger E. Hedlund (PhD, University of Madras; DMiss, Fuller Theological Seminary) was the professor of mission studies (research), Serampore College, from 1994 to 1997. He was based in India from 1974 to 2006 as a missionary, teaching in other reputed theological institutions such as Union Bible Seminary and SAIACS. He is the author of academic papers, reviews, essays, and twelve books as well as twelve edited volumes. His books include *God and the Nations: A Biblical Theology of Mission in the Asian Context* (1998, 2002) and *Christianity Made in India: From Apostle Thomas to Mother Teresa* (2017). His recent edited volumes include *Oxford Encyclopaedia of South Asian Christianity* (2012) and *Missiology for the 21st Century: South Asian Perspectives* (2004). He and his wife, June, are living in retirement in Redland, California, and he is engaged in writing their memoirs and family histories as well as book reviews and occasional essays.

Aruthuckal Varughese John (PhD, Madras Christian College, University of Madras) is a professor of theology and head of the Department of Theology and History, SAIACS, Bangalore. He received his PhD in philosophy in 2006 in the area of Kierkegaard studies as a fellow of the Indian Council of Philosophical Research. He has been a postdoctoral fellow (2016–20) with Langham International. Before joining SAIACS, he was a postdoctoral Kierkegaard House Foundation Fellow (2010–11) at the Howard and Edna Hong Kierkegaard Library, St. Olaf College, Minnesota. He has authored several articles in academic journals and edited volumes, including entries in the *Oxford Encyclopaedia of South Asian Christianity* (2011) and *South Asia Bible Commentary* (2015). He is the author of *Truth and Subjectivity, Faith and History: Kierkegaard's Insights for Christian Faith* (2012).

Manoja Kumar Korada (PhD, University of Mysore) hails from Odisha, India, and he currently lives with his family in Kottayam (India) and teaches at IPC Theological Seminary Kottayam. He has been involved in formal theological education for over two decades. Apart from presenting papers in national and international academic consultations, he has published his works, which include *The Rationale for Aniconism in the Old Testament: A Study of Select Texts* (2017). He also travels and trains pastors, laypeople, and grassroots-level workers in the field.

Arren Bennet Lawrence (PhD, Asia Graduate School of Theology) is an assistant regional secretary of Asia Theology Association and an adjunct New Testament professor at SAIACS, India. He is the author of *Legalistic Nomism: A Socio-rhetorical Reading of Paul's Letter to the Galatians* (2015), *Comparative Characterization in the Sermon on the Mount: Characterization of the Ideal Disciple* (2017), and *Approaches to the New Testament* (2018). He is editing *Exploring the New Testament in Asia: Evangelical Perspectives* (forthcoming) and *Friendship in the New Testament* (forthcoming) while he is also writing *Asia Bible Commentary on the Epistles of Thessalonians* (forthcoming). He is married to Joyce, and they are blessed with a daughter, Netanya.

Eric R. Montgomery (PhD, McMaster University, Canada) served as a pastor of education and discipleship for several years before relocating with his family to India. While in India, Eric served as a professor of New Testament and as the director of PhD studies at Evangelical Theological Seminary (Bangalore, India). He has contributed articles to the *Theologisches Wörterbuch zu den Qumranschriften*, the *Journal of Theological Studies*, and *Bibliotheca Sacra*. Eric and his family presently reside in Manila, Philippines, where he teaches at the International Graduate School of Leadership.

Andrew B. Spurgeon (PhD, Dallas Theological Seminary) is a professor of New Testament and intercultural studies at Singapore Bible College and an adjunct professor of world missions and intercultural studies, Dallas Theological Seminary. He is the publications secretary for Asia Theological Association and the general editor of the Asia Bible Commentary Series. He has authored numerous articles and five commentaries. His latest books are *Romans: A Pastoral and Contextual Commentary* (2020), *James: A Pastoral and Contextual Commentary* (2018), and *Twin Cultures Separated by Centuries: An Indian Reading of First Corinthians* (2016). Professor Spurgeon and his wife, Lori, live in Singapore, and their three adult sons live in Canada and the United States.

Johnson Thomaskutty (PhD, Radboud Universiteit Nijmegen) is an associate professor of New Testament, Union Biblical Seminary (Pune, India). Formerly, he served as a lecturer of New Testament and college chaplain at Serampore College (Hooghly, West Bengal). He is the author of *The Gospel of John: A Universalistic Reading* (2020), *Saint Thomas the Apostle: New Testament, Apocrypha, and Historical Traditions* (2018), and *Dialogue in the Book of Signs: A Polyvalent Analysis of John 1:19–12:50* (2015). His forthcoming works include *An Asian Introduction to the New Testament* (edited volume; 2021), *India Commentary on the Gospel of John*, and *Asia Bible Commentary on the Gospel of John*. He also contributed more than fifty peer-reviewed articles in national and international journals and books.

Prabhu Singh Vedhamanickam (PhD, Asbury Seminary) is a trained missiological anthropologist who has served God in various capacities and with different ministries like Evangelical Union, Ambassadors for Christ, and currently, SAIACS. At SAIACS, over a period of nearly ten years, he has served in various capacities, which include professor of anthropology and missions, head of the Missions Department, and founder of the Centre for Intercultural Studies. He also leads one of the largest research initiatives in the Global South, studying the Christward movements in North India. At present, he is the principal of SAIACS. He is also a trainer and consultant for several Indian and global agencies, particularly in issues related to gospel and culture.